STATES
OF EXILE

Polyglossia: Radical Reformation Theologies

Edited by Peter Dula, Jennifer L. Graber, Chris K. Huebner, and J. Alexander Sider

A series intended for conversation among academics, ministers, and laypersons regarding knowledge, beliefs, and the practices of the Christian faith. *Polyglossia* grows out of John Howard Yoder's call to see radical reformation as a tone, style, or stance, a way of thinking theologically that requires precarious attempts to speak the gospel in new idioms. It is a form of theological reflection that blends patient vulnerability and hermeneutical charity with considered judgment and informed criticism. The books in this series will emerge out of conversations with contemporary movements in theology, as well as philosophy, political theory, literature and cultural studies.

STATES OF EXILE

ALAIN EPP WEAVER
Foreword by Daniel Boyarin

Visions of Diaspora, Witness, and Return

 **Herald Press**
Scottdale, Pennsylvania
Waterloo, Ontario

Library of Congress Cataloging-in-Publication Data
Weaver, Alain Epp.
  States of exile : visions of diaspora, witness, and return / Alain Epp
Weaver.
   p. cm.
Includes bibliographical references and index.
ISBN-13: 978-0-8361-9422-7 (pbk. : alk. paper)
1. Emigration and immigration in the Bible. 2. Emigration and immi-
gration—Religious aspects—Christianity. 3. Population transfers.
4. Christianity and culture. 5. Christianity and politics. I. Title.
  BS680.E38W43 2008
  261—dc22
                                        2007045374

Unless otherwise indicated, the Bible text is from the *New Revised
Standard Version Bible*, copyright © 1989, by the Division of Christian
Education of the National Council of the Churches of Christ in the USA,
and is used by permission.

Cover photo of British graffiti artist Banksy's 2005 painting of a girl
holding onto balloons on the concrete walls around Jerusalem.

To order or request information please call 1-800-245-7894 or visit
www.heraldpress.com.

For Samuel Rafiq and Katherine Noor

Contents

Foreword

States of Exile: Visions of Diaspora, Witness, and Return by Alain Epp Weaver is a new kind of political theology (indeed, very different from the usual usages of that term). This theology of political practice is growing out of a set of deeply ethical, practical political religious choices for living, for a life. Epp Weaver, together with his wife and children, spent more than a decade among the Arab Christians of the Middle East and especially in occupied Palestine. They were practicing political ethics and absorbing the pain and the voices of those among whom they dwelt, expanding that circle of empathy to include Muslims and Jews as well. The book is thus a politically grounded set of reflections on exile and return set in the context of Jewish exile and return, the exile of the Palestinians that it occasioned, and modes of possible return and redemption for those same dispossessed of Palestine.

Deeply inspired (as I am) by John Howard Yoder's profound theological thinking about diaspora as a practice of religious communal life and his rethinking of the Radical Reformation's theological response to living Jews, Epp Weaver nevertheless makes an important step beyond Yoder. In recognizing that the "not in charge" for which Yoder calls is only a temporal, not a theological not in charge, Epp Weaver writes, "The church in exile, as a church which is politically not in charge, should be theologically not in charge as well." Meanwhile, Yoder's remarkable rethinking of a theology of the Jews for Christians "is flawed precisely to the extent that it fails to cede theological control of the Jewish-Christian conversation." There may be no doubt that a benevolent and respectful colonization is preferable to a harsh and derogatory one, but colonization it remains, and this Epp Weaver realizes.

Among the most disturbing aspects of Yoder's theological colonization of Judaism is his insistence that the so-called "abandonment" of a missionary vocation constituted a Constantinianization of Judaism on the part of the Mishna and the succeeding rabbis. Not recognizing that the whole notion of mission in the sense of a converting mission is deeply antithetical

9

precisely to the principle of a theological stance of not being in charge, Yoder paradoxically accepts as Constantinian that which most surely stands against and resists Christendom. The Jews have abandoned mission to the church, Yoder claims, and thus played into the hands of the Constantinian church and become Christians (in the most negative sense).

In my own writings on Paul, I have argued that there are parallel missions in rabbinic Judaism and Christianity, that the genius of Christianity is to care for all the people of the world (and let us grant it its best sense, the one envisioned by Yoder). By contrast, the genius of rabbinic Judaism is to leave other people alone. In seeking to imagine a Judaism (non-rabbinic it would seem) that doubles the Christian missionary impulse and practice (while, in a kind of Orwellian speech, calling the rabbinic practice "Christian"), Yoder precisely evacuates the kind of mutual critique and thus mutual learning possible between the two *different* communities.

This critique is thus of an entirely different order than Yoder's critique of Zionism, in which a sport of modern Judaism (unfortunately, a majority sport) has taken on a project that is distinctly related to some versions of a Christian imagination of territory conquered for God and also of an exclusivism that seeks to deny the legitimacy of others in the land. Epp Weaver understands all this and exposes and analyzes it brilliantly as a way to revise and thus recover Yoder's deeply significant and moving kerygma for both radical Christians and Jews.

Everything fits together (although not overly smoothly, surely not glibly) in this book: the examination of Yoder's theology of the creed and the call for Christian churches to pay attention to the Palestinian refugees and their call to return home. Epp Weaver is a true disciple of Yoder. The testimony, witness, to the Zionist oppression of the Palestinians is of one piece with the question of the Nicene Creed in this book. The theological witness of this book is powerful and moving, challenging and rich.

If, in some ways, Yoder was vulnerable to the charge of producing a Jewish interlocutor who was comfortable for him (a charge only partially valid in my view), Epp Weaver has certainly, through listening to Jews but not simply accepting what they have to say en bloc and uncritically, engaged in a project of producing Christian theology that many Jews, not only this one, I hope, will want to listen to and engage.

Daniel Boyarin
University of California at Berkeley
February 2008

Acknowledgments

Most of the essays in this book were written while I was serving with Mennonite Central Committee (MCC) in various locations in the Middle East. From 1992 to 1996, and then from 1999 to 2006, my wife, Sonia, and I were blessed with the opportunity to live and work alongside Palestinians and Israelis, and later Jordanians and Iraqis as well. To say that I learned much more than I gave may sound like a cliché, but I can find no better way to state the case. In Gaza, Jerusalem, Amman, and the West Bank village of Zababdeh, I learned from Palestinian Christians about the blessings and challenges of being Christ's church as a minority community and of witnessing to the Prince of Peace while living under military occupation and in exile within or outside of one's land. Meanwhile, many Israelis and Palestinians, be they Jews, Christians, or Muslims, inspired and humbled me by their dedication to nonviolent resistance and their conviction that the binational reality of Palestine-Israel is an opportunity to be embraced instead of a fate to be feared. I hope this book in some limited measure does honor to the *sumud*, or steadfast witness, of the Palestinian church and to the courageous commitment of Israeli and Palestinian peace workers.

Numerous persons provided invaluable critique of earlier versions of these individual chapters, including Kathryn Tanner, Paul Griffiths, Daniel Boyarin, Stanley Hauerwas, Dipesh Chakrabarty, Nur Masalha, Patricia Shelly, Peter Ochs, Michael Cartwright, Calvin Shenk, J. Denny Weaver, Mark Thiessen Nation, Dwight Hopkins, William Schweiker, Kevin Hector, Malika Zeghal, David Burrell, Don Rogers, Cedar Duaybis, Samia Khoury, David Mark Neuhaus, Timothy Seidel, Christi Hoover Seidel, Sriprakash Mayasandra, Bassem Thabet, Jan Janzen, Rick Janzen, J. Daryl Byler, Bill Janzen, John Rempel, Gerald Schlabach, Zoughbi Zoughbi, John Roth, Bob Herr, Judy Zimmerman Herr, Ed Nyce, Paul Robeson Ford, Antonia Daymond, the participants in the Race and Religion and Middle East History and Theory workshops at the University of Chicago,

Scott Holland, Elizabeth Yoder, Eitan Bronstein, Naim Ateek, Jonathan Kuttab, and Peter Dula. Their incisive comments and responses sharpened my thinking and provoked new ideas. Special thanks are due to Chris Huebner, whose sharp editorial eye helped immeasurably. All remaining infelicities of style or incoherence of argument should of course be attributed to me, not to the many people who have so graciously read through parts of this manuscript.

I am profoundly grateful to MCC colleagues with whom I had the pleasure of living and working and who were invariably generous with their time and insights. In particular, Jan and Rick Janzen, directors for MCC's Europe and Middle East program, have not only been close friends and trusted colleagues, but have championed the importance of self-critical theological analysis within MCC.

My parents, Anthony and Dianne Epp, and my parents-in-law, Mary and Denny Weaver, have been a consistent source of love, encouragement, and support to my family and to me during our years of MCC service and graduate study. I am deeply indebted to them.

Over the past two decades Sonia Weaver has been a constant companion on three continents. Sonia always challenges me to be a clearer thinker and writer and to communicate my ideas simply and directly. This book would not have been possible without her. We have shared joys and sorrows, along with the excitement and the uncertainties of life and work in the Middle East. This book is dedicated to our children, Samuel Rafiq and Katherine Noor, both born at *mustashfa al-mutalla'* in Jerusalem, who have embraced multiple moves and new schools, homes, and cultures without complaint and with good humor and a sense of adventure.

Chapters of this book appeared in an earlier form in various journals and books. The author and publisher gratefully acknowledge permission to reprint from these publications:

Chapter 1, originally published as "John Howard Yoder's 'Alternative Perspective on Christian-Jewish Relations'" in *Mennonite Quarterly Review* 79/3 (July 2005): 295-328.

Chapter 2, originally published as "On Exile: Yoder, Said and a Theology of Land and Return" in *CrossCurrents* 52/4 (Winter 2003): 439-61. A slightly revised version appeared in *A Mind Patient and Untamed: Assessing John Howard Yoder's Contributions to Theology, Ethics, and Peacemaking*, ed. Ben C. Ollenburger and Gayle Gerber Koontz, 161-86. Telford, Pa.: Cascadia, 2004.

Chapter 3, originally published as "Further Footnotes on Zionism, Boyarin, and Yoder" in *CrossCurrents* 56/4 (Winter 2007): 41-51.

Chapter 4, originally published as "After Politics: John Howard Yoder, Body Politics, and the Witnessing Church" in *Review of Politics* 61/4 (Fall 1999): 637-73.

Chapter 5, originally published as "Missionary Christology: John Howard Yoder and the Creeds" in *Mennonite Quarterly Review* 74/3 (July 2000): 423-39.

Chapter 6, originally published as "Parables of the Kingdom and Religious Plurality: With Barth and Yoder towards a Nonresistant Public Theology" in *Mennonite Quarterly Review* 70 (July 1998): 410-41.

Chapter 7, originally published as "Memory against Forgetting: The Church and the End(s) of Palestinian Refugee Rights" in *Cornerstone* 44 (Spring 2007): 2-5; also in *The Forgotten Faithful: A Window into the Life and Witness of Christians in the Holy Land*, ed. Naim Ateek, Cedar Duaybis, and Maurine Tobin (Jerusalem: Sabeel Ecumenical Liberation Theology Center, 2007), 185-91.

Chapter 8, originally published as "Breaking Down the Iron Wall of Separation: Reflections on Nonviolence in Palestine-Israel" in *Challenging Christian Zionism*, ed. Naim Ateek, Cedar Duaybis, and Maureen Tobin, 200-7. London: Melisende, 2006.

Chapter 9, originally published as "Engaging 'Terrorism': The Case of Israel/Palestine" in *Conrad Grebel Review* 20/2 (Spring 2002): 48-64.

Chapter 10, originally published by Edinburgh University Press as "Remembering the *Nakba* in Hebrew: Return Visits as the Performance of a Binational Future" in *Holy Land Studies: A Multidisciplinary Journal* 6/2 (November 2007): 125-44.

Introduction

Life in exile is liminal existence, a state in which one is, in the words of the late Palestinian-American critic Edward Said, perpetually "out of place," de-centered.[1] Exile names a *political* condition—the physical reality of stateless refugees, of violent dispossession, of enforced homelessness. Yet exile also names a state of being, a critical mode of standing apart from dominant ideologies, of being scattered in the world yet ultimately not belonging to it. For Said, these two states of exile—the political and the critical—were intimately intertwined.

This book represents my attempt to reflect on exile theologically in a way that follows Said's lead in taking seriously different states of exile: the material state of displacement and dispersion; the critical state of not being slavishly bound to ideologies and of being receptive to the possible inbreaking of productively disruptive difference; and even the possibility of a political state of exile, an "exilic state"—referred to in the following chapters as a binational, or "diasporized" state—that breaks down nationalist assumptions about exclusivist connections between people and territory. These reflections emerge most immediately from my work alongside Palestinians whose individual and collective lives have been indelibly marked by exile, shaped by stories like this one:

> Our town was occupied on May 12, 1948. . . . We lived under occupation for fourteen days. On May 26, the military governor sent for the leading men of the town; at military headquarters, he informed them quite simply and coldly that Beisan must be evacuated by all of its inhabitants within a few hours. My father pleaded with him, "I have nowhere to go with my large family. Let us stay in our home." But the blunt answer came, "If you do not leave, we will have to kill you."[2]

And so Naim Ateek, today a Palestinian Anglican priest and theologian, became a refugee at the age of eleven. His family, like the other

15

Christian families of Beisan, was put on buses by the Israeli military and sent to Nazareth, while at the same time, Beisan's Muslim inhabitants were sent across the Jordan. Ateek's experiences of violent displacement are by no means unique. The Lutheran bishop of Jerusalem, Munib Younan, notes that his is "a family of refugees." His father's family was driven from Bir al-Sabi' (Beersheva), his mother's family was displaced from West Jerusalem, and his wife Suad's family was driven from Kfar Bir'im.[3] At the age of eleven, Riah Abu El-Assal, the current Anglican bishop of Jerusalem, joined his family in fleeing from their Nazareth home for the relative safety of Beirut. One year later, Riah and his older sister Suad managed to sneak back into what was now Israel.[4]

Elias Chacour, Archbishop of the Galilee for the Greek Catholic (Melkite) Church, was a young boy when, in November 1948, his family and neighbors were ordered by the Israeli military to leave their village of Kfar Bir'im. The villagers were told that the evacuation was only temporary and that they would be allowed to return when the fighting was over. Chacour and his mother were taken to the nearby town of Jish, but his father and older brothers, along with other villagers, were trucked to the Jordanian border, where Israeli soldiers shot above their heads to drive them across the border. Although the family later reunited in Jish after the older men had sneaked back under the cover of night, Bir'im's residents were not allowed to return. On September 16, 1953, the Israeli air force and army bombarded and leveled the town. Today only the church and its bell tower remain standing, its former inhabitants prevented from moving back.[5]

These individual histories of exile and dispossession, one must stress again, are not exceptional, but are in fact representative of the experiences of hundreds of thousands of Palestinians who became refugees during the events of 1948 that Israelis call the War of Independence but that Palestinians name as *al-Nakba*, the Catastrophe. For Palestinians, theological reflections on exile are thus not exercises in a theoretical celebration of the nomadic, but are rooted in the material realities of their lives: in the refugee camps and the more than 500 villages destroyed in 1948, and since then in uprooted olive orchards, in farmland confiscated for settlement construction, in blocked passage and permits denied at military checkpoints, and in a wide variety of other military and quasi-legal mechanisms used to estrange Palestinians from their land.

This Palestinian dispossession has gone hand in hand with the Zionist project of return to the land. From its inception in the late nineteenth century, Zionism portrayed Jewish life in diaspora as inherently unstable and abnormal, even dangerous, an argument that would become grimly convincing in the wake of the Holocaust. Return to the land (*ha-shiva le-Eretz Yisrael*) meant becoming a secure, independent nation like other European nations, a "return to history" (*ha-shiva la-historia*) in which history is written and defined by nation-states. Return, in this framework, required the "ingathering of the exiles" (*kibbutz galuiot*) and the "negation of the diaspora" (*shelilat ha-galut*). As cultural critic Ella Shohat explains, to return was to travel along a trajectory "from diaspora to redemption" (*mi-gola le-geoola*), a trajectory in which "Zionism formed a redemptive vehicle for the renewal of Jewish life on a demarcated terrain."[6]

Zionist leaders recognized early on that this return, this creation of a Jewish homeland in Palestine in the mold of the nation-states of Europe, with national hegemony over circumscribed territory, would require the expulsion of Palestinians—what the Zionist leadership called "transfer." "I am for compulsory transfer; I do not see anything immoral in it," David Ben-Gurion told the Jewish Agency Executive in June 1938.[7] As Jacqueline Rose perceptively insists, "Zionism . . . always knew the violence of its own path."[8] "Homecoming" for Jews, including exiled refugees escaping the genocidal ravages of the Nazi regime, was tied, in this vision, to the homelessness of Palestinians, with exile and return locked in a zero-sum game.[9]

Diaspora, Witness, and Return

Running through the essays in this book are interrelated questions: Must return for one people result in the exile of another? Does Babylon stand in irreducible opposition to Zion? Or can exile and return instead be conceptualized as dynamically interrelated? Is such a rethinking of exile and return perhaps required if Palestinians and Israelis are to be truly at home in the land? To answer these questions I have sought to give a theological account of how we might come to think of exile and return together instead of in binary opposition to one another and of what implications such rethinking has for the witness of the church and for life in the land. As I have grappled with these matters, I have found no better guide to the promises and perils of exile than the late John Howard Yoder. Some of the essays here directly engage his work (chapters 1, 3, 4, and 5), but Yoder's influence, it will quickly become clear, hovers behind the work as a whole, particularly his understanding of the "not in charge" character of the church's witness.[10]

Relatively well-known is Yoder's ecclesiological vision, developed over several decades, of the church dispersed in mission to seek the *shalom* of the world by practicing a particular "body politics" not wed to the power of empire or the state. Yoder's work provocatively pushes Christians to recover what he identified as the church's Jewish calling to live and witness as an exilic community, a community that both lives in Babylon and is "out of place" in it. Less appreciated is the extent to which Yoder understood exile to be not simply the *site* but also the appropriate *manner* of the church's witness. To follow Yoder's lead in doing theology *in* exile, Christians must develop theological practices *of* exile, cultivating a way of life and a manner of witness that is "not in charge," that does not seek to control theological conversations but instead fosters receptivity to the unexpected movements of God's Spirit.[11]

Diaspora, Witness, and Return, the three sections into which this book is divided, refer to intertwined states of being. The church in diaspora is called to be a witnessing church, a church that builds houses and plants trees in the cities of its dispersion even as it remembers Zion and dreams of a future return. Genuine return, meanwhile, is not ultimately a departure from diaspora, the restoration to a pure origin, but instead involves a homecoming in which exile shapes the meaning of home. Learning to return to the land in an exilic fashion, to live lightly in the land, is an integral part of Christian witness. Diaspora and exile should not be set, then, in irrevocable opposition to return. Instead, faithful Christian witness demands that we think of exile and return together, as inseparable dimensions of life as God's people in the world. The sections of this book thus do not follow upon one another in linear progression but instead represent different lenses through which to view the church's complex witness.

A Christian reflection on diaspora must emerge from an engagement with Scripture while also carefully attending to the concrete realities of exile faced by contemporary refugees. The essays in part 1 tackle this dual task. In chapter 1, I critically reflect on Yoder's revision of the Jewish-Christian schism in which he described Jews and Christians as sharing a calling to the exilic vocation of seeking the peace of the cities into which they have been scattered (Jer 29:7). This vision of exile as a site of mission and as a political way of being in the world directly and indirectly informs all of the essays in this book. However, Yoder's revision of the Jewish-Christian schism, while opening up promising possibilities for the discovery of a shared vocation, also displays the difficulties Christians have in attempting not to be in charge of the encounter with Judaism. Although Christians can properly be challenged by Yoder to learn from Judaism's history of exilic existence, I claim that they must also move beyond Yoder by cultivating an exilic manner of theologizing that allows a positive space for Jewish-Christian difference.

In the next two chapters I bring the scriptural vision of God's people in exile, called to work for the peace of Babylon, into conversation with the concrete realities of exile and dispossession in Palestine-Israel. Can the Jeremian calling to God's people be received as good news by displaced persons? For example, can Palestinians who have been violently dispossessed embrace exile as vocation? Does this positive account of exile speak to the dreams and desires of Palestinians for return, for a sense of home, for a secure place in the land? Can it speak to the Zionist dream of a secure place for the Jewish people in the land?

To answer these questions, I first examine in chapter 2 how the Palestinian-American critic Edward Said treated exile. While insisting on the horrors of displacement and uprootedness, Said also emphasized that exile opens up critical perspectives that undercut uncritical attachments to nationalist ideologies of exclusion. By bringing Said into conversation with Yoder, we can discover the importance of working toward an exilic politics of land and return, toward a way of being in and returning to the land that is not dependent on the erasure and displacement of difference but that instead welcomes that difference as an integral component of landedness.

The major problem with dominant forms of Zionism, I argue in chapter 3, is that they are bound up with policies and practices of separation and dispossession. Through an engagement with critics of Yoder on the question of Zionism and an analysis of how the landmark Jewish statement on Christianity, *Dabru Emet*, treats Israel, I probe tensions within and limits to Zionism. While Yoder's critics suggest that his championing of a politics of exile inevitably leads to an abdication of all responsibility for life in the land, I argue that an exilic consciousness can inform a particular way of life in the land, one not bound by the exclusivist connections between territory and demographic hegemony made by nationalist ideologies. Daniel Boyarin's notion of "diasporized states," I suggest, helps point the way toward more inclusive forms of landedness.

In part 2 I explore different dimensions of an *exilic* form of the church's witness. What does it mean for the life of the church not only to live without political control but also to relinquish theological control? An exilic witness is one that is "not in charge," a style of mission defined by the radical dependence of the church on God alone, a dependence that requires a cultivated receptivity to the surprising movements and disruptions of God's Spirit. In chapter 4, through an examination of how John Howard Yoder related to creedal orthodoxy, I explore the missionary christology that sustains and shapes the church in exile. From Yoder, the church dispersed in mission learns that the confession of Christ's lordship requires immersion into the languages and philosophies of the cities of the church's exile so that the church might not only testify to, but also encounter, the risen Christ within ever-new thought worlds.

How the church properly seeks the *shalom* of the cities of its dispersion is the question addressed in chapter 5. In other words, what shape does the church's political witness properly take? Here again, Yoder proves to be an invaluable guide to the theological convictions that undergird the body politics of the gathered community—the church's witness to the wider world through its own internal practices—as well as ad hoc participation in the state, in nonviolent action, and in multiparty coalitions.

Part of the church's exilic witness, I argue in chapter 6, consists of its openness to God's word breaking in from outside its walls. Drawing on Karl Barth's discussion of "secular parables of the kingdom," I contend that Christians have good reasons to expect to encounter Jesus amongst the non-Christians with whom we live and work. Through the witness of these parables of the kingdom, the church is both confirmed in its mission and judged for its unfaithfulness and called to reformation.

In part 3, Return, I focus on what an exilic politics of land and return means for the particular case of Palestine-Israel. Whether one thinks that conferences at Camp David, Annapolis, or elsewhere might yet yield a durable and equitable two-state accommodation to the Palestinian-Israeli conflict or agrees with the small yet growing number of Palestinians and Israelis who believe that proponents of peace and reconciliation must begin envisioning and working for a future of mutuality within one state, nurturing a binational perspective has become a pressing imperative.[12] Whether in the context of one state or two, the Palestinian other, the Jewish other must no longer be viewed as a threat to be walled off or erased, but as an integral part of one's own identity. Nationalist projects of separation and domination might prove successful for years, even decades, at managing ethnic and national conflict, but they will not create lasting security or the conditions for genuine reconciliation.

An exilic consciousness within the land stands opposed to nationalist projects of separation that seek to establish exclusive connections between people and territory instead working for more complex spaces that embrace difference. In the case of Palestine-Israel, this means striving for a diasporized state—or, one might say, a state of exile—in which Palestinians and Israelis alike might sit securely under vine and fig tree (Mic 4:4), a reconciliation of mutual interdependence within one body, be that within some form of one binational state or within a confederation of two states.

The church, I claim in chapter 7, should operate as an agent of memory against ideologies and practices of historical amnesia. Specifically, the church must not be complicit in the erasure of the histories of Palestinian refugees but should instead join with Palestinians and Israelis who work for a return to the land in which Palestinians and Israelis live in mutuality and equality.

When Israeli peace activists join together with Palestinian communities that are nonviolently resisting the encroachment of bulldozers, walls, and fences, they augur this coming future of mutuality, parabolically embodying the Ephesian vision of reconciliation and the demolition of dividing walls of hostility. This politics of bridge-building, or reconciliation-amidst-difference, I argue in chapter 8, stands against the iron wall politics of separation that has guided mainstream Zionism since its inception and that continues to animate Israeli policies in the present.

Fostering practices of bridge-building requires avoiding and unmasking deceptive forms of language used to divide. In the case of Palestine-Israel, no rhetoric is more commonly used to demonize than that of terrorism. I therefore turn in chapter 9 to a critical analysis of the ways in which the discourse of terrorism stigmatizes violence by some parties while obscuring or legitimizing the violence of others. After examining the obfuscating effects of the language of terrorism, I then propose particular practices of truth-telling, advocacy, and nonviolence that the church can undertake and join amidst the multifaceted violence of Palestine-Israel, practices that contribute to a future of justice, reconciliation, and equality.

Commemorative return visits by Palestinians and Israelis to the sites of Palestinian villages destroyed in 1948 are examples of practices that prefigure and build toward a binational future of reconciliation and mutuality. In chapter 10 I look at the acts of performative memory staged by the Israeli Zochrot Association, a group dedicated to remembering the Palestinian *Nakba* in Hebrew. Through the acts of memory organized by Zochrot, a binational future is sacramentally enacted in the present. The return performed by these visits is not a recapturing of an imagined pristine past, but is instead about creating and proleptically embodying heterogeneous spaces.

I conclude by returning in the epilogue to the interrelationship between exile as a political reality and as an exilic mode of theological witness, considering the importance of attending carefully to the breaches in the walls that both the church and the nation-state erect. Taking my cue from a passage in Gillian Rose's *Mourning Becomes the Law*, I argue for the importance of complex, heterogeneous spaces and for an ecclesiological politics that embraces such spaces as sites of provocative promise rather than threats against which defensive barriers must be built.

Homecoming

"I come from there and remember." So begins "I Am from There," one of the many poems in which Mahmoud Darwish grapples with the tensions and promises of exile and return.[13] For Darwish—born in al-Birwah in what is now Israel, later exiled to Lebanon, and today back in Palestine yet still separated from the village of his birth (living in the West Bank town of Ramallah)—exile and return are states of being inextricably bound up with one another. The refugees in Darwish's poems remember and dream of home, but the experience of exile has marked them enough that they do not expect—or perhaps even desire—a return in the form of the recovery of an unblemished past.

"I have learned the words of blood-stained courts in order to break the rules," Darwish writes. "I have learned and dismantled all the words to construct a single one: Home." Darwish's understanding of home—like Said's, like Yoder's—is one that "breaks the rules." Dismantling and reconstructing ideologies in which home identifies an exclusivist, carefully policed territory, one can then construct a new understanding of home, of return, that allows for greater complexity, for the welcome embrace of others, for the reception of the provocative Word from without. It is toward such a rich vision of home, toward the *shalom* of the city, that a theology in and of exile struggles, and it is in the hope for a future in which Palestinians and Israelis might dwell in such a home that these essays are written.

Diaspora

1

On Not Being in Charge
John Howard Yoder's Revision of the Jewish-Christian Schism

Christian reflection on exile—as a political reality and as a critical mode of reflection—begins with Scripture, with the story of God's people weeping by the waters of Babylon, remembering Zion and struggling, yet eventually learning, to sing praises to God in a strange land (Ps 137). Exile is not simply a theoretical perspective but names the concrete experiences of displacement, dispossession, and violence of millions upon millions of refugees, migrant workers, and others. Theological reflection on exile needs to begin with the concrete realities of exile, both the exiles of today and the story of exile told in Scripture. The church dispersed in mission throughout the world, with no permanent homeland save for God's reign, must thus turn to the story of the people first called Israel in order to learn from Israel's experience in exile, insisting on binding its own discernment about how to live and witness faithfully to God in the strange lands of the world to Israel's story and to the contemporary ruptures and forced dislocations that so many refugees have undergone.

Few theologians have reflected as carefully and as extensively on what the church should learn from the Jewish experience of living and witnessing as God's people in the exilic situation of "not being in charge" as did the late John Howard Yoder.[1] The church, having too readily throughout its history become "at home" amidst empires and nation-states, has to turn to the Jewish experience of exile, both within Scripture and beyond, to rediscover its calling to seek the peace of the cities of its exile (Jer 29:7). Yoder's conviction that the church needs to take lessons from the Jewish experience of exile in turn led him to revisit and ultimately revise traditional Christian teaching about Judaism.

25

Christians have often made claims repudiating the abiding character of God's covenant with the Jewish people. For example, Roy Kreider, a Mennonite mission worker with Messianic Jews in Israel with whom Yoder corresponded as an administrator for Mennonite Board of Missions in the 1950s and 1960s, claimed that "Jews are no longer covenant people except as individuals make covenant with God through Jesus Christ."² Such an assertion was representative of what Yoder termed the "resolutely anti-Jewish" "supersession thesis," according to which "Christians have replaced the Jews as the people holding the right understanding of the Abrahamic and Mosaic heritage and as the bearers of the salvation history" (*JCSR*, 147). Yoder countered this "supersession thesis" with a re-reading of Scripture and of postbiblical Jewish and Christian history in which he argued that the Jewish-Christian schism "did not have to be." Just as Israel's history of radical reliance on God alone culminates in Jesus and the messianic community gathered around him, so, Yoder argued, does a "free church" reading of Scripture and ecclesiology converge with a Jewish embrace of diaspora as vocation.

One of the many problems with traditional Christian theologies that repudiate Judaism is that they take control of theological encounters, limiting God's freedom to remain true to God's promises and walling off the possibilities of disruptive difference. Such a strategy of control runs counter to theologies nurtured in exile. The church in exile, as a church that is politically not in charge, should be theologically not in charge as well—sustained solely, and constantly surprised, by the movement of God's Spirit. However, an analysis of Yoder's "one basic alternative perspective" on the revision of the Jewish-Christian schism suggests that his treatment of Jewish-Christian relations is flawed precisely to the extent that it fails to cede theological control of the Jewish-Christian conversation (*JCSR*, 35). While Yoder commendably highlights the convergence of some Jewish and some Christian understandings of how God's people should live in exile, he does not provide a positive theological account of Jewish-Christian difference, of the possibility that Christians might be genuinely surprised by new discoveries in their encounters with Jews.

Appreciating the promises and pitfalls of Yoder's reworking of the Jewish-Christian schism is, I believe, vital for Christians concerned about living faithfully in exile. After outlining Yoder's revision of the schism and considering critiques of his approach, I conclude by reflecting on the difficulties and unavoidable tensions in attempts not to be in charge of the Christian-Jewish encounter.

Trust in God, from Abraham to Paul

Key to Yoder's understanding of exile is a particular reading of Scripture as the story of God's people responding to the call to depend on God alone. Scripture, in both its Old and New Testament witness, testifies to God's gathering of a people who learn radical reliance on God alone and whose mission consists in dispersal into the world to seek the world's peace and salvation by living as a faithful community. A scriptural trajectory thus connects Abraham's faith in God to God's provision for the tribes in their wandering, Israel's radical reliance on God alone in holy wars to an always-present critique of kingship as way of becoming like other nations, Jeremiah's urging the exiles to seek the peace of the cities where they dwell to Jesus' admonition to his followers to go out in mission into the world.

Israel's fundamental identity "was not defined first by a theoretical monotheism, by cult or *kaschrut*, nor by the Decalogue. It was rather defined by the claim of the tribes to 'have no king but [Y]HWH/Adonai,'" a claim that developed from the Abrahamic and Mosaic trust in God and that stood in uneasy tension with, and at times pointed toward the rejection of, Israelite monarchy. Abraham's trust in God initiates a new stream of history that will culminate in Jesus: "What begins in Abraham, and crests in Jesus, is not merely a different set of ideas about the world or about morality: it is a new definition of God. A God enters into relations with people who does not fit into the designs of human communities and their rulers" (*JCSR*, 243).

Israelite kingship (or, to be anachronistic, "statehood") was, in this telling of the biblical narrative, something of an anomaly, subject to critique from within the scriptural witness that points back to Israel's reliance on God.[3] Connecting the holy war traditions and the call to depend on God alone with the Jeremian acceptance of exile, Yoder explained that this trust in God "opens the door to his saving intervention. It is the opposite of making one's own political/military arrangements. Jeremiah's abandoning statehood for the future is thus not so much forsaking an earlier hope as it is returning to the original trust in [Y]HWH" (*JCSR*, 71). The exile thus represents, not a disruption in God's plans for his people, but rather an opportunity to return to radical dependence on God. "The move to Babylon was not a two-generation parenthesis, after which the Davidic or Solomonic project was supposed to take up again where it had left off. It was rather the beginning, under a firm fresh prophetic mandate, of a new phase of the Mosaic project" (184).[4]

Exile meant a return to an ethic, theology, and spirituality of "not being in charge," of embracing "*Galut* [diaspora] as vocation."[5] This reality of "not being in charge" continued even with the return of some exiles to the land and with the nation-building projects of Ezra and Nehemiah, for their return to life and worship in the land was accomplished without kingship or sovereignty, under the protection of pagan imperial power.[6]

This scriptural trajectory of God's sustaining a people who live without being "in charge" continues into the New Testament. "Jesus' impact in the first century," Yoder contended, "added more and deeper authentically Jewish reasons, or reinforced and further validated the already expressed Jewish reasons, for the already established ethos of not being in charge and not considering any local state structure to be the primary bearer of the movement of history" (*JCSR*, 171). Affirming the dominant trends in biblical scholarship, Yoder argued that "nothing in the Christianity of the apostolic canon is anti-Jewish, or even un-Jewish or non-Jewish, unless it be read in the light of later Christian prejudice" (60). Traditional theological oppositions between the "law" of the Old Testament and the "grace" of the New fail to capture the complexity of the scriptural witness. Jesus, he claimed, did not set aside the Law, but rather "increased its wholeness, its bindingness, its breadth and depth" (151).

A proper reading of Paul, meanwhile, has him proclaiming that in Christ we have "the fulfillment and not the abolition of the meaning of Torah as covenant of grace" (*JCSR*, 97). Pacifist Christians, who might slip into anti-Jewish and Marcionite oppositions of the violent God of the Old Testament with the loving God of the New, are reminded by Yoder that "Jesus did not reject anything Jewish in calling for love of enemy"; Jesus' call to enemy-love should be viewed as the development of an "original intent . . . . within the Torah itself, which points to the renunciation of violence and the love of enemy" (70).[7]

Not only should Jesus not be viewed as setting aside Judaism, but Paul, who has routinely been portrayed as opposing Judaism by supporting table fellowship with Gentiles and encouraging mission to Gentiles, should be understood as a Jewish contributor to a vibrant Jewish conversation. Paul was part of a "debate that had been going on already generations earlier, a debate provoked within Diaspora Judaism before Jesus, by its extensive success in attracting to the synagogue community sincere seekers of non-Jewish blood" (*JCSR*, 50). Jewish communities in exile had been engaging in mission to Gentiles for centuries as the life of the gathered community attracted God-fearing Gentiles.[8] Paul's openness to table fellowship with Gentiles and his approach to dietary laws should not be portrayed as anti-Jewish, but rather as one voice in a Jewish debate. "What Saul or 'Paul' did was not to found another religion but to define one more stream within Jewry," a stream that "had been prepared for by the phenomenon of 'Jeremiah,' i.e., by the acceptance of *galut* as mission centuries before" (32, 33).

Early Christianity as a Jewish Movement

Just as the New Testament witness should be understood in large degree as part of a Jewish conversation, so should the early church be viewed as one strand in a variegated Jewish tapestry. Yoder disputed the notion of a "historical parting of the ways" between two clear distinct entities, one named Judaism and the other Christianity. The trope of "two ways" to describe Christianity and Judaism fails to do justice to a complex reality in which "the real cultural reality" of the first and second centuries "must have been much more like the branches of the Nile in its delta" (*JCSR*, 116). Rather than arguments between Jews and Christians, one had intra-Jewish conversations and debates about two main issues: first, "about one very Jewish but also very theological question, namely, on whether the presence of the Messianic Age should be conceived of as future or also already as present"; and second, differences in degree or tonality "in the attitude towards the incorporation of the Gentiles into the faith of Abraham" (48-49, 59).[9]

In the midst of this complex reality, "To be a Jew and to be a follower of Jesus were not alternatives" (*JCSR*, 55).[10] Yoder's argument here anticipated recent scholarly trends such as the efforts by Daniel Boyarin and others to disturb the image of a clean break between Judaism and Christianity in the second century, mapping instead complex conversations and arguments (extending, some would argue, well into the fifth century) that resist easy binary analysis.[11]

If increasingly influential historical scholarship bolsters this contestation of the "parting of the ways" model, however, Yoder drew surprising and provocative theological conclusions from his historical analysis for Jewish-Christian relations. For example, consider Yoder's claim that "there was no such thing as normative Judaism in the first century of our era" (*JCSR*, 47).[12] This claim can be read as a historical description, a recognition that no one stream within Judaism could claim hegemony during that period. However, Yoder clearly wanted to press more challenging points. First, if there was no such thing as normative Judaism, then the Jewish-Christian schism simply "did not have to be." Rather, one could imagine histories in which Jewish and non-Jewish followers of *Yeshua* [Jesus] would have remained in conversation with Jews who did not recognize Jesus as the messiah. Second, if the Jewish-Christian schism did not have to be, then it does not have to be today: "What happened *historically* cannot be excluded *theologically*. If it cannot on historical grounds be excluded for then, it cannot on theological grounds be forbidden for tomorrow" (53).[13] A survey of the contemporary landscapes of Judaism and Christianity uncovers such diversity that the "spectrum of differences *within* each of the faith communities is now broader than the distance between their centres; the terrain of their overlap may again become substantial" (62).[14] Just as there were a variety of Judaisms in the first centuries of the Common Era, so today there are a plurality of Judaisms and Christianities (111-12).

Yoder believed that highlighting the plurality of "Judaism" then and "Judaism" and "Christianity" today would facilitate a contemporary rapprochement between Jews and Christians, as Christians come to understand themselves as part of a Jewish conversation and debate. Yoder's critics, however, worry, as will be discussed more fully below, that his account is a new way of negating the theological significance of rabbinic Judaism. By denying that there was or is a "stable and autonomous" entity called "Judaism," was Yoder calling Jews and Christians to understand themselves as members of one conversation who must learn from one another what it means to be Israel? Or was he denying the normativity of rabbinic Judaism only to assert as normative a Judaism that proclaims Jesus as Lord, dispensing with as theologically insignificant any aspects of rabbinic Judaism that did not mirror the marks of free church Christianity?[15]

Rabbinic Judaism as the Way of Jesus

How should Christians understand the centuries-long life and witness of Jewish communities that did not and do not acknowledge Jesus as the messiah? Some of the best theological minds of the twentieth century tackled this question by revisiting the question of election. Karl Barth and Dietrich Bonhoeffer, among others, explicated with hermeneutical and theological depth how "the election of Israel is irrevocable" (*JCSR*, 150). While expressing admiration for this approach, Yoder for the most part (one imagines deliberately) avoided discussion of election when considering the theological significance of rabbinic Judaism for Christians. Instead, he sketched an alternative history of church and synagogue in which Jewish communities living as minorities within a

"Christianized" empire were the communities that kept alive the Jeremian way of life that was "not in charge," the way of life Jesus had come to fulfill, the way of life that depended upon God rather than the sword for its preservation. Thus Yoder can provocatively write that "for over a millennium the Jews of the diaspora were the closest thing to the ethic of Jesus existing on any significant scale anywhere in Christendom" (81-82).[16]

The exilic location of Jewish communities allowed them to maintain a Jeremian mode of embodied witness. Rabbinic Judaism is "the way of life . . . which makes sense of exile as the way it is going to have to be" (77). This way of life has key sociological and theological markers. On the sociological front, Yoder identified the following traits of rabbinic Jewish communities:

- The phenomenon of the synagogue; a decentralized, self-sustaining, non-sacerdotal community life form capable of operating on its own wherever there are ten households;

- The phenomenon of Torah; a text around the reading and exposition of which the community is defined;

- The phenomenon of the rabbinate; a non-sacerdotal, non-hierarchical, nonviolent leadership elite whose power is not civil but intellectual, validated by their identification with the Torah. (171)

These practices were interwoven with a theological vision of radical dependence upon God, a vision that, "from Jeremiah until Theodore Herzl," was "the dominant Jewish vision." The key components of this vision of Jewish pacifism/quietism include the conviction that "since God is sovereign over history, there is no need [for God's people] to seize (or subvert) political sovereignty in order for God's will to be done"; the beliefs that only the *Meschiach* [Messiah] will establish the righteous social order and that attempts by Maccabees and Zealots to do so had not been blessed by God; and an acceptance of suffering both as a punishment for sins and as a way of sanctifying God's name ("the death of the righteous 'sanctifies the Name,' i.e., makes a doxological contribution, on the moral scales of history, which our avoidance of suffering, even if unjust, would obviate") (*JCSR*, 191).[17]

This theological and sociological shape of diaspora Jewish communities was not simply a "pragmatic expedient" in the face of the temple's destruction and the people's enforced exile, but, more profoundly, it stood in continuity with the Jeremian embrace of life in diaspora as the calling for God's people in the world.[18] Diaspora Jewish communities embodied "mission without provincialism, cosmopolitan vision without empire" (*JCSR*, 75). The church's entanglement with empire—the mistake of Constantinianism— thus goes hand in hand with a loss of the church's "Jewish rootage" and an accompanying loss of the church's "vision of the whole globe as under God," a "sense that Torah is grace and privilege," and a "readiness to live in the diaspora style of the Suffering Servant" (152).[19]

The sociological and theological marks of diaspora Jewish communities bear a striking resemblance to the defining characteristics of Anabaptists, radical reformers, and the proponents of the "free church": the radical reformers engaged in a retrieval of "certain Jewish aspects of original Christianity" (105). Anabaptists and Mennonites revived within Western Christianity the Jeremian legacy of "not being in charge," so for them, as for Jews, "every foreign land could be their home, yet every homeland remained to them foreign" (109).[20] Like Jews, Anabaptists and Mennonites lived amidst European Christendom as "a visible counter-community, distinct from the structures of clan, city, and state" (136). Like Jews, Anabaptists and Mennonites thus sometimes faced violent persecution and occasionally enjoyed "the privileged status of that hard-working minority population which kept to itself, worked hard, paid its rents and taxes, and was appreciated by the rulers who protected them" (110). As minorities, Jews and the radical reformers were "unembarrassed about particularity," finding no scandal in the fact that their beliefs and practices diverged—sometimes dramatically—from that of the wider society (108). Jews, Anabaptists, and Mennonites, moreover, discovered that by living as a committed minority they could effectively seek the peace of the Babylons into which God had led them: "Not being in charge of the civil order," Yoder underscored, "is sometimes a more strategic way to be important for its survival or its flourishing than to fight over or for the throne" (172).

Theologically, Jews and Anabaptists shared multiple emphases in common. Exploring these convergences could provide a "key to a renewed modernity in our witness," helping Christians to articulate with greater depth "what has gone wrong with Christendom" (46). Yoder's description of rabbinic Judaism as non-sacerdotal, nonhierarchical, and decentralized mirrored his ecclesiological vision of a nonhierarchical process of "binding and loosing," built on a particular understanding of the "priesthood of all believers," and his persistent critique of what he termed ritualism as opposed to sacrament as social process. "Byzantine dogmatics and episco-pal politics, ritualism and establishment," Yoder claimed, "are the main-stream mistakes most easily identified by the cultured critics of our time." Jews and free church Christians offer an alternative to these "mistakes" that could appeal to these "cultured critics" (46).[21]

Yoder identified additional convergences between Jews and Anabap-tists beyond the supposed shared critique of "ritualism and establishment." For example, both affirm "a possibility in principle—not an achievement in fact—of human behavior that pleases God" (122). This affirmation is not the product of a Pelagian belief in human goodness, but rather springs from a conviction about God's ability to work through God's creatures: to say "that obedience is possible is a statement not about me nor about human nature, but about the Spirit of God" (123). However, just as obe-dience is possible, so is disobedience. Jews and Anabaptists share an under-standing that God's people can—and do—engage in idolatry, that they can "abandon" God, even if God does not abandon them. Noting "the Jewish-ness of the very idea of apostasy," Yoder observed that "for the radical reformers . . . the Church, any church, including their own, is radically defectible" (140, 123).

God's election (although Yoder did not use the language of election) of the people Israel—the Jewish people and the church—is not a guarantee of faithfulness or a divine stamp of approval on the actions of the elect. If "mainstream" churches "do not consider it as seriously possible that God might have been abandoned by the people claiming to act in his name," Jews and Anabaptists take the possibility very seriously (137). "Indefectibility belongs . . . only to [God's] promise," Yoder insisted, "never becoming negotiable as our appropriation of it." The apostasy and idolatry of God's people do not prevent God from being faithful to God's people; the divine, covenantal promise is indefectible, an always-extended gift to those who repeatedly spurn it (140).[22]

Non-Missionary Judaism as a Product of Christian History

The Jeremian call to seek the peace of the city into which God has brought God's people is a missionary call. By embodying an alternative way of life through faithful practices, the people of Israel attract others to God's vision of *shalom* for the world. Diaspora Jewish communities from the exile onward had welcomed, to varying degrees, "God-fearing" Gen-tiles attracted to the people's worship. The loss of this missionary spirit is a de facto Christianization of Judaism (not, in this context, a compliment):

The abandonment of the missionary vision and action is a kind
of backhanded adjustment, not to the Gentile world in general,
but to Christianity. *Non-missionary Judaism is a product of
Christian history.* For Jews to be non-missionary means that they
have been "Christianized": they have accepted a slot within a
context where telling the Gentiles about the God of Abraham is
a function that can be left to the "Christians" (*JCSR*, 106).

Yoder viewed some parts of the development of Talmudic Judaism as
reflective of a forsaking of missionary identity. "The Mishna backed
away," Yoder claimed, from a "continuing missionary openness" (153).
Restrictions in the Mishna on intervisitation and table fellowship, from
this perspective, are characterized as purely defensive reactions to the new
missionary vitality of messianic Jewish/Christian communities. Efforts to
draw and police border lines on the previously fluid terrain of Jewish
identity aimed at separating non-messianic Jew from messianic Jew and
in the end contributed to a weakened sense of missionary calling as God's
people seeking the peace of the city.

While loss of missionary vitality was an initial adaptation to
Christianity by Judaism, more recent forms of Judaism's Christianization
include (a) "the reciprocal acceptance of the Jewish minority and the
Christian 'establishment'" in which, according to Will Herberg's model,
Protestantism, Catholicism, and Judaism represent "three kinds of equally
legitimate, socially functionally theism"; and (b) assimilation to the ideology
of the nation-state in the form of Zionism. "If assimilation into pluralism signified the rounding out of the Christianization of western Jewry," Yoder
maintained, "the development of Zionism is its culmination" (106-7).[23]
Zionism and Judaism's assimilation into Western pluralism are both symp-
tomatic of a "refusal to admit a call to be different" (a refusal that plagues
the church as well), a refusal that constitutes "a denial of the Jewish vision
on religious and moral grounds" (85). However, just as the church can be
called back to faithfulness from compromises with empire, so can contemporary Judaism return to the Jeremian calling to embody a different form
of political life amidst the world's Babylons. "If," Yoder suggested, "the
successes and the excesses of Israeli nationalism have provoked a small but
clear backlash of anti-nationalistic critique, even in the midst of belea-
guered Israeli society, that is a powerful extension of the much older story
I was telling about Judaism as the oldest and the toughest 'peace church'"
(86).[24]

A Biased Reading?

Yoder anticipated criticisms that his was a biased, selective reading of Scripture and of Jewish history. "Is it not bias[ed] for us even to have an opinion as to who 'the Jews' 'ought' to be?" Yoder imagined critics asking. "Or who they are? Is it not both bad historical method and bad inter-community dialogue to choose one's own picture of who the Jews must properly be, what image of Judaism one considers representative?" As will be seen below, Michael Cartwright and Peter Ochs, the Christian and Jewish scholars (respectively) who edited Yoder's posthumous collection of essays, both level variations of precisely this charge. To such criticisms, Yoder responded that "the problem of bias and selectivity" cannot be avoided, with "any reading of what can be called 'Jewish'" bound to be "a debatable selection" (*JCSR*, 113-14). Faced with "the vast melee of Jewish experience," Yoder made no apologies for reading Jewish history in such a way that "Yochanan is more representative than Menachem, Abraham Joshua Heschel than David Ben Gurion, Arnold Wolf than Meir Kahane, Anne Frank than Golda Meir. What goes on here," Yoder insisted, "is not that I am 'co-opting' Jews to enlist them in my cause. It is that I am finding a story, which is really there, coming all the way down from Abraham, that has the grace to adopt me" (115).

Jewish-Christian Difference and a Theology of Exile

Yoder's protests to the contrary notwithstanding, some sympathetic critics—including Michael Cartwright, Peter Ochs, and Daniel Boyarin—insist that in fact Yoder does "co-opt" Judaism to the extent that his argument threatens to reduce rabbinic Judaism to a mirror of free church Christianity, leaving no room for the otherness of Judaism and implicitly denying that Christians have anything to learn from Jews about what it means to be the people Israel aside from what they (should) already know, namely, the diaspora way of living in the world. Yoder's theology of Judaism, in other words, remains "in charge" to the degree that it forecloses the possibility of genuine Jewish-Christian difference. While Yoder showed that Jewish and Christian understandings of the life of God's people in exile can converge, his theology was insufficiently *exilic* insofar as it was not open to disruptive difference. The tensions within Yoder's position, I believe, can be traced to his decision not to address the question of election, not to provide a theological account of God's enduring relationship with the Jewish people. I turn now to an analysis of some of the critiques of Yoder's revision of the Jewish-Christian schism, critiques of the points of tension that Ochs has called the "burdens" of Yoder's approach. (I will leave aside criticisms of Yoder's discussion of Zionism and the promise of the land for now, but will turn to those in chapter 3.) These tensions within Yoder's work are instructive in that they display the challenges of articulating a theology of the Jewish-Christian encounter that neither erases difference nor reifies it.

Misrepresentation/Dislocation of Rabbinic Judaism

One perceived "burden" of Yoder's approach identified by Ochs is a misrepresentation and dislocation of rabbinic Judaism. Take, for example, Yoder's appraisal of Jewish pacifism. Ochs endorses Yoder's effort to correct "Christian tendencies to identify Jesus' pacificism [*sic*] with his non-Jewish vision, as if 'Old Testament' Judaism were a Judaism of war, opposed to Christianity's post-Jewish peace."[25] At the same time, however, Ochs understands the de facto nonviolence of diaspora Jewish communities to be a "limited pacifism" rather than a thoroughgoing pacifism, "a condition to be pursued within the limits of the earthly needs and realities of a landed people and a political entity."[26] Jews, from Ochs's perspective, should not be "pacifists," but instead "non-non-pacifists."[27] Both Yoder and Steven Schwarzschild, his close Jewish interlocutor, Ochs argues, overstate the case for Jewish pacifism, wrongly turning the rabbinic "sages' striving for peace into a conceptually clear and distinct 'pacifism' that will sound to them less like Hebrew and Rabbinic thinking than like Greek and Modern thinking."[28]

Just as Yoder overstated the case for the nonviolence of rabbinic Judaism, so, to Ochs's mind, does he claim too much for the "missionary" character of rabbinic Judaism: "Even when it had missionizing tendencies, early Rabbinic Judaism was simultaneously protective of Israel as a separate people."[29] While not denying evidence that some rabbinic concern about mission emerged as a reaction to Christian missionizing, Ochs worries about a possible "delegitimizing" of "Mishnaic Judaism: judging its legal teachings and its protective care for the people Israel as mere reactions against the ascendancy of Christianity."[30] Cartwright states the charge more forcefully: "Yoder's narrative," he contends, "*dislocates* the *Mishnah* from Jewish existence by characterizing it as largely defensive and therefore implying that (for the most part) Rabbinical Judaism constitutes a mistake."[31]

Cartwright's and Ochs's concerns here appear to me to be about the potential effect or implications of Yoder's argument, more about what

Yoder left unsaid than about what he said. Yoder, for example, never wrote that "Rabbinical Judaism constitutes a mistake," but Cartwright fears that Yoder's characterization of *some* of the Mishna as defensive will lead to a Christian refusal to see the Mishna as vital to Jewish identity. Yoder did not claim that the Mishna was "largely defensive," but in fact noted that the parts of the Mishna about which he had concerns constituted only a small portion of Mishnaic material.[32] However, one must grant that Yoder was silent about the positive theological significance of the Mishna and the entire textual tradition of rabbinic Judaism, a silence that understandably creates worries about those traditions being dislocated in Yoder's revisionist work.

Monological Reading of Scripture?

Cartwright's and Ochs's concerns about Yoder's understanding of rabbinic Judaism relate to their fear that Yoder, with his strong emphasis on the exilic motif within Scripture, engaged in what they call a "monological" hermeneutic that failed to do justice to the multivocality of the biblical text. According to Cartwright, "Yoder's ever-present vigilance against the spectre of the biblical text becoming a 'wax nose' tended to foster a monological hermeneutic that sought to *limit* the range of possible meanings of the text of Scripture (when registered within the Jewish tradition)."[33] Ochs connects this hermeneutical issue with what he views as Yoder's logic of "twos," his "tendency to draw stark distinctions between true and false judgments," between pacifism and non-pacifism, mission and non-mission, exile and landedness.[34] As an alternative to this "logic of twos," Ochs suggests a "logic of threes," a logic of "relationality rather than of warring essences," while Cartwright urges Christians to learn "to read Scripture polyphonically," a skill he notes can be learned by paying attention to rabbinic modes of interpretation.[35]

Ochs, ironically more clearly than Cartwright, sees that this critique touches on christological matters, noting that Yoder's "tendency to uncompromising judgments" reinforces and is reinforced by "a doctrine of fulfilled or messianic time: that in Jesus Christians have the potential to live in fulfilled time."[36] Christological convictions—for example, that Jesus is the promised Messiah in whom and through whom nonviolent witness is made possible—inevitably and properly shape the Christian's reading of Scripture, with Christians interpreting the multilayered strands of the biblical text in light of God's revelation in Jesus. This interpretation need not be "monological." In fact, one could argue, contra Cartwright and Ochs, that the radical, free church mode of scriptural interpretation favored by Yoder, in which Scripture is properly read and interpreted by the gathered community, is one that best gives play to the polyphony of Scripture. Part of the problem here is that Ochs and Cartwright fail to appreciate the already-polyphonic character of Yoder's understanding of exile, something that will be fleshed out in greater detail in the next two chapters in which I examine how "exile" can in fact shape forms of "landedness."

Tradition, Theological Boundaries, and the Conditions for True Dialogue

In agreement with much current historical scholarship, Yoder correctly recognized that "Judaism" and "Christianity" are constructions created by the imposition of what Daniel Boyarin calls "border lines" within the fluid terrain of Jewish reality in late antiquity.[37] While Cartwright and Ochs do not, for the most part, question Yoder's description of variegated streams of Judaism in late antiquity—including messianic movements—they disagree with the practical and theological implications Yoder drew from this historical insight, namely, that the "schism," the border lines, not only "did not have to be" then, but do not have to be today.

What Cartwright and Ochs correctly identify as problematic about Yoder's approach is its de facto erasure of theological boundaries between Judaism and Christianity today, encompassing them both under the rubric of the Jeremian exilic vision. "Jew" and "Gentile," Cartwright claims, are, for Yoder, "(unstable) sociological constructions to be overcome, not constitutive identities that have stability that inheres in traditioned practices, narratives, etc."[38] This approach to tradition is severely damaging to the cause of genuine dialogue. Yoder erred in rejecting "the assumption of theological boundaries between Judaism and Christianity," boundaries that are essential for appropriate theological competition.[39] This apparent denial of difference between Judaism and Christianity could be viewed as a covert missionary strategy, one that surreptitiously "Christianizes" Judaism by reducing it to a trajectory culminating in Jesus.

Yoder "displaces the necessity for contemporary Jewish-Christian dialogue," Cartwright argues, by eclipsing "the difference between Christians and Jews in the name of a common destiny," the destiny of an exilic Jeremian witness.[40] Constructing a Judaism with which he can converse, Yoder leaves no room for Jewish difference, for an otherness that could instruct Christians about what it means to be the people of God.[41] Yoder's "openness to new forms of Jewish-Christian sharing is closed down," in

Ochs's assessment, "when he claims already to know in advance what that sharing should be."[42] As Christians relate to Jews, argues Cartwright, "the distinctiveness of their respective vocations and narratives of peoplehood must be preserved as these children of Abraham attempt faithfully to live out their theological understandings of covenant."[43] Is Judaism valuable only insofar as it embodies the exilic shape that Christian existence should take? Or instead, does not the entire matrix of traditioned Jewish practices also differ from Christianity in ways from which Christians might learn through true dialogue about what it means to be God's people in the world?[44]

Boyarin, too, worries about the apparent erasure of difference between Christian and Jew in Yoder's work. Yoder's embrace of Judaism as the first peace church, Boyarin fears, is a "gesture of 'appropriation' that reads so many Jews somehow right out of Judaism," with only those Jews who embrace the vision of diaspora as mission being accredited as "Jewish."[45] "Yoder's way beyond supersession is for us to begin to imagine ourselves as one thing, as one community, to disinvest ourselves in difference," Boyarin observes. Recognizing that efforts to draw clear boundaries between "insider" and "outsider" routinely go hand in hand with politics of dispossession and death, Boyarin is on one level attracted to this position. "While I still see value in difference per se, in the maintenance of communal and cultural religious tradition, perhaps more than Yoder does, when such maintenance begins to produce so much harm in the world, then perhaps we need to let go, however painfully, of it." But then he hesitates: "Perhaps, perhaps, perhaps not."[46] Should there not ultimately be, Boyarin rightly asks, a positive place for difference?

Toward a "Not-in-Charge" Theology of the Jewish-Christian Encounter

Boyarin's correct insistence on the importance of affirming Jewish difference points back to the issue that Yoder bracketed in his revision of the Jewish-Christian schism, namely, election. Assuming, as Christians do, that the Old Testament promises to Israel are fulfilled in Jesus, and assuming, with Paul, that the church has been grafted into Israel (Rom 9–11), how should Christians theologically understand rabbinic Judaism? I conclude by reflecting on the challenges of developing a theology of Judaism that does not seek to control the Jewish-Christian encounter.

Over the past half-century a wide variety of Catholic and Protestant churches have begun to rethink and repudiate theologies that claim that

God's covenant with the Jewish people has been abrogated and that rabbinic Judaism must therefore only be characterized negatively. One way to rethink the church's teaching on Judaism has been to suggest that there are two covenants through which God offers salvation to humanity, one for Jews and another for Gentiles. The problem with this approach is twofold: not only is it difficult to impossible to square it with the essential Christian proclamation that salvation for all of humanity comes through Jesus, it also represents another way of seeking to take charge of the Jewish-Christian encounter—except this time not through erasure of Jewish-Christian difference, but instead through the reification of that difference.

Traditional theologies of repudiation and two-covenant theologies thus both fall prey to the temptation to take control, to set up guards against disruptive difference. Not only do theologies of replacement deny the possibility of being provocatively and instructively unsettled and decentered in the Christian encounter with Judaism, but so also do two-covenant theologies that imagine Jews and Christians each having separate, self-enclosed vocations. "If Israel is replaced by the church," Scott Bader-Saye explains, "then there is no need for Christians to listen to the contemporary witness of Judaism. Likewise if Israel and church are traveling separate, parallel paths to God, then their callings are different enough to mitigate the significance of Israel's witness for the gentile journey."[47]

The challenge of a "not-in-charge" theology of Judaism will be to think of the convergence and difference of Christians and Jews in dynamic terms. Christians must learn, as Michael Cartwright correctly insists, to "practice a politics that not only recognizes the ongoing existence of Jews as part of our theology of history, but also accepts the burdens of learning *from Jews* some of what it might mean to be the people of God, if—as we want to continue to claim—Abraham is our father."[48] For there to be such learning, one must acknowledge difference, for as Kendall Soulen observes, "reconciliation does not mean the imposition of sameness, but the unity of reciprocal blessing."[49] This difference, however, unfolds in an ongoing, dynamic interplay within the unity of being the people of God together. Two people, bound together through the unsettling action of God's Spirit that shapes and empowers them to witness to God in the exiles of the world, while challenging and learning from one another about what it means to be God's people: that is the task and the promise of an exilic theology of the Jewish-Christian encounter.

2

An Exilic Politics of Land and Return
The Case of Edward Said

*We travel like other people, but we return to nowhere. As if traveling
is the way of the clouds. We have buried our loved ones in the
   darkness of the clouds, between the roots of the trees.
And we said to our wives: go on giving birth to people like us
   for hundreds of years so we can complete this journey
To the hour of a country, to a meter of the impossible. . . .*

*We have a country of words. Speak speak so we may know the end of
   this travel.*

                               —Mahmoud Darwish

The Palestinian poet Mahmoud Darwish quoted in the epigraph captures
well the ambiguities of exile: travel without end; the pain of disconnec-
tion and the nostalgia of memory; the realization, encoded in the closing
demand to "Speak speak," that for a people who have "a country of
words," return from exile, the end of travel, will more likely than not be
textual rather than physical.[1] Darwish thus shows the reality of millions
of Palestinians exiled from their land, living without fixed destination,
and sustained by the tenuous hope of return.

    How should Palestinian exile, and exile more generally, be under-
stood theologically? How should Christians understand the dreams of
many exiles, dreams that often appear hopeless, of return to their homes?
John Howard Yoder would probably have objected to starting with such
general questions—they might have struck him as too "methodologistic,"
beginning theological reflection with abstract questions rather than with
God's story in Scripture and the church.[2] Nevertheless, as discussed at

length in the previous chapter, the drama of exile, especially as displayed in Jeremiah's call to the exiles to seek the peace of the city in which they find themselves (Jer 29:7), played a key role in shaping Yoder's reading of Scripture, his ecclesiology, and his missiology. As early as 1973 Yoder was probing the fruitfulness of the theme of exile for theology, considering exile and exodus as two faces of liberation.[3] Exile, while painful, opens up a new chapter in the history of the radical reliance of the people of God on God alone. God's people, for Yoder, are called to a nonviolent dependence on God that eschews the sovereignty of the sword in favor of embodying an alternative politics amidst the Babylons of the world.

Yoder tentatively wondered about the relevance of this exilic, Jeremian vision for displaced peoples. Was there "something about this Jewish vision of the dignity and ministry of the scattered people of God which might be echoed or replicated by other migrant peoples?" he asked. "Might there even be something helpful in this memory which would speak by a more distant analogy to the condition of peoples overwhelmed by imperial immigration, like the original Americans or Australians, or the Ainu or the Maori?"[4] Yoder recognized the potential affront of his question, I believe, and thus phrased it carefully. Nevertheless, the provocation remains: can those who have been violently uprooted from their lands embrace as good news the prophetic admonition to build houses and plant gardens in exile?

Yoder's appropriation of Jeremiah's call to the exiles holds significant promise for a hermeneutics of Scripture, for an interpretation of church history, and for the articulation of a nonviolent ecclesiological politics. However, can the call to seek the peace of the city of one's exile also be heard as good news, even if only by distant analogy, by the millions upon millions of people in the modern period who have been violently uprooted by imperial and colonial practice? What does Jeremiah's call mean for a return to one's land, for justice for the exiled refugee? Are justice and return endlessly deferred, postponed until the eschaton?

I propose to tackle these questions through an examination of the way the motif of exile functions in the thought and politics of the prolific and provocative Palestinian-American critic Edward Said, whose writings display the agonies and the promise of exile. Said offered a multifaceted appraisal of exile: while insisting on its harrowing character, he also expounded at length on the critical epistemological and moral possibilities opened up by exile. I contend that an exilic consciousness of not being fully at home in one's home so long as injustice endures can contribute to a the-

ology of living rightly and justly in the land. This view from exile, Said's
work teaches us, poses a challenge to exclusionary politics that would deny
a just place in the land for both Palestinian and Israeli.[5]

An initial caveat: Said, given his relentless critique of religion, his
stark opposition between religious (bad) and secular (good) criticism, and
his desire to keep religion in proper bounds, might appear an odd thinker
to bring into conversation with Yoder, someone who operated within an
explicitly theological horizon, who lived under the authority of God's
Word and the church, and who resisted liberalism's attempts to confine
the church's witness.[6] Apart from noting the similarities in the wide-ranging, amateur character of their intellects, what theologically useful observations can possibly come of bringing Yoder into conversation with such
an aggressive, even dogmatic, secularist?[7] Clearly, Said's treatment of religion is problematic at many levels. Nevertheless, I maintain that in Said's
appropriation of exile we find a distant analogy to Jeremiah's vision for
the people of God in exile and that exploring these distant analogies, what
Karl Barth called "secular parables of the kingdom," provides provocative material for reflection as Christians seek to articulate theologies of
exile, land, and return.[8]

The Moral Task of the Exilic Intellectual

Palestinian existence is at root one of exile. Dispersed geographically
and separated by borders, Palestinians nevertheless form "a community,
if at heart a community built on suffering and exile."[9] In the Arab-Israeli
war of 1948, in what Palestinians call the *Nakba* (Arabic for 'catastrophe'), well over 700,000 Palestinians fled in fear from the fighting or were
driven from their homes by the Israeli military forces that proceeded to
destroy more than 500 villages. Many of these refugees and their descendants now live in United Nations-administered camps throughout the
Middle East, denied the possibility of returning to their homes and properties.[10] Some of these uprooted Palestinians remained in what became the
State of Israel, classified as "present absentees" under the Absentee
Property Law of 1950 and prevented from returning to their land.[11] Tens
of thousands more Palestinians, many of them already refugees, became
refugees once more in 1967, driven out of Mandate Palestine across the
Jordan River by Israeli forces.

Since 1967, for Palestinians in the occupied territories of the West
Bank, East Jerusalem, and the Gaza Strip, dispossession has taken a variety of forms. The Israeli civil administration confiscates land from

Palestinians for the construction of colonies that are illegal under international law. Israeli bulldozers destroy Palestinian homes and rip up Palestinian orchards and vineyards. The Israeli Interior Ministry uses a variety of pretexts to strip Palestinians of identity cards that allow them to live in their Jerusalem homes, while thousands of Palestinians born in the Occupied Territories who went abroad for work, study, or family reasons are barred from re-entry. Roadblocks and walls separate Palestinian from Palestinian, making travel between the West Bank and the Gaza Strip impossible, while travel within the north and south of the West Bank is strictly regulated through a complex permit system and network of checkpoints.[12]

Palestinians are thus continually ripped out of their contexts and find themselves travelers in a strange world. "The Palestinian is very much a person in transit," Said noted. "Suitcase or bundle of possessions in hand, each family vacates territory left behind for others, even as new boundaries are traversed, new opportunities created, new realities set up."[13] If exile creates "new opportunities," it also is profoundly alienating. "Exile is a series of portraits without names, without contexts. Images that are largely unexplained, nameless, mute."[14] Without continuity of place, Palestinians experience no continuity of identity. "Palestinian life is scattered, discontinuous, marked by the artificial and imposed arrangements of interrupted or confined space, by the dislocations and unsynchronized rhythms of disturbed time," Said explained, "where no straight line leads from home to birthplace to school to maturity, all events are accidents, all progress is a digression, all residence is exile."[15]

De-centered, out of place, Palestinian life becomes one of travel without fixed destination: "Our truest reality is expressed in the way we cross over from one place to another," Said insisted. "We are migrants and perhaps hybrids in, but not of, any situation in which we find ourselves. This is the deepest continuity of our lives as a nation in exile and constantly on the move."[16] Rupture of continuity is the fate of the defeated, while the victors, the powerful, remain in place. "Continuity for *them*, the dominant population," Said noted, as opposed to "discontinuity for us, the dispossessed and dispersed."[17] Said's emphasis on the Palestinians' "privilege of obduracy," their steadfastness (*sumud*), the declaration that "here we are, unmoved by your power, proceeding with our lives and with future generations," is a way of desperately trying to hold on, amidst the transit of exile, so that the de-centeredness of exile does not become dissolution.[18]

Said strenuously objected to any attempts to romanticize exile. "Exile is one of the saddest fates," he wrote. "There has always been an association between the idea of exile and the terrors of being a leper, a social and moral untouchable."[19] For Palestinians, the experience of exile has not only been physically and emotionally painful, but it has had negative effects on individual exiles and on the exiled community as a whole. "Our collective history *fil-kharij* ('in the exterior') or in the *manfa* and *ghurba* ('exile' and 'estrangement') has been singularly unsuccessful," Said judged, "progressively graceless, unblessed, more and more eccentric, de-centered, and alienated."[20] Exile can turn people inward, generating a form of sectarian withdrawal that shuns those outside the community. Exile is a "jealous state" that can create "an exaggerated sense of group solidarity, and a passionate hostility to outsiders, even those who may in fact be in the same predicament as you."[21] Ripped out of place, the exile often seeks solace in uncritical commitment to political parties and institutions, a tendency that Said, as a perpetual critic of the Palestine Liberation Organization, carefully resisted.

Meanwhile, those who resist the temptation to subscribe blindly to political programs face the temptation of individualistic withdrawal away from all communities. Exile is marked by "the sheer fact of isolation and displacement, which produces the kind of narcissistic masochism that resists all efforts at amelioration, acculturation, and community. At this extreme," Said warned, "the exile can make a fetish of exile, a practice that distances him or her from all connections and commitments."[22]

Critiquing attempts to find a moral within exile, Said demanded that the brute reality of life in the refugee camp be given priority over literary treatments of exile in any critical evaluation of forced displacement. "Exiled poets and writers lend dignity to a condition legislated to deny dignity—to deny an identity to people," Said maintained. "To concentrate on exile as a contemporary political punishment, you must therefore map territories of experience beyond those mapped by the literature of exile itself. You must first set aside Joyce and Nabokov and think instead of the uncountable masses for whom UN agencies have been created."[23] Literature and religion run the risk of downplaying the horrors of exile in the interests of extracting new insights from exile itself. In contrast, Said countered:

> On the twentieth-century scale, exile is neither aesthetically nor humanistically comprehensible: at most the literature about exile objectifies an anguish and a predicament most people rarely experience first hand; but to think of the exile informing this literature as beneficially humanistic is to banalize its mutilations, the losses it inflicts on those who suffer them, the muteness with

which it responds to any attempt to understand it as "good for us." Is it not true that the views of exile in literature and, moreover, in religion obscure what is truly horrendous: that exile is irremediably secular and unbearably historical?[24]

Here Said's critical evaluation of exile would appear to run directly counter to Yoder's exilic theological appropriation of exile. Said's caution about an aesthetic or religious amelioration of exile's pains serves as a needed reminder that we must not lose sight of the fact that exile does not simply name a concept but designates a condition in which millions of people live. Romanticized treatments of exile are neither theologically nor politically persuasive.

Can nothing, then, be learned from exile? Said's own writings suggest otherwise. Just as Yoder articulated a missiological vocation for the people of God in exile, so Said argued that exile opens up an intellectual and moral space that provides for the intellectual a place from which to resist co-optation into becoming an apologist for power and creates a discomfort with being settled in one's home so long as injustice forces homelessness on others.

For Said, exile is the proper *place* for the critic, the intellectual. "If you think about exile as a permanent state, both in the literal and in the intellectual sense, then it's a much more promising, if difficult, thing. Then you're really talking about movement, about homelessness in the sense in which [Georg] Lukàcs talks about it in *The Theory of the Novel*—'transcendental homelessness'—which can acquire a particular intellectual mission that I associate with criticism."[25] While exile "is an *actual* condition," it also functions in Said's thought as "a *metaphorical* condition." Developing a distinction between insider and outsider intellectuals reminiscent of Yoder's contrast between the Constantinian and free churches, Said differentiated between those on the one hand who belong fully to the society as it is, who flourish in it without an overwhelming sense of dissonance or dissent, those who can be called yea-sayers; and on the other hand, the nay-sayers, the individuals at odds with their society and therefore outsiders and exiles so far as privileges, power, and honors are concerned.[26]

The responsibility of the intellectual is to offer a critique from exile. "Exile for the intellectual in this meta-physical sense," according to Said, "is restlessness, movement, constantly being unsettled, and unsettling others. You cannot go back to some earlier and perhaps more stable condition of being at home; and, alas, you can never fully arrive, be at one with your new home or situation."[27] Even those who have not experienced the pain of

being physically uprooted from their homes can be marginal to the powers
(of the academy, government, the news media, etc.) that reward uncritical
support for policies that oppress, exclude, and dispossess. "Exile means that
you are always going to be marginal. Exile is a model for the intellectual
who is tempted, and even beset and overwhelmed, by the rewards of accommodation, yea-saying, settling in."[28] Furthermore, the exilic intellectual
should not succumb to a morose despair. "The intellectual in exile is,"
according to Said, "necessarily ironic, skeptical, even playful—but not cyn-
ical."[29]

Even more than to Georg Lukàcs's notion of "transcendental homelessness," Said's positive appropriation of exile for his construal of the
intellectual vocation owed a debt to the reflections of the German Jewish
theorist Theodor Adorno on "dwelling." In his autobiographical reflections, *Minima Moralia*, Adorno asserted:

> Dwelling, in the proper sense, is now impossible. The tradition-
> al residences we grew up in have grown intolerable: each trait of
> comfort in them is paid for with a betrayal of knowledge, each
> vestige of shelter with the musty pact of family interests. . . . The
> house is past . . . it is part of morality not to be at home in one's
> home.[30]

Adorno's insight, amplified by Said, is that particular economic and
political configurations make the condition of having a home, of landedness, possible. It is "part of morality," then, to recognize how these economic and political systems also exclude others from the condition of
landedness. In the case of Palestine-Israel, this insight can be employed
to suggest that no one, neither Palestinian nor Israeli, can truly be at
home in the land so long as the structures that generate homelessness are
perpetuated.

Adorno, having grasped the impossibility of dwelling securely, given the
knowledge of the conditions that make such dwelling possible, looked to
the text, to literary production, for new dwelling. "In his text, the writer sets
up house. For a man who no longer has a homeland, writing becomes a
place to live." However, text provides only elusive comfort, for "in the end,
the writer is not even allowed to live in his writing."[31] Said developed
Adorno's argument, claiming that the intellectual, in her writing, "achieves
at most a provisional satisfaction, which is quickly ambushed by doubt, and
a need to rewrite and redo that renders the text uninhabitable."[32] A comparison to Yoder proves useful at this point: while doubt and existential

agony drive Said's exilic intellectual to rewrite her text again and again, for Yoder the exilic community—the church—is driven not by doubt but by the workings of the Holy Spirit to engage continually in the theological, missionary task of bringing the gospel into new thought worlds. Lacking any theological horizon, Said could only view the *poeisis* of the text as production and construction, whereas for the church the textual task of revising and renewing its proclamation of the gospel occurs within the framework of *pathos*, of a suffering receptivity to the word of the triune God.[33]

Said did, it turns out, "redeem" exile by stressing its moral possibilities. The exile, because she is not at home in her home, can resist accommodation to the powers, intellectual and political, that exclude and dispossess. Is this critically laudable aspect of exile, however, compatible with a struggle to end the physical condition of exile? Specifically, in the case of Palestinian refugees and other Palestinians who have lost their lands, can one work for *al-awdah* (return) and not lose the moral perspective granted by exile? We are thus returned to our earlier question of whether or not Yoder's exilic politics can speak to a theology of landedness, of justice in the land. To help us answer these questions, I now examine how Said discussed the matter of return.

On the one hand, return was clearly not *only* a metaphorical concept for Said. In a volume of essays examining Palestinian refugee rights and ways to press for return and compensation, Said expressed dismay with what he viewed as the current Palestinian leadership's historical amnesia and willingness to forgo the demand for return. What Palestinians must do, Said urged, is to "press the claims for return and compensation in earnest with new leaders." Said cited as exemplary the work of the Badil Resource Center and the Palestinian researcher Salman Abu Sitta, praising their efforts to develop concrete plans and campaigns for the actual return of refugees.[34]

On the other hand, Said also discussed return in a more metaphorical fashion and warned against establishing an easy symmetry between exile and return that would threaten to undermine the moral insights cultivated in exile. "All of us speak of *awdah*, 'return,'" Said reflected, "but do we mean that literally, or do we mean 'we must restore ourselves to ourselves'? The latter is the real point, I think, although I know of many Palestinians who want their houses and their way of life back, exactly. But is there any place that fits us, together with our accumulated memories and experiences?"[35] Exile, by separating people from place, threatens to tear people from their history, de-centering and disorienting them to the point of threatening their identity. What return would then mean is a "return to oneself, that is to say, a return to history, so that we understand what exactly happened, why it happened, and who we are. That we are a people from that land, maybe not living there, but with important historical claims and roots."[36]

The greatness of Palestinian poet Mahmoud Darwish, according to Said, consists in his refusal in his poems to provide the reader with an easy return, with simple closure. Darwish's work "amounts to an epic effort to transform the lyrics of loss into the indefinitely postponed drama of return. . . . The pathos of exile is in the loss of contact with the solidity and the satisfaction of earth: homecoming is out of the question."[37] A return that forsakes the moral insights of exile, a return that reaches back to retrieve a pristine past without concern for the human cost, must be avoided. The Zionist project of a return to bring closure to Jewish exile stands for Said in marked contrast to the positive dimensions of Palestinian exile. Darwish, Said contended, captures the key dimensions of the exilic experience, dimensions vital to the critical intellectual's task: "Fragments over wholes. Restless nomadic activity over the settlements of held territory. Criticism over resignation. . . . Attention, alertness, focus. To do as others do, but somehow to stand apart. To tell your story in pieces, *as it is*."[38] The openness of exile presents more powerful political and moral possibilities for the intellectual than the closed symmetry of Zionist return. The broken story of Palestinian exile occurs "alongside and intervening in a closed orbit of Jewish exile and a recuperated, much-celebrated patriotism of which Israel is the emblem. Better our wanderings," Said went on to suggest, "than the horrid, clanging shutters of their return. The open secular element, and not the symmetry of redemption."[39]

An Exilic Politics of Land and Return?

Said's positive appropriation of exile as a critical posture provides, I believe, a positive answer to Yoder's question about whether or not Jeremiah's vision for the exilic community might speak by distant analogy to other dispossessed peoples. Pressing questions remain, however. Can Yoder's exilic politics of the church as the nonviolent body of Christ in diaspora speak to the call for justice and right living in the land, to the desire, indeed the justice, of people returning to their homes? Gerald Schlabach, in a friendly challenge to Yoder's Jeremian reading of Scripture and church history, provides a helpful reminder of the Deuternomic admonition to live rightly in the land (cf. Deut 6–9).

European-American Christians, particularly those in urban and suburban settings whose livelihoods are not dependent on the cultivation of the land, could be tempted to confuse Jeremiah's vision for life in exile with the rootless virtual reality of much postmodernist thought. Such confusion would be self-deceptive in that it would obscure the ways in which general North American prosperity has been built at the expense and on the land of its original inhabitants, and it would further avoid the desire of many exiled peoples to return to live justly in the land. Schlabach sharply observes that "we do no favor to any dispossessed people if we think of land only in a figurative rather than an earthy sense."[40]

If, however, we do not avoid the challenges of return and justice, can we envision a politics of return, a politics of living rightly in the land, that does not simply replicate injustice and create new exiles in the wake of return? Traditional Zionist discourse about a Jewish return from exile not only depends on a binary opposition between exile and return but also involves the erasure of the indigenous Arab Palestinian presence and the positing of an "empty land" in which the drama of the return from exile might unfold.[41] In practice, this discourse translated into the expulsion of hundreds of thousands of Palestinians from their homes and continues to underwrite Palestinian dispossession today. After surveying the polemic against diaspora in mainstream Zionist thought, I will argue that striving for a future in Palestine-Israel not bound up with the violent uprooting of others paradoxically entails the articulation of *an exilic politics of land and return*. "Christians can live rightly in the 'land' that God gives," Schlabach suggests, "only if they sustain a tension with landedness itself."[42] Part of this tension is not being fully at home in the land so long as others are excluded from the benefits of landedness, with exile allowed to shape understandings of home.

"The binarism of homeland/exile is central to Zionism," according to Laurence Silberstein, who delineates a series of binary oppositions issuing from the root opposition of exile to homeland:

> homeland as a source of security, stability, refuge, nurturing, safety/exile as site of danger, insecurity, instability, threat, anxiety; heimlich/unheimlich; homeland is good/exile is bad; homeland is productive/exile is parasitic; homeland is conducive/exile is not conducive to redemption through labor; homeland is welcoming/exile is hostile; homeland is life-giving/exile is life-threatening; homeland is creative/exile is stultifying; homeland

is nurturing to Jewish national culture/exile is destructive; homeland is unifying/exile is fragmenting.[43]

These binary oppositions present life in exile as an intolerable condition whose only cure can be found in immigration to the homeland. The
Hebrew word for immigration to Israel, *aliyah*, or "ascent," encodes the
negative valuation that Zionism accords life in diaspora. Those who grow
disenchanted with life in Israel, meanwhile, are classified as *yoridim*, or
"those who descend."

Zionism, in most of its traditional forms, thus meant the "negation of
the diaspora" (*shelilat ha-galuth*).[44] "The fulfillment of the Zionist dream,"
Silberstein explains, "depends upon acts of deterritorialization and reterritorialization. . . . Jews and Jewish culture must be deterritorialized from diaspora spaces and reterritorialized in the spaces of the homeland." Silberstein
also perceptively notes that the "reterritorialization" of Jewish immigrants
into Mandate Palestine eventually involved the "deterritorializing and reter-
ritorializing of large numbers of Palestinian Arabs, particularly during the
1948 War."[45] Israeli political theorist Amnon Raz-Krakotzkin argues persua-
sively that the traditional Zionist negation of the diaspora went hand in hand
with a negation of a prior Palestinian presence in the land. "The definition
of Zionist settlement as an expression of 'shelilat hagalut' [negation of dias-
pora] and 'shivat haam' [the return of the nation] to its homeland," Raz-
Krakotzkin contends, "prevented relating to the collective yearnings of the
local Arab population and its perspective. It [also] undoubtedly made it
impossible to turn the fact of this collective's existence into an essential foundation for establishing a new Jewish identity."[46] Raz-Krakotzkin argues that
the Zionist valorization of a "return to history" accepted the Christian and
Enlightenment perception that exilic existence had been an exclusion from
history, an exclusion from grace.[47] The Zionist return to history, sadly, has
mirrored much of the Christian West's violent and exclusivist practice. Raz-
Krakotzkin suggests that "the historical conception of shelilat hagalut, the
emptiness of Jewish time that separates the loss of sovereignty over the land
and its renewed settlement, is completed in a direct way through the image
of the land—the place for the realization and resolution of history—as an
'empty land.'"[48] The distance between conceiving of the land as empty and
actually emptying the land of its indigenous inhabitants proved unfortunately short.

To counter Zionist discourse and practice of dispossession, Raz-
Krakotzkin proposes to recover exile, or *galut*, as a critical concept. Exile
as a concept represents an "absence, the consciousness of being in an

incomplete present, the consciousness of a blemished world." The absence, moreover, involves a lack of justice for Palestinians. To return from exile, then, must mean justice for the dispossessed. To yearn for redemption is to engage in political activity "that values the perspective of the oppressed, the only perspective from which a moral stance can develop."[49] A recovery of exile as a critical concept demands that Israeli Jews incorporate the consciousness of exiled Palestinians into their own longing for return. As Silberstein explicates Raz-Krakotzkin's position, "By identifying with and assuming responsibility for, attending to, and responding to 'the consciousness of the conquered Palestinian,' the Jew recovers the 'principles embodied in the theological concept of galut.'"[50]

A recovery of exile as a critical concept for political theory or for a theology of the people of God seeking *shalom* for all will be critical not only of exclusivist Zionist practice but also of any narrow nationalism, including Palestinian nationalism, that would threaten to exclude others from sharing in God's gift of landed security. In this critique Edward Said would again be an ally. While typically viewed as a champion of Palestinian nationalism, Said did not view Palestinian statehood as an end in itself, but rather as one potential way for bringing landed security to all in Palestine-Israel. In his later years, in fact, Said became increasingly critical of political arrangements in Palestine-Israel based on separation. "The idea of separation is an idea that I'm just sort of terminally opposed to," Said explained, "just as I'm opposed to most forms of nationalism, just as I'm opposed to secession, to isolation, to separatism of one sort or another."[51] Politics of separation too easily becomes a politics of apartheid, with one group enjoying benefits and privileges denied to the other.[52] As an alternative to the politics of separation, Said offered the model of the binational state in all of Mandate Palestine, a state in which Jews and Palestinians live as equal citizens. In a fascinating interview with Ari Shavit of the Israeli newspaper Ha'aretz, Said connected his appropriation of Adorno's critique of home with his support for a binational state. "Adorno says that in the twentieth century the idea of home has been superseded," Said began.

> I suppose part of my critique of Zionism is that it attaches too much importance to home. Saying, we need a home. And we'll do anything to get a home, even if it means making others homeless. Why do you think I'm so interested in the binational state? Because I want a rich fabric of some sort, which no one can fully comprehend, and no one can fully own. I never understood the idea of this is my place, and you are out. I do not

appreciate going back to the origin, to the pure. Even if I were a Jew, I'd fight against it. And it won't last. Take it from me, Ari. Take my word for it. I'm older than you. It won't even be remembered.

Shavit replied to Said, "You sound very Jewish," to which Said playfully and somewhat provocatively responded, "Of course. I'm the last Jewish intellectual. . . . The only true follower of Adorno. Let me put it this way: I'm a Jewish-Palestinian."[53]

Said and Raz-Krakotzkin both articulate in similar ways an exilic politics of land and return, a politics embracing the challenge of living rightly in the land while nonviolently struggling for a return to the land by the dispossessed, yet maintaining an enduring tension with landedness. The late Palestinian-Israeli writer Emile Habiby summed up the necessary tensions of an exilic politics of land when he spoke of a "freedom of longing for the land within the land."[54] This "longing for the land within the land," suggests Raz-Krakotzkin, can be "a new starting point of all who dwell in the land, a basis for their partnership."[55]

John Howard Yoder, focused as he was on the church's calling to embody a nonviolent politics amidst the Babylons of the world, was wary of attempts to theorize the shape of the ideal state, deeming such efforts as surreptitiously Constantinian attempts to identify the state rather than the church as the primary bearer of the gospel of reconciliation, renewal, and redemption.[56] Yoder probably would have been skeptical of the enthusiasm with which Said promoted the binational state. That said, Yoder did not shy away from ad hoc engagements with the state, encouraging Christians to target particular abuses rather than offering up grand political schemes. Moreover, Yoder's understanding of the people of God as a political body living nonviolently amidst empires while seeking their peace and welfare is compatible with the exilic politics of land and return articulated by Raz-Krakotzkin and Said, even as it also operates within an eschatological horizon, a horizon that animates Yoder's vision with more reasons for hope than can be provided by the secular proponents of an exilic politics like Said and Raz-Krakotzkin.

Christians, together with others, must embrace the challenge of living rightly in the land: this can include calling for just distribution of land and working nonviolently for landed security for refugees. However, part of living rightly in the land will mean living lightly. Christians, as citizens of the heavenly city on pilgrimage in the Babylons of the world, will not use violence to establish justice in the land or to bring about a return to the land. Rather than pursue the sovereignty of the sword, they will pray unceasingly and work nonviolently, impelled by a "longing for the land within the land," for the day when all of God's children will dwell securely within the land God so graciously gives.

3

Zionism, Separation, and Diaspora Consciousness in the Land

How should Christians evaluate the Zionist vision and project of establishing a Jewish state, however understood, in Palestine? Some Christians, like those committed to a premillennial dispensationalist reading of Scripture, warmly embrace Zionism, convinced that the ingathering of the Jewish people into the new State of Israel represents a key moment in the run-up to Jesus' triumphant return. Other Christians, in contrast, have been wary about attributing theological significance to Zionism or have even been sharply critical. As noted in the first chapter, John Howard Yoder conceptualized Zionism as a Jewish counterpart to the Constantinian temptation besetting the church, viewing it as a retreat from the Jeremian vision of the people of God seeking the peace of the cities of its exile. In the previous chapter, I asked if Yoder's exilic theology offered an adequate theology of land and return for dispossessed refugees, concluding that one can build on Yoder's work in order to articulate an exilic consciousness within the land, an unsettling and unsettled form of landedness and return. In this chapter, I turn more explicitly to the question of how a theology in exile can speak to the question of Zionism.

Displacing the Land? Critiques of Yoder's Exilic Politics

Both Zionism and Constantinianism, according to Yoder, abandon the mission of seeking the city's peace through life as a creative, nonviolent minority that knows that it is "not in charge," choosing instead to take charge of, and responsibility for, history, using violent force if necessary to establish security and peace.[1] Peter Ochs and Michael Cartwright, while not defending every manifestation of Zionist ideology and practice, believe that Yoder's critique of Zionism left him unable to articulate a positive theological vision for care of and responsibility for "the land of Israel." Cartwright faults Yoder for breaking the triad of Torah, land, and people, arguing that "Yoder's conception of Judaism displaces land and/or Zion in the course of accentuating the possibilities for a *diaspora* peoplehood."[2] Yoder's framework, Cartwright contends, precludes the possibility of a middle ground "between an ancient foreshadowing of modern nationalist sovereignty" in *eretz yisrael* and "Israel's forced separation from it in this world."[3] According to Cartwright, this dichotomized opposition between the Davidic project on the one hand and the Mosaic or Jeremian projects on the other means that for Yoder "*any attempt* to include responsibility for the land of Israel" must be decried as a form of Constantinianism.[4] Yoder thus "effectively disengages from the deeply rooted complex of Jewish theological claims that see the land of *eretz yisrael* as the locus of the sacred and thereby displaces the theological unity of election, covenant, and God's promise of redemption from exile."[5]

Ochs concurs with Cartwright's assessment, insisting that Jews bear a particular responsibility for the land, a responsibility for which Yoder's exilic politics fails to account. Jews, Ochs contends, would not "expect the radical reformers to bear the same responsibilities for landedness that Jews bear, just as much as they would not expect most Jews to bear the same responsibility for pacifism that the radical reforms bear."[6] From Ochs's perspective, Yoder's work—along with that of the early-twentieth-century German Jewish playwright Stephan Zweig, whom Yoder approvingly cited—tends "to avoid the embarrassment, burden and unreasonable complexity of Israel's landedness." Yoder, Ochs believes, did not see a middle ground "between an ancient foreshadowing of modern nationalist sovereignty in [the land of Israel] and Israel's forced separation from it in this world."[7] Ochs agrees that if "political Zionism as it is embodied in the conservative elements of Israel's Jewish government" were "the only form of landedness, then we would have reason to be sympathetic to both Zweig's and Yoder's efforts to prophesy against it." But, Ochs asks, might there not be other forms of "Israel's landedness"?[8]

Dabru Emet and the Ambiguities of the Jewish State

What positive vision of Israel's landedness would Ochs and Cartwright then champion? While they do not provide an explicit answer in their commentaries on Yoder's work, one can piece together part of what their answer might be from the landmark statement in Jewish-Christian relations, *Dabru Emet* (Speak the Truth), which Ochs co-authored together with Michael Signer, David Novak, and Tikva Frymer-Kensky.[9] A brief yet fecund treatise signed by hundreds more Jewish leaders and rightly welcomed by many Christians as opening a new era in Christian-Jewish conversation about what it means to be the people of God together, *Dabru Emet* responds not only to Christian confessions of sins of omission and commission against Jews and Judaism but also to Christian theological efforts to revise and repudiate traditional teachings of contempt for Judaism while affirming the abiding character of God's covenant with the Jewish people. In light of these "dramatic and unprecedented" developments, the authors ask, what may Judaism say about Christianity?

The authors identify eight affirmations Jews can make about Christianity, including that "Jews and Christians worship the same God" and that "Jews and Christians must work together for peace." Some Jewish critics of the document felt that it gave too much theological legitimacy to Christianity, while others feared that it too readily dissociated Christianity from Nazism. Many Jews, however, welcomed the statement, and it was appropriately received by Christians as a theological gift. My focus here, however, is not on the full riches of this document, a statement rightly hailed as representing a positive way forward in Jewish-Christian relations. Rather, I will look solely at *Dabru Emet's* third section, an affirmation of Christian respect for the Jewish claim on *eretz yisrael*. This passage, I believe, is particularly instructive for the present discussion of what is meant by a theological embrace of Israel's landedness. It reads:

> **Christians can respect the claim of the Jewish people upon the land of Israel.** The most important event for Jews since the Holocaust has been the reestablishment of a Jewish state in the Promised Land. As members of a biblically based religion, Christians appreciate that Israel was promised—and given—to Jews as the physical center of the covenant between them and God. Many Christians support the State of Israel for reasons far more profound than mere politics. As Jews, we applaud this support. We also recognize that Jewish tradition mandates justice for all non-Jews who reside in a Jewish state.[10]

Championing Israel's landedness or preserving the Torah-people-land triad, one deduces from this paragraph, thus means supporting, for "reasons far more profound than mere politics," a Jewish state, albeit one that practices "justice for all non-Jews."

David Burrell has correctly described this section as the statement's "one discordant note," arguing that its "keywords" are all "fatally ambiguous."[11] The ambiguities concerning the land in *Dabru Emet*, I contend, are the same ambiguities one finds in Ochs and Cartwright's call for a positive vision of Israel's landedness or for a preservation of the triad of Torah, land, and people. Specifically, the ambiguities reside in the definition of Jewish state. If Zionism is understood as a project to establish a Jewish state, then understanding these ambiguities is essential to understanding tensions within Zionism.

Zionism and the Politics of Separation

What does *Dabru Emet* mean when it speaks of a Jewish state? This key term is simply left undefined: it is left unclear as to whether it means a state the majority of whose citizens are Jewish, a state somehow infused with Jewish values, or a state that upholds, protects, or otherwise supports Jewish religious law. If the term Jewish state is opaque in *Dabru Emet*, it has at least one transparent meaning in contemporary Israeli politics, namely, the creation and preservation of demographic hegemony within a circumscribed territory. Oren Yiftachel has called this political regime an "ethnocracy," a regime that "facilitates and promotes" a process of the "expansion and control" of a dominant nation over contested territory and resources.[12]

Snapshots of Israeli political discourse of the left as well as the right suggest the separationist focus of this ethnocratic polity. Take, for example, the blunt election slogan of Ehud Barak, the former Labor Party leader, in his successful bid to be Israel's prime minister in 1999: "Us here, them there." Barak raised this same banner during subsequent peace negotiations with the Palestinians. Barak's failure in his re-election campaign against Ariel Sharon should not be interpreted as the defeat of these separationist policies. They continued in the form of Sharon's unilateral separation, or disengagement plan, which, when Sharon lapsed into a coma, morphed into Ehud Olmert's convergence plan.

Regardless of the policy name or the political party in power, the strategic goal of this separationist policy has been fundamentally the same, a goal summed up by Olmert in 2003 when he served as deputy prime minister as "Maximum Jews, minimum Arabs."[13] This demographic imperative has a territorial corollary: seize as much land and as many aquifers as possible while absorbing a minimal number of Palestinians. These strategic demographic and territorial goals give birth to a policy of *hafrada* (separation). Israel's concrete walls and electrified fences, its networks of checkpoints, its roadblocks, its expanding settlement regime and connecting settlement roads—all separate Palestinian from Israeli, while also severing Palestinians from each other and from land and natural resources, leaving them circumscribed by what historian Rashid Khalidi has aptly termed an "iron cage."[14]

Israel's separationist policies, it should be clear, are not attempts to resolve the Palestinian-Israeli conflict: they are about managing it. In 2004 Dov Weisglass, top aide to then-Prime Minister Sharon, stated bluntly that the "disengagement" plan was a way to put the peace process in "formaldehyde."[15] Nor, one might add, are Israel's current practices of separation particularly new. Indeed, one could argue that they are integral to any Zionist project in which Zionism is understood in nation-statist terms, that is, in exclusivist terms linking demographic concerns and territorial control: space must be created, borders must be drawn in which one national group will have hegemony over resources—moves that spell dispossession, expulsion, and at times death for others.[16]

Jewish State/Binational State?

Is the ethnocratic regime just described what *Dabru Emet* has in mind when it speaks approvingly of Christian affirmation of a Jewish state? Presumably not, for the statement stresses the importance of "justice for all non-Jews in a Jewish state," and the separationist practices of the Israeli state, bound up with Palestinian dispossession, are difficult-to-impossible to square with the demands of justice. If not, however, then one is left with the question of what *is* meant by Jewish state. One can re-focus this question, I suggest, by asking if the Jewish state affirmed by *Dabru Emet* might be compatible with a future of one binational state in all of the land of Palestine-Israel, a country in which Palestinians and Israelis would live in mutuality and equality. Could the positive vision of Israel's landedness that Ochs wishes to champion be a binational one? If not, why not?

These questions are not idle hypotheticals. The irony of the present-day manifestation of the Zionist project of separation is that even as its walls and fences sever, they also bind Palestinians and Israelis together as they erase the territorial basis for a two-state solution based on the 1949 Armistice Line (the so-called Green Line). If the wall has been marketed as a security measure, its appeal to the center-right and the center-left in Israeli policy circles has in large measure been the promise of controlling the demographic threat posed by Palestinians, with its attendant danger of a gradual creep toward a binational reality. However, by building a barrier leaving Palestinians in discontiguous, land-locked islands doomed to economic stagnation, Israel unwittingly brings a binational future closer. As Meron Benvenisti, former deputy mayor of Jerusalem, observes, a binational state is not a nightmare of the future; it is the current reality, with one sovereign state, Israel, ruling over all the land between the Jordan River and the Mediterranean Sea, a state in which over 3.5 million Palestinians are denied basic rights of citizenship, whose mobility is tightly constrained, and whose economic future is bleak.[17]

A binational reality founded on the walls and fences of a separationist ideology will not, of course, be stable. It will not ultimately bring security to Israelis (and it certainly brings insecurity to Palestinians). It will not provide a basis for resolving the conflict. A juncture has been reached, I would therefore suggest, where a shift in perspective becomes necessary. What if, one might ask, the possibility of a binational future was viewed, not as a horrific prospect to avoid at all costs or a fate to which Palestinians and Israelis have been doomed, but rather as an opportunity for rapprochement? What if the best way to secure Israel's landedness and to preserve the triad of Torah, people, and land was not through policies and practices of separation but rather through some type of binational framework?[18]

Diaspora Consciousness in the Land

The work of Daniel Boyarin will, I believe, prove to be an invaluable resource in helping make this shift in perspective. Boyarin's notion of "diasporized states" points away from nation-statist projects with their obsessions with demographic control and border policing and toward "a notion of identity in which there are only slaves but no masters." This diasporized state is a political model in which one's identity is shaped through one's opening to and encounter with the other, one that is a decisive "alternative to the model of self-determination, which is, after all, in itself a western, imperialist imposition on the rest of the world."[19] Furthermore, Boyarin's work helps us better understand that Yoder's proposed Jeremian politics is a way of living faithfully in the land, not, as his critics suggest, a way of abdicating responsibility for landed existence. While Ochs suggests that a model of Israel's landedness not reducible to "a very modernist notion of national-political-ethnic sovereignty" is possible, it is Boyarin, with his politics of diaspora, who points the way toward a binational future of mutuality and interdependence that transcends modernist nationalisms. Boyarin's work helps us to see that a diaspora politics is not about a flight from the land, but is instead about articulating a concrete way of living faithfully in the land, a way not captive to exclusivist ideologies of separation.

Boyarin is concerned with reading the biblical narrative in ways that undermine triumphalist appropriations of Scripture and that subvert readings of Israel's history that underwrite ideologies and practices of dispossession. Boyarin highlights how Scripture places a question mark over narratives of conquest: "The stories of Israel's conquest of the land, whether under Abraham, Joshua or even more prominently, David, are always stories that are more compromised with a sense of failure of mission than they are imbued with the accomplishment of mission."[20] Boyarin understands dominant forms of Zionism as relinquishing key elements of Jewish practice and identity. The mainstream forms of Zionism, with their "negation of the diaspora," their rejection of the "feminized" Jew of the diaspora in favor of the new "masculine" pioneer of the *yishuv*, represent "a cultural capitulation that does not honor Jewish difference."[21]

Boyarin, therefore, wants to uncouple Judaism from Zionism understood in nation-statist terms. Now, Cartwright and Ochs might well wish to accuse Boyarin of falling prey to the mistake of which they accused Yoder, namely, breaking the triad of Torah-people-land. Boyarin, after all, claims that while "ethnicity and religion are inseparable in Judaism," there is no "necessary connection between ethnicity, religion and territoriality."[22] One reading of Boyarin would have him maintaining only an eschatological/relativizing function for the promise of land: the mistake of Zionism, in this reading, is that it seeks to force into the present what traditionally has functioned as a future hope. "Diasporic Jewish identity has been founded on common memory of shared space and on the hope for such a shared space in an infinitely deferred future," Boyarin observes. "The tragedy of Zionism," he continues, "has been its desperate . . . attempt to reduce real threats to Jews and Jewishness by concretizing in the present what has been a utopian symbol for the future."[23]

Note, however, that just as Boyarin seems to uncouple Judaism from land, or to leave the promise of the land solely as a "utopian symbol for the future," he proceeds to point to ways in which land might be re-integrated into Jewish self-understanding. A people, he notes, "can be on their land without this landedness being expressed in the form of a nation-state, and landedness can be shared in the same place with others who feel equally attached to the same land!"[24]

This suggestive passage indicates that for Boyarin diaspora and land are not two categories to be thought of in opposition to one another. We should be clear that for Boyarin diaspora does not translate into total estrangement from *eretz yisrael* or from any other particular lands. Diaspora as a political-theoretical category allows Boyarin to name an alternative form of politics that poses a decisive challenge to politics both of nationalist sovereignty and of indigenousness.

Boyarin develops this understanding of diaspora as a *political* vision in his book, *Powers of Diaspora*, co-authored with his brother, Jonathan. The Boyarins propose taking "diaspora provisionally as a 'normal' situation rather than a negative symptom of disorder."[25] This means countering Christendom and Zionist historiographies that equate "history" with state control and that view Jewish life in diaspora as somehow "ahistorical."[26] By privileging diaspora as a political category, the Boyarins embrace "a dissociation of ethnicities and political hegemonies."[27] Diaspora functions as an alternative to "territorialist nation-statism," to "a global and universal logic" that "seeks to fix ethnically (genealogically and culturally) homogeneous groups within nonoverlapping, neatly bounded, and permanent boundaries."[28] As Daniel observes in *A Radical Jew*, it also undercuts "the uncritical valorization of indigenousness (and particularly the confusion between political indigeneity and mystified autochthony)." These political lessons of diaspora are first learned from Scripture: "The biblical story is not one of autochthony but one of always already coming from somewhere else. . . . Israelite and Jewish religion is perpetually an *unsettlement* of the very notion of autochthony."[29]

To counter the separationist projects of nationalisms in their various forms, be they settler-colonial nationalisms or indigenous nationalisms, Boyarin proposes what he calls the "diasporized" state, an important supplement to Yoder's treatment of diaspora.[30] As discussed above, Cartwright and Ochs both accuse Yoder of failing to propose a third way between exile from the land and nationalist sovereignty in the land. The notion of a diasporized state—what we might call a diaspora or exilic consciousness within the land, one in which sharing the land with others is a normal state of affairs—is a signpost toward this third way. Yoder himself, I believe, makes some gestures in this direction when he insists that "those peoples are qualified to work at the building of the city who build it for others, who recognize it not as their own turf but God's," and when he asserts that claims to possession should be judged on whom they exclude or expel.[31]

What would this diasporized state mean for Palestinians and Israelis? What does it mean for an appraisal of Zionism? This vision would certainly stand in opposition to Zionist projects built on separation and tied to shoring up demographic control behind tightly circumscribed borders. Instead, it would champion a vision of an "Israel in which individual and collective cultural rights would become an essential part of its structure, no longer coded as a Jewish State, but as a binational, secular, and multicultural one."[32] One should also hasten to note that the politics of a diasporized state would undercut not only separationist forms of Zionism but also any other nationalisms, including Palestinian nationalism, understood as projects making simple equations between demography and territory, and aimed at establishing hegemonic control over state mechanisms. In the current context, however, in which Israel controls all of Palestine-Israel from the river to the sea, a move toward a diasporized reality will require a "renunciation of near-exclusive Jewish hegemony,"[33] for "only conditions in which power is shared between religions and ethnicities will allow for difference within common caring."[34]

In the introduction to *Border Lines*, Boyarin asks poignantly: "If we are for ourselves alone, what are we?"[35] Boyarin addresses this question to fellow Jews, but it is a question that Christians can and should address to other Christians, Palestinians to other Palestinians, etc. Boyarin's understanding of diaspora as an alternative form of politics helps us to affirm the particularity of difference while also affirming that identity is not self-enclosed but constituted through encounter with others. The shared life of two peoples, the reconciliation of two peoples, does not mean the erasure of difference between the two. Peace is not about homogenizing or obliterating difference, but rather about breaking down dividing walls of hostility and about the formation of bridges and bonds between those who remain different.

At a time when levels of mistrust and hostility between Israelis and Palestinians are perhaps higher than ever before, it might seem naïve or utopian to offer a vision of a binational future as an opportunity for reconciliation based on justice and mutual recognition. I would nevertheless suggest that a point has been reached where utopia and realism converge, for the alternatives to a binational future of equality and mutual concern are grim indeed. With a two-state solution based on the 1949 Armistice Line (the Green Line) overtaken by facts on the ground, one is left with either an indefinite continuation of the current distorted binational reality founded on a discriminatory, separationist ideology, or an embrace of the ideologies of expulsion. The hope for a future of justice, peace, and reconciliation in the context of a binational state might seem like a frail hope, but it is, I believe, a hope that Palestinians and Israelis alike will, over the coming years, find increasingly realistic and attractive.

For those who nurture this frail hope, the recovery of non-separationist, pre-1948 forms of Zionism will be essential, with the work of such visionary proponents of binationalism as Martin Buber and Hannah Arendt gaining renewed importance.[36] Ideologies of separation have failed to bring security to Israelis or Palestinians, and they have certainly failed to establish justice or secure peace. Fostering a diaspora consciousness within the land, contrary to the worries of Ochs and Cartwright, will prove essential for assuming faithful responsibility for the land and will thus be vital in the slow, painful move away from a politics of separation and hostility toward a politics of mutual dependence and care.

Witness

4

Missionary Christology as Subversive Proclamation
Creedal Orthodoxy and Diaspora Witness

The church in diaspora is a church in mission. Jesus sends the church out into the world to "make disciples of all nations, baptizing them in the name of the Father and of the Son and of the Holy Spirit" (Matt 28:19). Exile is the *site* of mission, the name for the innumerable places to which the church is sent by her Lord. However, a peculiar thing happens as the church embarks on this exilic mission. As Christians in mission learn new languages, become immersed in new thought worlds, we discover that the Spirit of the God incarnate in Jesus has preceded us. While we thought we were going out to share information about Jesus with others, we gradually realize, as we seek to confess our faith in Jesus in ever-new situations, that we do not possess or control our proclamation of Jesus but that our prior expectations and certainties about Jesus' identity are subverted. The church in exile is "not in charge" politically, but even more so, it is not in charge theologically: exile is thus not only the *site* of mission but also a *style* of mission.

Countless churches, to be sure, have undertaken mission in the exact *opposite* of a not-in-charge style. When the church has been wedded to or has colluded with imperial or colonialist designs or with the hegemonic or expansionist projects of the nation-state, it has sought to take charge of mission, to impart information about Jesus to targets of evangelization, rather than being open to encountering and being judged and transformed by the risen Christ within the cities, the languages, and the philosophies of its exile.

The faithful church in exile—as opposed to the triumphalist church that seeks to turn exile into a permanent homeland—is sustained by a missionary christology, by a confession of Christ's lordship that calls the proclaiming church itself into question. It is within the context of the church's mission that we should evaluate John Howard Yoder's relationship to the ecumenical creeds of Nicaea and Chalcedon. Some believers church theologians, like J. Denny Weaver, have sought to enlist Yoder in their critique of the creeds, which they view as inadequate for sustaining Christian discipleship.[1] Others, in contrast, like A. James Reimer, accuse Yoder of having succumbed to historicist assumptions and use Yoder as a foil against which to define their own defense of the creeds.[2] Still others, like Craig Carter, have claimed Yoder as a defender of creedal orthodoxy.[3] What has not been adequately appreciated in these debates about how best to exegete Yoder is the missionary concern that animated Yoder's christological reflections.

Yoder in many ways can be appropriately described as a missionary theologian.[4] It should come as no surprise, then, that throughout the anthology of Yoder's ad hoc christological reflections, be they from his major works like *The Politics of Jesus* or from articles in obscure journals and his memoranda to colleagues, one can discern a consistent theological pattern, a pattern that can aptly be called "missionary."[5] This mapping of Yoder's distinctive missionary christology is not primarily an exercise in rescuing Yoder's theology from superficial misreadings. Rather, understanding Yoder's approach to the creeds is important because it illuminates the interrelationship between christology and the shape of the church's diaspora witness.

The Functional Validity of the Creeds

Yoder followed a two-pronged strategy of appealing to Nicaea and Chalcedon in ecumenical conversations while simultaneously relativizing the centrality of those creeds for the mission of the church. If Yoder did not assume the a priori bindingness of the creeds, he did freely reason from the creeds in the context of ecumenical conversations over pacifism and Jesus' normativity for ethics. At the same time, however, he relativized the significance of the creeds by highlighting their cultural specificity and by arguing that a missionary theology might appropriately reformulate christological definitions as the faith entered new cultural contexts.[6] Yet even as Yoder relativized the centrality of the orthodox creeds, he also insisted that any christology confessing Jesus as normative for discipleship would have to struggle with the same type of questions as did the creeds and would necessarily be a "high" christology, a christology that confesses Jesus' unity with God's being and work in the universe. The New Testament, Yoder contended, provides several examples of a missionary faith invading and transforming new cosmological worldviews with the confession of the Jewish Jesus as Lord. Yoder's own presentation of the politics of Jesus, moreover, consisted of a missionary attempt to make the gospel comprehensible to a world guided by historicist assumptions, while at the same time subverting historicism by identifying Jesus with the God of the creation and the apocalypse.

Seeking to convince his theological interlocutors for whom the creeds were fundamental touchstones that creedal orthodoxy implicitly demands Jesus' normativity for ethics, Yoder reasoned from the creeds to show that a theological ethics that understands Jesus' life and teachings as definitive of what it means to live a human life will be "more radically Nicene and Chalcedonian than other views."[7] To deny Jesus' normativity in the ethical sphere was to veer off into one of two heretical directions. If Jesus "is a man but not normative," Yoder demanded, "is this not the ancient ebionitic heresy?" If, however, "he be somehow authoritative but not in his humanness, is this not a new gnosticism?"[8] While Yoder understood that the creeds pass over Jesus' life, teaching, and ministry, leaving a potentially problematic gap between Jesus' birth and death, he also recognized the surplus of meaning within the creeds. While many Christians, wittingly or unwittingly, have taken the gap within the creeds as grounds for dismissing the normativity of Jesus' life and ministry for Christian discipleship, nothing prevents contemporary theologians from reasoning from the creedal identification of Jesus as true man and true God that such normativity logically proceeds from creedal affirmations.

What Nicaea and Chalcedon properly affirmed in the postbiblical era, and what New Testament material such as John's logos christology proclaimed before that, was the identity of Jesus and God. This identity extended beyond the formal affirmation of the full humanity and full divinity of Jesus to an identity of God with the *shape* that Jesus' humanity took. "His humanity matters not only as how he came to us—the clothing he had to wear to get to us. The revelation of the obedience that God wants of us also matters."[9] Through his kenotic way of life, Jesus discloses the being of God. Yoder's commentary on John's gospel explains the nature of the identity of God and Jesus:

> The eternal WORD condescending to put himself at our mercy,
> the creative power behind the universe emptying itself, pouring

itself into the frail mold of humanity, has the same shape as Jesus. God has the same shape as Jesus, and he always has had. The cross is what creation is all about. What Jesus did was local, of course, because that is how serious and real our history is to God. But what the cross was locally is universally and always the divine nature.[10]

The creedal defense of God's incarnation in Jesus should not be viewed as a divine seal of approval of human nature as it stands. Rather, the incarnation meant that "God broke through the borders of our standard definition of what is human, and gave a new, formative definition in Jesus."[11] Yoder did not dismiss the creedal effort to establish an identity of substance between the Father and the Son, granting that the use of Greek metaphysical categories could be viewed as an attempt to safeguard the normativity of God's revelation in Jesus. "The functional validity of the *homoousios*," Yoder contended, "is that it may be understood as a way to affirm Jesus' normativeness in the face of assumptions which claim normative autonomy for contrary understandings of 'nature' and 'reason.'"[12]

Even while granting the potential validity of creedal formulations of Jesus' consubstantiality with the Father along with attendant claims of Christ's preexistence, Yoder was concerned that "Christ" should never become an airy abstraction. He insisted that "any 'larger' claims for Christ as pre-existent, as creator or cosmic victor, must not be disengaged from the man Jesus and his cross."[13] Throughout his career, Yoder stressed that Christians must not separate Jesus from the context of first-century Judaism in Palestine. The identification of the man from Nazareth with the preexistent logos, or with the second person of the Trinity, must not come at the expense of his Jewishness. "If we recognize that *christos* means *meschiach*," Yoder argued, "we can never untie our thought, or our life, from the Jewishness of those first-century events which we celebrate as Easter and Pentecost, which made people apply the titles of *meschiach* and *kyrios* to a rebel rabbi whom the Sanhedrin had hounded and the Romans had killed."[14]

True, the *form* of the creeds drained narrative content from the *homoousios*, with the attendant risk that the ethical and political character of the incarnation might be driven into the background. However, if the form of the creeds moved "farther and farther away from the Gospel story," this did not mean that the creeds did not in fact defend "a biblical concern in non-biblical language."[15] An emphasis on Jesus' Jewishness is thus not incompatible with a simultaneous affirmation of Christ as preexistent, as active in creation. The ethical and political character of Jesus' ministry as a first-century Jew thus need not be played off against ontological affirmations of the identity of Jesus with the second person of the Trinity. Rather, the ontological affirmations of Jesus' divinity gain substance through a consideration of Jesus' historical mission.

The postbiblical doctrine of the Trinity could thus be affirmed by Yoder so long as it secured the confession of Jesus' lordship and his normativity for ethics. Against theologians like H. Richard Niebuhr, for whom the doctrine of the Trinity relativized the claims of Christ by differentiating between revelation in the Son and the transcendence of the Father, Yoder countered that a properly trinitarian theology does not involve a claim of three different kinds of revelation (which he associated with the Sabellian, or modalist, heresy), but rather helps Christians affirm "that God is most adequately and bindingly known in Jesus."[16] "The point of the doctrine of the Trinity," Yoder explained, "is not to affirm distinctions or even complementary differentiations between Father, Son, and Spirit, but rather to safeguard the unity of these three ways in which we know God. It was not to relativize Jesus or to cut the later church loose from his normativeness."[17]

If one refuses to see the three persons of the Trinity as differing modes of God's self-expression, but rather sees them as persons who interpenetrate one another in divine community, then one will not play off God's transcendence against God's self-incarnation but will rather insist that God's incarnation in Jesus is the key by which to understand God's transcendence. As Arne Rasmusson observes, the doctrine of the Trinity means "that we must talk about God so that God the Creator is none other than God as we meet God in the life and destiny of Jesus Christ and in the continuation of Christ's life through the Spirit in the existence of the church. There is no other God behind this God."[18]

That Jesus provides Christians with the normative key for understanding God's transcendence does not mean, it should be stressed, that the transcendent God is not "mysterious." Christians affirm that Jesus Christ is the full and normative revelation of God's being and purpose. That revelation, however, comes to us as a gift—a gift that is never our possession and that always eludes our attempts to comprehend it fully. God's mystery may not be appealed to in order to relativize the claims of Jesus upon our lives. But since Christ participates in the Creator's transcendence, Christians never have full access to what "Christ" means and are therefore impelled to be open to God's ever new and always surprising activity. Any new insights into Christ, however, must always be tested against the biblical narratives about Jesus.

The Bindingness of the Creeds?

Yoder did not grant the creeds a particularly privileged role in theological construction. Adherence to the principle of *sola scriptura*, Yoder believed, demands that all postbiblical doctrines be subjected to ongoing critical scrutiny. "In what sense," he asked, "are we bound to doctrinal definitions of the fourth century, or the fifth, or the sixteenth? Is it only in the sense that they are useful documents of how the church struggled to keep the centrality straight in the language of their time? Or do we, without thinking, take over . . . the idea that there is a certain amount of postbiblical dogmatic substance that all Christians have to believe?"[19]

A prime example of Yoder's ambivalence about the centrality of the creeds for contemporary Christian identity can be found at the end of his essay "Christ, the Light of the World." Disputing with those who, in their attempts to justify violence, set up "other lights" beside or in opposition to the light of Christ, Yoder stressed that a basic question for Christian ethical and theological reflection was "whether to set up beside the Jesus of the canon and the creeds some other specific sources and content of ethical obligation." Here Yoder appeared to equate unproblematically the Jesus of the canon with the Jesus of the creeds. However, immediately after having seemingly granted the creeds authority, Yoder argued that ecumenical conversation proceeds best with sole reference to the Jesus of the New Testament witness and without an a priori commitment to particular ecclesiastical or creedal heritages.[20] The ambiguity points to a critical question: Are the creeds universally *essential* for a proper reading of the Jesus story, or should they be viewed in a missiological lens as culture-specific attempts to present the claims of Jesus in a Hellenistic context?

At times Yoder left himself open to the charge that he considered the creeds to be *incompatible* with the New Testament. Consider, for example, his contrast of the Hellenistic categories in which Nicene christology was framed with modern and biblical thought forms:

> If we look back at the politics that were played between 325 and 431, at some of the theologians' methods and motives, at the personal quality of Constantine, or if we ask in what sense he was a Christian when he dictated this dogma, then we have to be dubious about giving this movement any authority. If we call into

question the acceptance of Hellenistic thought forms foreign to the way the Bible thinks, which fit neither with the Hebrew mind nor, for that matter, with the modern mind, then again we have to challenge whether the creed does us much good.[21]

This contention exposes an ambiguous, perhaps suspicious, attitude toward the creeds on Yoder's part. However, one must note the reasons for this suspicion. Yoder did not claim that the Nicaea lacked validity because it took shape under Constantine. Nor did he believe that the gospel could not be validly translated into "Hellenistic thought forms." Although an unsympathetic and cursory reading of this one passage apart from the rest of the Yoderian corpus might suggest that Yoder was making precisely both of these claims, in fact, as will be shown below, he explicitly denied them. Suffice it to say for now that the claim that "Hellenistic thought forms are foreign to the way the Bible thinks" is not equivalent to a declaration of biblical and creedal incompatibility: foreignness is not reducible to radical opposition.

A thorough reading of Yoder's writings will show that his suspicion of the creeds centered not on a belief in the fundamental incompatibility of Hebraic and Hellenistic thought forms, but rather on the question of whether or not Greek ontological categories adequately meet the demands of dynamic missionary christology today. If Yoder appealed to creedal formulations in his polemic against those who would relativize Jesus' normativity, he also refused to make Nicene-Chalcedonian categories foundational for contemporary Christian identity. Nicaea and Chalcedon, Yoder granted, "may represent valid enculturation in the face of the intellectual challenges of their own world." But, he continued, "to affirm that is not the same as to make those post-Constantinian formulations the baseline from which to go on to the rest of the world."[22] The creeds should not be granted the same authority as the Bible, nor should they be made the exclusive lens through which Christians interpret Scripture. "The doctrine" of Nicaea "is not supernatural truth, supernaturally communicated for its information value." The creeds are instead valid as culture-specific attempts to proclaim Jesus' lordship in a Hellenistic idiom. They reflect "the serious struggle of people, within their language and their culture, with their commitment to an absolute God and to a normative Jesus."[23] However, Christians need not be bound to creedal formulations as they carry the gospel into new linguistic and philosophical worlds.

Missiological concerns drove Yoder's questioning of the correctness

of upholding christological formulations based on Greek ontological categories as normative for all Christian thought. "Would Islam have taken
on the belligerent shape it did," he asked, "if it had not been for the ease
with which trinitarian language could be interpreted as forsaking monotheism? Might the missionary encounters with the Hindu world, or with
traditional religious cultures, have taken a different shape if the gospel
texts had been the springboard, if the ontological definities [sic] of *physei*
and *ousiae* and *hypostaseis* had not had to be part of the message?" The
gospel, Yoder recognized, will generate a scandal in any missionary situation. He wondered, however, if the particular scandal generated by an
insistence on the *substantial* identity of Jesus and God placed the scandal
in the right place.[24]

While not jettisoning the creedal concept of *homoousios*, Yoder did
argue that the proper way to discuss Jesus' unity with God was in terms
of his motivations and actions. New Testament affirmations of "the unity
of Jesus with the Father" were "not discussed in terms of substance but
of will and deed." Such a unity, which makes visible "Jesus' perfect *obedience* to the *will* of the Father," has ethical and political implications. In
Jesus, "God takes the side of the poor," and in Jesus, God the King
"rejects the sword and the throne, taking up instead the whip of cords and
the cross." If God so acts through Jesus, then "those who would belong
to and obey God" must do likewise.[25] Yoder's questioning of the missiological usefulness of stressing the substantial unity of Jesus with the Father
was not equivalent to a rejection of metaphysics and ontology. For example, as noted above, Yoder claimed that the love that led to the cross
reveals the divine nature. Furthermore, as we will see below, Yoder argued
that Jesus' call is ontologically founded in the transcendent God at work
in the world from creation to apocalypse.

The Pattern of a Missionary Christology

If Yoder de-centered the fourth-century creeds in the context of theological work, insisting on keeping Jesus, and Jesus alone, at the center of
theological reflection, he also emphasized that any Christian theology will
inevitably face questions structurally similar to those addressed in Nicaea-
Chalcedon if it seeks to uphold Jesus' normativity. "The development of
a high Christology," Yoder underscored, "is the natural cultural ricochet
of a missionary ecclesiology when it collides with whatever cosmology
explains and governs the world it invades."[26] That the creeds were the
product of a Hellenistic reading of the biblical text and took shape under

the imperial rule of Constantine did not fatally compromise the creeds as a faithful missionary translation and proclamation of Christ's lordship. Critics of the creeds would be mistaken, Yoder argued, were they:

- to suggest that the missionary invasion of the Hellenistic semantic world, which led to such a translation, could have been or should have been avoided by remaining biblical in semantics or ontology;

- to suggest that developments toward a high Christology had not already begun within the apostolic canon itself, or

- to interpret such developments as intrinsically contradictory to the Jewish message of the first generations.[27]

Yoder thus forthrightly denied that one can unproblematically remain "biblical" in one's vocabulary and that the creeds stood in inherent tension or even contradiction to the biblical narrative. To the contrary, Yoder insisted:

> I am not espousing a permanent ethnocentrism . . . , with Hebraic thought forms always sacred and safe and Greek always pagan. My objection is not to entering the Hellenistic thought world as a cultural arena. Jews had been doing that long before Jesus and Paul. Paul did it again, with no sacrifice of his Jewishness or his faithfulness to Jesus. What is to [be] reject[ed] is the subsequent abandonment of Jewish substance, as the "apologetes" succeeded the apostles and the goal of insight displaced that of obedience.[28]

From Yoder's perspective, apologists like Justin Martyr detached "the message of Jesus from its Jewish matrix" in an attempt to make Christianity philosophically credible.[29] However, this critique of Justin's apologetics did not issue from a sweeping claim that Hellenistic ontological categories necessarily stand in opposition to the Jewishness of Jesus. One can challenge the missionary usefulness of insisting on Nicene-Chalcedonian phraseology in order to speak to the modern world about the unity of Jesus and God. That challenge, however, need not translate into a rejection of the creeds on the grounds that they are supposedly incompatible with "the Jewish message of the first generations."

The New Testament, Yoder recognized, contains several attempts at providing ontological foundations for Jesus' call to discipleship. The canon does not present its readers with one homogeneous cosmology, but rather with a multiplicity of confessions of Christ's lordship within different cosmological frameworks. The writers of Hebrews, Philippians, and Colossians all made similar theological moves—moves that Yoder summarized in a sixfold missionary strategy that he contended any serious theology would adopt.[30]

First, the New Testament authors became at home in the new linguistic world, internalizing its philosophical and cosmological categories. Second, rather than fit Jesus into a ready-made slot in the cosmology, these writers placed Jesus above that worldview. "By confessing that Messiah has been placed by God above and not within the cosmology and culture of the world they invade," Yoder explained, "the messianic Jewish witnesses also affirm that under his lordship that cosmos will find its true coherence and meaning." Christ's lordship over any particular cosmological system involves the subjugation of the transpersonal principalities and powers that order and enslave human existence. Under Christ's rule, "the powers are not merely defeated in their claim to sovereignty and humbled; they are also enlisted in the original creative purpose of the service of mankind and the praise of God."[31] Just as the New Testament writers subordinated their inherited systems to the lordship of Christ, so too should contemporary theologians insist that the Jewish Jesus transcends and reconstitutes contemporary cultural and cosmological visions. For Yoder, this theological strategy was a call for "a renewal of the missionary arrogance (arrogance need not be a pejorative term) that dares to claim that Jesus, proclaimed as Messiah and Kyrios, transcends rather than being transcended by each new cosmos as well."[32]

Third, in Colossians, Hebrews, and Philippians "there is in each case a powerful concentration upon being rejected and suffering human form, beneath the cosmic hierarchy, as that which accredits Christ for this lordship." Fourth, salvation comes to be interpreted time and again as participation in the life of Jesus: "What we are called to enter into is the self-emptying and the death—and only by that path, and by grace, the resurrection—of the Son." Fifth, each of the writers moved to identify Jesus with God. "Behind the cosmic victory, enabling it," these biblical theologians proclaimed "what later confession called preexistence, co-essentiality with the Father, possession of the image of God, and the participation of the Son in creation and providence." Finally, these authors all affirmed that those who believe in the gospel "share by faith" in Jesus' victory over sin and the powers.

The creedal affirmation of the *homoousios*, that God the Father and God the Son are of the same substance, can be understood as following this missionary pattern. The creeds' authors, at home in the Hellenistic linguistic world, molded philosophical categories in new ways so as to proclaim that Jesus transcends and thereby subverts the philosophical cosmology of the Hellenistic world. The creeds, therefore, *need not* be viewed as a shift of focus away from the earthly, Jewish, political Jesus (even given the gap within the creeds between Jesus' birth on the one hand and his death and resurrection on the other), but as an attempt, by identifying the human Jesus with the one God through the concept of the *homoousios*, at securing the normativity of Jesus' humanity for his disciples.[33]

If Christians today find it difficult to affirm the identity of Jesus with God in terms of Greek ontological categories from the fourth century, any serious attempts to proclaim Jesus' normativity will nevertheless have to grapple with how to describe the unity of Jesus and God. Critiques of the creeds for not fleshing out the ethical content of christology should not issue in a low christology in which Jesus becomes merely one light among others.[34] Only a high christology can provide the basis for discipleship to a nonresistant Jesus and an ecclesiology that renounces the violent ways of the world. "A high Christology is a prerequisite for the renewal of a believers' church," Yoder argued:

> Only if Christ is, both formally and materially, more and other than the distillate of the rest of our best wisdom, only if his call is imperative, his message irreducible to other equivalents we already knew about, only such a Christ could call individuals: a Waldo to itinerancy, a Schweitzer to the Gabon, a Bonhoeffer to "come and die." Only such a Christ can gather around him a community with any intelligible reason to differ from its neighbors, and resist rulers, and call others to join them in his train. Only such a Christ has anything to say above the melee of a pluralism in which every sect has equal time and the truth question cannot be put. Only if the call of Jesus is ontologically founded, connected to the arc from creation to apocalypse, can it give us the leverage to challenge our conformity to our own age.[35]

Far from advocating a thoroughgoing historicism (as some of his critics have feared), Yoder thus proclaimed a Jesus whose call is connected to the arc of the transcendent God who created the cosmos and will bring it to its conclusion.[36] Rather than succumbing to the reductionist assumptions of historicism, Yoder subverted historicism from the inside. Jesus' mission was certainly political, his work historical. But this earthly, historical Jesus was then—in an example of the "missionary arrogance" characterizing the New Testament witnesses—proclaimed by Yoder to rupture any historicist cosmology that would reduce Jesus and all of creaturely existence to the unfolding of material and historical processes. Christians know of the cosmos "that Jesus is both the Word (the inner logic of things) and the Lord ('sitting at the right hand')." The cosmos of material, historical processes are circumscribed within God's sovereignty, a sovereignty in which the human Jesus participated. "It is not," explained Yoder, "that we begin with a mechanistic universe and look for cracks and chinks where a little creative freedom might sneak in (for which we would then give God the credit): it is that we confess the deterministic world to be enclosed within, smaller than, the sovereignty of the God of the Resurrection and the Ascension."[37] Precisely because Yoder did not succumb to historicist assumptions but rather proclaimed God's transcendence of the historical process, he could envision a radically disruptive "apocalyptic politics" that embodies a vision of peace in a violent world.[38]

Because the church, as a missionary body, continually enters new cosmological and semantic worlds, christological reformulations should come as no surprise. The challenge for contemporary theologians speaking to a world guided by historicist assumptions will be not only to make Jesus' historical and political mission comprehensible, but furthermore to show how Jesus, "connected to the arc from creation to apocalypse," in fact transcends the historicist story that the heirs of the Enlightenment tell.[39] The writers of the Gospel of John and the epistles to the Hebrews, the Colossians, and the Philippians, as well as the shapers of the ecumenical creeds, can all be seen as searching for ways to proclaim Christ's lordship in different semantic and cosmological contexts. However, a missionary christology cannot rest content on the achievements of the past but must always search for ways to renew the proclamation of Jesus' lordship within new cultural worlds.

As the church in exile goes about its missionary task of proclaiming and receiving the gospel in always changing, always new linguistic and theological worlds, the creeds will certainly have their place. The creeds are part of "a fallible history and a confused history" (in other words, part of human history), Yoder argued. Still, he continued, "the creeds are helpful as fences," in that they help rule out things that should not be said about Jesus. For example, the creeds, in their affirmation of the co-essentiality of the Father and the Son, help rule out any claims which "other lights" might make to human allegiance. While the creeds are useful in this limited sense, Yoder continued, "affirming, believing, debating for, fighting for the creeds is probably something on which a radical Anabaptist kind of faith would not concentrate." However, Yoder concluded, "that gives us even less reason to join . . . in fighting against the Creeds."[40]

Both insisting on and fighting against the creeds are emblematic of the attempt to take theological charge of ecumenical conversations, a spirit of control that theologians of exile renounce. Not being in charge theologically thus means relinquishing the need to set the terms of theological conversation and debate, trusting that, because the call of Jesus is grounded in God's work from the beginning to the end, we will come to know more about God and about what it means to follow Jesus precisely through these conversations that we do not control.

5

The Body Politics of the Church in Exile

If the church is to seek the *shalom* of the *polis*, the city, of its exile, what modes of *political* engagement and action should it undertake? Taking Scripture as our guide, we cannot be content with any answer that reduces this question to a forced decision between participation and non-participation in state structures, electoral politics, or legislative lobbying. Consider Daniel, who together with Hananiah, Mishael, and Azariah served in the Babylonian court of King Nebuchadnezzar but who "would not defile himself with the royal rations of food and wine" (Dan 1:8). Daniel's witness to the God of Israel in Nebuchadnezzar's court does not allow itself to be forced into a static conceptual scheme that reduces the question of political witness to the issue, for example, of whether or not it is permissible for Christians to vote, to hold elective office, and so forth. Rather, it explodes such schemes by highlighting the complex and contingent character of Christian political witness. Daniel and his companions loyally serve the king, who consults with them "in every matter of wisdom and understanding," proving themselves more valuable than the king's magicians and enchanters (1:20). Yet they faithfully adhere to the practices of their faith, refusing to eat forbidden food and to prostrate themselves before an idolatrous image of the king (Dan 3).

Christians concerned about faithful political witness—that is, about appropriately heeding the call to work for the well-being of cities of our exile—learn from the story of Daniel that service to the state, engagement in what the world calls politics, can have a legitimate place. But we also learn that such service is contingent and conditional, and that the greatest service the church can give to the cities of its exile is to maintain the integrity of its practices, practices that sometimes bring it into conflict with those cities.

More insistently and with greater nuance than any other twentieth-century theologian, John Howard Yoder insisted on the *political* character of Christian practices, articulating how through those practices the church lives as a *polis* that embodies a missionary counter-example to the violent politics of the nation-state. However, even as he delineated the "body politics" of the witnessing church, Yoder, pushing beyond previous Mennonite attitudes, also provided theological justification for ad hoc Christian engagement with the state, including participation in nonviolent actions such as demonstrations and sit-ins as well as limited involvement in electoral and legislative politics.[1] Grasping the nuances of Yoder's understanding of the complex character of Christian witness will, I believe, be indispensable for Christians reflecting on how to meet the challenge of striving for the peace of the cities of our exile, be they Baghdad or Washington, Ottawa or Jerusalem.

Ecclesiology as Politics

"Communities that seek to live out alternatives to coercion and violence as the basis of political life can serve as substantive, witnessing counterpoints to the practices they reject," argues political scientist Thomas Heilke, advancing the provocative suggestion that the practices of Anabaptist communities since the sixteenth century offer viable alternatives to the moribund politics of the present age. As an alternative to utilitarian or Hobbesian models of political life, Heilke counsels "exploring the strange but vaguely known worlds of alternative communities in which human wholeness and authentically human action are still held out as possibilities."[2] Fundamental to Yoder's understanding of Christian political witness was his exploration of the "strange but vaguely known" *political* character of Christian practices. The church as a *polis* lives and worships as a community whose practices analogically anticipate the kingdom of God.[3]

The church's primary form of political witness, for Yoder, is its embodiment of a new, nonviolent way of life in the world. The task of the church is to live as the "firstfruits" of the kingdom: "The people of God is called to be today what the world is called to be ultimately."[4] Grasping this ecclesiological character of Yoder's politics is crucial for a correct interpretation of Yoder's understanding of Christian political witness, for only then can one locate his advocacy for Christian participation in nonviolent direct action and his granting of limited legitimacy to participation in the functions of the state as ad hoc engagements with the world by a church marked by its own political character.

The body politics of the church's corporate life consists of its modeling new ways of living for the wider society. "The church is herself a society," according to Yoder. "Her very existence, the fraternal relations of her members, their ways of dealing with their differences and their needs are, or rather should be, a demonstration of what love means in social relations."[5] The Hebrew and Greek words translated as church (*qahal* and *ekklesia*) originally referred to political, deliberative assemblies, suggesting that Christians concerned with political witness must first look to the life of the church, since the church "is more truly political, i.e., a truer, more properly ordered community, than is the state."[6] Any notion of the church as "apolitical" must be abandoned. Instead, Christians must ask about what type of politics the church embodies in its corporate life: "The difference between the church and state or between a faithful and an unfaithful church is not that one is political and the other not, but that they are political in different ways."[7]

Yoder identified at least five practices through which the church lives out a disruptive political witness that opens up new political possibilities for the wider society. First, in its insistence on the diversity of ministries, the church undermines hierarchical structures in society (1 Cor 13). Second, the church's practice of mutual admonition serves as a model of accountability for non-church organizations (e.g., Matt 18:15-20). Third, the church's practice of arriving at decisions through "convinced consensus" in an open meeting in which every member has a voice (1 Cor 14), what Yoder called the Rule of Paul, has secular analogies in town hall meetings and managerial and educational styles that place a premium on free deliberation. Fourth, baptism enacts interethnic acceptance that brings down dividing walls of class, race, language, and ethnicity. Finally, in the sharing of bread and wine at communion, the church lives out economic solidarity and support.[8]

Yoder chose the theologically neutral term practices for these functions of the church instead of more tradition-specific words like sacrament or ordinance. However, his understanding of Christian practices had a decidedly sacramental character: the practices are "actions of God, in and with, through and under what men and women do. Where they are happening, the people of God is real in the world."[9] However, these practices are all social processes that can be spoken of in solely nonreligious terms. Thus, according to Yoder,

> The multiplicity of gifts is a model for the empowerment of the humble and the end of hierarchy in social process. Dialogue

under the Holy Spirit is the ground floor of the notion of democracy. Admonition to bind or loose at the point of offense is the foundation for conflict resolution and consciousness-raising. Baptism enacts interethnic social acceptance, and breaking bread celebrates economic solidarity.[10]

The most fundamental way for the church to be political (as well as missionary) is for it to embody a particular way of life structured around central practices that might serve as models for the wider society.

These practices, to be sure, are normative rather than simply descriptive of ecclesial life. Christians *should* share their goods with one another, and this economic solidarity *should* be enacted in communion. The church *should* be a place where ethnic divisions are relativized. All Christians *should* be empowered to claim a particular ministry within the church. That too often in Christian history ministry has been relegated to a professionally trained elite; that churches have mirrored ethnic, racial, and class divisions; that Christians stand guilty of hoarding possessions rather than placing them within the economics of God's jubilee—these realities should be interpreted, not as shortcomings of the practices to which the church is called, but as moral failings demanding repentance, reformation, and renewal. "Any existing church is not only fallible but in fact peccable," Yoder recognized. "That is why there needs to be a constant potential for reformation and in the more dramatic situations a readiness for the reformation even to be 'radical.'"[11]

In addition to serving as a witness to a "watching world," the church, when it is faithful, also actively contributes to the well-being of the surrounding society. At its best, the church has created "experimentally new ways of meeting social needs which, once their utility has been proved, can be institutionalized and generalized under the authority of the secular power"; schools, hospitals, and international relief work are all examples of projects that began in the church, projects in which the state eventually joined.[12] Furthermore, the church contributes to society by the "conscientious participation"—as a counterpart to the conscientious objection to military service—of its members in various professions like teaching, city planning, and nursing, among others.[13]

Body Politics and the Temptation of Constantinianism

If the church was central to Yoder's understanding of Christian political witness, then Constantinianism named for him the perennial temptation and historical failures of the church to embody an alternative to the world's violent politics. Early in his career, Yoder stressed the otherness of the church, a theme to which he would return again and again through his writings. The church must not "assume responsibility for the moral structure of non-Christian society."[14] The temptation to assume such responsibility Yoder labeled Constantinianism, the recurring danger of shifting attention away from the task of building up the particular *polis* of the church in favor of constructing an ideal *polis* at some supposedly wider level.

The danger of Constantinianism arises within Scripture, within the history of God's people. Moments of liberation, such as the exodus, readily collapse into a politics-as-usual, with a genocidal conquest of the land and with God's people clamoring to be like other nations (e.g., 1 Sam 8). To avoid the lure of Constantinian compromise, the church has to keep alive a diaspora consciousness, to be faithful to Jeremiah's call to the exiles to seek the *shalom* of Babylon:

> The message of Jeremiah (chapter 29) demonstrates that for the community that lives in the memory of Exodus, the acceptance of Diaspora existence is not a lesser evil, not resignation where nothing else is possible, but the path of obedience, a safeguard of identity, protection against the "lying dreams" of those who would trouble the exiles with unreal promises of restored national pride. The command to "seek the peace of that city" is not a denial but a definition of the meaning for now of the Exodus and the covenant.[15]

The view from diaspora, Yoder insisted, can sustain the church in the face of a multifaceted Constantinian danger. Constantinianism named a reality much broader than the shift from minority religion to state religion under Emperor Constantine in the fourth century CE, although that shift was in some ways emblematic of the term. In all of its varieties throughout history, two basic elements recur. First, a Constantinian mindset holds that "the true meaning of history, the true locus of salvation, is in the cosmos and not in the church. What God is really doing is being done primarily through the framework of society as a whole and not in the Christian community." Second, Constantinianism assumes "that if we pitch in and help it will be possible as it would not be otherwise to achieve for the world that fullness of salvation that it was already on the way to achieving by itself."[16] These two elements are present wherever and whenever Christians look away from the church to a supposedly wider world for the primary locus of political witness.

The failure of Constantinianism in any of its guises is ultimately a failure of worship. A doxological understanding of history proclaims and confesses that God, not humanity, is in charge of the cosmos and that, through Jesus Christ, God has decisively defeated the powers of sin and death. The church is not ultimately called to manage the affairs of the world, to bend history in the right direction. Rather, as a body that is "not in charge," the church understands that its faithful worship and practice constitute its most profound political witness.

A vital dimension of the church's body politics in exile, according to Yoder, is the *voluntary* character of its witness. For Yoder, the importance of the Anabaptist rejection of infant baptism was at bottom a question of the church's integrity as a voluntary, alternative community, distinct from the rest of society at large. Neo-Constantinian arrangements, like the post-Reformation identification of particular churches with particular territories (*cuius regio, eius religio*), had to be opposed, for it made membership in the church mandatory, compromising the voluntariness of the church.

This emphasis on the voluntariness of the church, however, opened Yoder up to criticism from those who fear that such talk plays into the liberal capitalist privileging of individual choice. Oliver O'Donovan, for example, attacks Yoder's characterization of the church as a *voluntary society*, asking if Yoder, "in the name of non-conformism," was "not championing a great conformism, lining the church up with the sports clubs, friendly societies, colleges, symphony subscription-guilds, political parties and so on, just to prove that the church offers late-modern order no threat?"[17] Yoder's one-time colleague and (for the most part) fellow traveler Stanley Hauerwas tentatively seconds O'Donovan's critique of the language of voluntarism, stressing instead the nonvoluntary character of the church.[18] Furthermore, one could rightly ask if Yoder's repeated insistence on the voluntariness of the exilic church does not run up against the original biblical model of God's people in exile, a people who are first and foremost *chosen* by (rather than *choosing*) God.[19] Is not the church in exile fundamentally sustained by the fact that it is "a chosen race, a royal priesthood, a holy nation, God's own people" (1 Pet 2:9), rather than a voluntary association?

The language of voluntarism can certainly be corrupted into the rhetoric of capitalist consumption. However, these dangers, while ever-present, can be avoided. Yoder, I contend, advanced a nuanced understanding of the voluntary character of the church that escapes the reduction of the church to one consumer option among others. In order to grasp the nuance of

Yoder's approach, consider his insistence, in his essay "The Original Revolution," on "the duty of beginning now, first, with the creation of a new, voluntary, covenanting community in which the rejection of the Old is accredited by the reality of the New which has already begun." The rhetoric of "creating" a new, voluntary community might initially appear to justify O'Donovan's worries about the reduction of the church to the level of other voluntary associations. However, this language is counterbalanced by the latter half of the sentence, where Yoder claimed that the newness of the voluntary community is "accredited by the reality of the New which has already begun." The use of the perfect tense indicates that Yoder viewed the church as not simply the creation of individual agents, but rather as the dawning of that new eschatological order of being inaugurated in Jesus' cross and resurrection. The voluntariness of the church, then, consists of the human response to God's prior work in Christ: "The question for our time," Yoder explained, "in the world which awaits and aspires to revolution, is not whether the kingdom is coming but what we will do about it."[20]

The voluntary character of Christian discipleship correlates, then, not with a low view of the church but with a high view of grace. "To say that the kingdom is at hand, that the new world is on the way," Yoder argued, "is first of all to anchor our thoughts in the priority of grace. Before we can set out toward the New World, it must have—and by God's goodness, it has—come to us. We can only be on our way because of that prior coming. We do not go out to find or to build the kingdom but only to meet it."[21] Grace, then, while not excluding the individual's experience of regeneration, refers primordially to the ontological reality of God's establishment of the kingdom through Jesus Christ, a reality now only dimly perceived but that the church, in voluntary doxological response, partially embodies and anticipates.

Christ and the Powers: The Cosmological Context of Christian Political Witness

Yoder's primary understanding of Christian political witness, then, centered on the church as the embodiment of the "firstfruits" of the kingdom. Given this basic starting point, however, Yoder went on to outline ways in which the church can participate in broader nonviolent movements for social change as well as become involved in a limited fashion in electoral and legislative politics. How Yoder understood such forms of Christian political witness theologically depended on his understanding of the Pauline language of "principalities and powers."

Rather than dismiss Paul's use of such phrases as "principalities and powers" as reflections of an outdated cosmology, Yoder suggested that the biblical language of the "powers" might be grasped by contemporary readers under the term "structure." The concept of structure "functions to point to patterns or regularities that transcend or precede or condition the individual phenomena we can immediately perceive." One could thus perhaps speak of the powers as the "spirits" of different institutions.[22]

Yoder stressed the goodness of the powers as part of God's creation while also emphasizing their fallenness in their rebellion against God. The powers are "part of a good creation," but "they have absolutized themselves, and they demand from the individual and society an unconditional loyalty."[23] Without structures to order human lives, there would be neither history nor society. The powers are thus indispensable parts of God's good creation. As fallen, however, the powers aggrandize themselves, demanding from humans the worship due only to God. Lost amidst the powers, humankind is nevertheless preserved through the powers. The powers thus encode for Yoder "the simultaneous recognition of humankind's fallen condition and the continuing providential control."[24]

If the powers are good creations of God, then human salvation will not consist in the abolition of the powers, but rather in their subjugation. The rebellious self-glorification of the powers is broken through the work of Christ. Jesus was subject to the powers, "but morally he broke their rules by refusing to support them in their self-glorification."[25] Through Jesus' death and resurrection, the powers have been decisively defeated. As the church follows Jesus in discipleship, it participates in that triumph. "The Powers have been defeated," Yoder claimed,

> not by some kind of cosmic hocus-pocus, but by the concreteness of the cross; the impact of the cross upon them is not the working of magical words nor the fulfillment of a legal contract calling for the shedding of innocent blood, but the sovereign presence, within the structures of creaturely orderliness, of Jesus the kingly claimant and of the church who herself is a structure and a power in society.[26]

The defeat of the powers, then, comes not in the form of their abolition, for that would mean the abolition of history and society. Rather, it comes through the embodiment, in concrete historical existence, of an alternative form of power, one that glorifies not itself but God.

While the powers have been defeated in the cross and resurrection,

their rebelliousness continues: only at the eschaton will the triumph of
Christ over the self-glorifying powers be made fully manifest, the world
transformed to live according to the nonviolent power disclosed through
Jesus. In the interim, however, the powers remain a simultaneously indispensable and oppressive part of human existence, even as they are subject to and constrained by Christ's lordship.

The state is thus a created and rebellious power.[27] Beyond this basic
definition, however, Yoder refused to offer a detailed metaphysics or
ontology of the state, arguing that Scripture in general and Romans 13
in particular do not provide an account of what the "good" state does
or does not do. Instead, Paul in Romans was concerned with urging
Christian subordination to the Roman state. Yoder's argument hinged
on a distinction between *institution* and *ordering*. "God is not said to
create or *institute* or *ordain* the powers that be," Yoder explained, "but
only to *order* them, to put them in order, sovereignly to tell them where
they belong, what is their place."[28] The state, then, is "accepted in its
empirical reality, as something that God can overrule toward His
ends," but such acceptance does not imply "any ratification of [the
state's] moral standards or political purposes, or any theory of the
proper state."[29]

Questions regarding the form of the ideal state, Yoder believed, are
not only foreign to Scripture but inappropriate for the Christian: "To ask,
'What is the best form of government?' is itself a Constantinian question.
It is representative of an already 'established' social posture. It assumes
that the paradigmatic person, the model ethical agent, is in a position of
such power . . . that it falls to him to evaluate alternative worlds and to
prefer the one in which he himself . . . shares the rule."[30] Early Christianity
was in no such position, since it did not rule the empire. Romans 13, then,
should not be read as a blueprint for an ideal state, but rather as pastoral
counsel to a church that did not expect to control or shape the actions of
the state.

Yoder resisted the dualistic assumption that God had revealed different norms for the church and for the state. *Both* church and state, according to Yoder, stand under Christ's lordship, and both are ultimately called
to love, although only the church has christologically based reasons for
conforming to God's nonviolent love. Establishing such a dualism, Yoder
argued, "implicitly denies both missionary and ecumenical concern, since
in effect 'Christ is Lord for us but not for them.'"[31]

If one cannot construct a theory of the ideal state from a Christian perspective, one can ask to what ends God bends the state. In an early article, Yoder asserted that God uses the state to maintain the order needed for the church to live as a witness to a new form of social relations: "In the order of conservation, He uses the violent state to punish evil with evil to preserve a degree of order in society and leave room for His higher working in the order of redemption, through nonresistant self-giving love in Christians."[32] That God so bends the state to divine ends does not mean that God has revealed an independent morality for the state, nor does it give divine sanction to Christian participation in wielding the sword. While the state subordinated to Christ's lordship may use force for the purpose of maintaining order within society, "the state never has a blanket authorization to use violence. . . . Only the absolute minimum of violence is therefore in any way excusable."[33]

The Politics of Nonviolent Direct Action

How, then, should Christians relate to the powers, in particular the power of the state? Yoder's answer was twofold. First, Christians are called to be subordinate to the state, the locus classicus being Romans 13:1-7. Fleshing out what subordination to the state means leads to a consideration of Yoder's appraisal of nonviolent resistance and civil disobedience. Second, Christians can witness to the state by using "middle axioms" that call on the state to live up to its own stated ideals. Let us examine these in turn.

From Yoder's perspective, Christians must be subordinate as Jesus was subordinate to the state. To *any* state: Christian subordination does not depend on the state's goodness or justice. "No state can be so low on the scale of relative justice that the duty of the Christian is no longer to be subject," Yoder declared. At the same time, however, "no state can rise so high on that scale that Christians are not called to some sort of suffering because of their refusal to agree with its self-glorification and the resultant injustices."[34]

Refusal and subjection: at issue in this seemingly paradoxical prescription was Yoder's reading of Romans 13. The language of subordination, Yoder realized, could easily be problematically distorted to encode a demand for blind obedience to all that the state might command. Christians must therefore differentiate between subordination and obedience. "Subordination is significantly different from obedience": the Christian might be called to disobey the state, but by being prepared to accept the punishment for such disobedience, would remain subordinate to it. A non-Christian example helps to clarify the distinction between subordination and obedience: Israelis who refuse to serve in the military but instead willingly go to jail thus disobey the state while remaining subordinate to it. In the Christian's case, the rationale for this subordination is christological. "We subject ourselves to government," Yoder explained, "because it was in so doing that Jesus revealed and achieved God's glory."[35]

This distinction between subordination and obedience is also operative in Yoder's defense of Christian participation in nonviolent actions in violation of the law. So, for example, Palestinian Christians in the town of Beit Sahour who refused to pay taxes to the Israeli military government in the 1980s refused to *obey* the laws of the state, but in their nonviolent acceptance of the state's punishments for this disobedience, they were *subordinate* to that state.

Earlier Mennonite theologians like Guy Hershberger had rejected Christian participation in nonviolent resistance on the grounds that such actions were coercive and thus deviations from Jesus' example of nonresistant love. Yoder stood in this tradition of theological reasoning, while pushing beyond it in significant ways. That Yoder dramatically modified Hershberger's blanket rejection of Christian participation in nonviolent resistance should be clear from careful attention to his choice of words. Hershberger believed that both "nonviolence" and "pacifism" encoded attitudes toward power that threatened to lead the Christian away from biblically based nonresistance toward coercive forms of political involvement.[36] Yoder, in contrast, freely used nonviolence and pacifism with positive connotations and sought through his ecumenical contacts to build bridges between Mennonites and other Christian pacifists. One should not, Yoder insisted, deny the "inherent close relations Mennonites could well have to peace movements, on grounds of criticisms (humanistic optimism, irrealism about sin and power) which would apply even more to military alternatives."[37]

Nonviolent action need not be conceptualized exclusively in terms of coercion but can instead be viewed as a way to appeal to the conscience of the enemy. "The purpose of the sit-in is not to coerce the 'adversary' but to communicate to him, to 'get through to him,' to bring to his attention moral dimensions of his behavior which he had not recognized."[38] So, for example, Palestinian efforts to organize boycotts of Israeli goods illegally manufactured in the Occupied Territories and to spearhead divestment campaigns need not be understood as coercive attacks against Israel, but they can instead be seen as appeals to Israel to end its discriminatory and repressive practices.

Even as he defined the terms by which Christians might engage in nonviolent action, Yoder expressed awareness that many advocates of nonviolence view it solely as a coercive tactic. Yoder found the rhetoric of nonviolence as a "war without violence" to be problematic from a Christian perspective:

> If Christians are concerned that the continuation of this revolutionary movement be Christian, nonviolent, redemptive, their concern will be to continue to concentrate upon the identification and removal of one abuse at a time, rather than on theoretical sketches of the new order toward which we must move.[39]

Nonviolence is always in danger of becoming problematic for Christians to the degree that its practitioners become obsessed with effectiveness. Yoder did not deny that faithfulness will, ultimately, bear fruit: in ecumenical conversations he regularly engaged in thought experiments with proponents of war about the potential effectiveness of particular nonviolent strategies, urging, for example, that proposals such as Gene Sharp's vision of a nonviolent national defense be taken seriously.[40] Potential short-term effectiveness aside, however, Yoder insisted that Christians cannot anticipate what success faithful action will enjoy. "Results are not calculable," Yoder emphasized. "We cannot calculate how obedience and success are connected, even though in the long run the right way is the most effective."[41]

A doxological vision of history grounded in the resurrection and lordship of the crucified Christ undergirded Yoder's confidence that faithfulness to the way of nonviolent love was ultimately in accordance with the direction of the universe: "The cross of Christ is the model of Christian social efficacy, the power of God for those who believe."[42] This claim is rooted not in utilitarian, cost-benefit analysis but in the eschatological triumph of the Lamb as envisioned by the seer of the Apocalypse. Because the Lamb has conquered, Jesus' disciples can follow him without an obsessive need to control history, without constant calculation of the cash value of their actions, but rather with the confidence that discipleship runs with the grain of the cosmos.

"The relation between our obedience and the achievement of God's purposes," Yoder claimed, "stands in analogy to the hidden lordship of him who was crucified and raised."[43] Accordingly, Yoder classified the achievements of the nonviolent protest movements under the rubric of "sign," thus pointing to the parabolic character of such actions. Because Christians confess that the crucified Christ is the hope of the world, they can see nonviolent action as a part of the inbreaking of God's kingdom into the world: "A sit-in or march is not instrumental, but it is *significant*. Even when no immediate change in the social order can be measured, even when people and organizations have not yet been moved to take a different position, the efficacy of the deed is first of all its efficacy as sign."[44] So, for example, when groups of Israeli Jews and Palestinians gather in commemoration and remembrance at the ruins of a Palestinian village destroyed in 1948, or when Israeli activists join with the villagers of Bil'in in the West Bank in nonviolent attempts to prevent the construction of the separation barrier, their primary importance is their efficacy as signs, signs of a possible coming future of mutual interdependence and solidarity rather than walls, separation, and repression.

However, even as Yoder provided a theological rationale for how the church can participate in nonviolent coalition politics aimed at improving social and political structures by removing one abuse at a time, he cautioned that such participation must never be the basic form of Christian witness to the world. "The church is not *primarily* an instrument to speak to or for the masses about how those masses might transform the social and political structures to which they are subject," Yoder cautioned. "Her pulpit is no podium and her preacher should be no demagogue." Fundamentally, the church is to be a new political entity, analogically anticipating, celebrating, and partially embodying the coming kingdom.[45]

Appeals to the State

If the church and its practices stood at the center of Yoder's understanding of Christian politics, he also saw a legitimate place for electoral engagement, lobbying efforts for or against particular pieces of legislation, and advocacy for or against specific government policies. While Christians engage in these activities on an ad hoc basis, and while Yoder considered them to be secondary forms of political witness, he nevertheless affirmed them as potentially valid ways to witness to Christ's lordship.

Yoder opened the door for limited Christian participation in the state apparatus. He most likely had Hershberger in mind when he argued that "those who think participation in the legislative and elective processes to be major involvement in the wielding of the sword are probably mistaken."[46] Christians do not compromise their nonresistance either by voting or even by running for legislative office. Whether a candidate committed to Jesus' way of love in social relations would have a realistic chance of winning a major legislative election, and whether Christian participation in the legislative process would be good stewardship of one's individual talents, are secondary questions whose answers would depend on contingent, historical factors.[47] Yoder consistently questioned statist assumptions that the primary form of political involvement is direct participation in the mechanisms of power. However, that Yoder could conceive of Christian participation in legislative politics without compromise of nonresistance was a significant modification of, even departure from, previous understandings of the implications of nonresistance.

Placing both church and state under the norm of Christ, Yoder removed the foundation of a dualistic withdrawal from the world. Christians cannot be content to allow the state to operate according to a supposedly ordained standard of justice but must witness to state officials in the hopes that the state might more closely approximate the norm of love. By not expounding a dualistic ethic for church and state, Yoder challenged the "existence or the knowability of a fixed standard of justice in the realm of unbelief" and thereby affirmed that the only norm willed for humanity by God is nonviolent love. "What holds down the performance and the standards that apply in the world," Yoder maintained, "is the weight of sin, not a divinely revealed lower order for secular society."[48]

If both church and state stand under the lordship of Christ and Christ's norm of nonviolent love, an ontological reality recognized only by the church, how can Christians appeal to state officials to improve their policies? Yoder answered with his proposal of "middle axioms." These middle axioms involve taking the "pagan" language of the state—terms such as liberty, equality, democracy, and human rights—as the basis for appeals to the state to better its performance. Middle axioms are simply "the fruitful use of the self-justification language of the rulers, whoever they be, as the instrument of our critical and constructive communication with them."[49] By employing the state's own "pagan or secular terminology" in her witness to the state, the Christian simply uses the language of the state as an ad hoc norm for nudging the state closer to the standard of nonviolent love. The ad hoc character of the witness is crucial: no metaphysical value is ascribed to the middle axioms outside of Christ.[50] They could conceivably be employed under any state: "No tyrant can be so low on the scale of righteousness that the Christian could not appeal to him to do at least a little better."[51]

As suggested at different points in this chapter, Christian political witness in Palestine-Israel can and does take a variety of forms, from nonviolent direct action to protests that function as signs of a coming future. Christians seeking the peace of Palestine-Israel can and do undertake a variety of middle axiom appeals. We call on actors such as the United States, Israel, and the Palestine Liberation Organization to abide by the terms of international treaties and conventions that they all explicitly or implicitly recognize, such as the Fourth Geneva Convention, seeking to convince these parties that attacks on civilians, the construction of colonial settlements in occupied territories, and various forms of collective punishment run counter to the obligations of those treaties. We can argue from United Nations resolutions that refugees should be allowed to return home and from International Court of Justice rulings that the walls and fences of the separation barrier should be dismantled. Or we can pragmatically reason that the long-term security of Palestinians and Israelis will be secured, not through schemes of partition and separation, but through the slow, painstaking work toward a binational future that is already a reality in distorted form.

However, these types of appeals are always contingent and provisional, driven not by a conviction that God's reign is coterminous with international law or UN resolutions, but instead issuing from the Christian freedom to call on the world's powers to live up to their own professed convictions. A more basic way that Christians in the United States, Canada, and elsewhere in the world can help seek the peace of Palestine-Israel will be to accompany the often ignored and forgotten Palestinian churches, churches that are fragile yet resilient, small but immeasurably significant. Through their worship and ministries, these churches witness to a politics of bridges instead of walls, of reconciliation instead of separation.

In an age when the bureaucratizing tendencies of the nation-state have increasingly come to define politics, when the "political" has become equated with the "effort to sustain a hegemonic, territorial sovereign entity, embodied in a physical collective of human beings and articulated to action for its own self-preservation," Yoder's understanding of Christian political witness inevitably provokes.[52] His work spurs us to recover a vision of the church that, through its worship and its practices, embodies a particular politics. As Christians scattered in diasporic witness throughout the world seek the peace of the world's cities, Yoder's work will serve as a disruptive reminder, continually needed, that true political witness and action cannot be reduced to the circumscribed boundaries of the nation-state and that through the practices of the church and the wall-demolishing action of God in Jesus Christ, new political possibilities emerge.

6

Parables of the Kingdom
Encountering Jesus Outside the
Walls of the Church

Exile, as Edward Said observed, can lead to an insular turn inward, with the erection of defensive walls to guard against difference and to buttress identity. However, these walls are inherently unstable, and the foreign world they have been built to keep out always manages to enter. These intrusions, these disruptions, can be experienced as threats—threats to identity, threats to faithfulness—and undoubtedly often the threats are real. For the church to engage in the practices of baptism, communion, the diversity of ministries, binding and loosing, and discernment under the Holy Spirit inevitably and properly entails the drawing of provisional boundaries: faithful practice requires decisions about what constitutes unfaithfulness.

But the intrusion of the world into the church is not always a threat to faithfulness. Threats from the outside can be salutary, judging and disrupting the church's unfaithfulness. Sometimes the world's intrusion into the church carries with it promise and opportunity: promise that the church will continue to encounter the risen Christ in all of the cities of its exile and the opportunity for learning and reformation in light of this encounter. The church dispersed in mission, sustained by God's ever-surprising Spirit, expects to encounter Jesus outside its walls. Scripture attests that Jesus' identity and mission become known in liminal spaces, in the borderlands: in his immersion in the waters of the ancient border river into the land of promise (Matt 3:13-17); in his encounter with the Syro-Phoenician woman whose persistence uncovers the reality that Jesus' mission is broader than previously anticipated (Mark 7:24-30); and in his parabolic identification of the Samaritan, the religious outsider, as the good neighbor (Luke 10:25-37). Sent out into the world by Jesus, the church should expect to continue to meet Jesus in the borderlands.

God's people in exile live amongst and work alongside people who do not confess Jesus as Lord, from ardent secularists to indifferent agnostics to committed believers of other faiths. Through its practices, the church is in some way set apart from these neighbors, co-workers, and fellow citizens. At the same time, however, one of the practices that the church should cultivate, if it truly believes that Jesus Christ is one with the Father and reigns over all of history and creation, is an open receptivity to encountering Jesus outside itself in the words and deeds of its non-Christian neighbors. Through these encounters the church receives a deeper understanding of its mission in the world. As the Swiss theologian Karl Barth explained, "The Church, recognizing God's voice in this alien voice from without, lets itself be called to itself thereby, lets itself be reminded of its particular ministry with all its promise."[1]

Barth called these "alien" voices to which the church must pay heed "parables of the kingdom," that is, parables that Christians encounter *extra muros ecclesiae*, outside the walls of the church. In this chapter I examine in depth the christological basis of these "parables of the kingdom" and the conditions for their reception by the church. Being receptive to God's word spoken outside of the church requires that we develop a non-triumphalist understanding of Christian witness, a not-in-charge manner of mission open to the promise of productively unsettling encounters with non-Christians.

Resisting the Domestication of Difference

Barth, I contend, helps us think through how the church should understand its experience of learning from non-Christians by providing a distinct alterative to theological and philosophical ways of conceptualizing religious and ideological difference that in the end serve to domesticate and erase that difference. One dominant approach in modern theological thought, from Immanuel Kant to John Hick and other so-called pluralist theologians and philosophers, has been to view different religions (Christianity included), along with secular ideologies, as expressions of a common core of either ethical conviction or inner experience.[2] From this perspective, it is held that Christians can learn from non-Christians because they are fundamentally the same. These approaches also appear to have the advantage of fostering social peace in polities torn apart by religious and ideological animosities: uncovering a deep unity is imagined to be the path to securing social harmony.

Such approaches are deeply flawed, however. First and foremost, they all involve a christological devaluation, a pointing away from claims that the Jewish Jesus is one with God and Lord over heaven and earth and toward supposedly more universal claims. Furthermore, such superficially pluralist theologies, while professing to affirm difference, in fact serve profoundly conservative ends, demonstrating a real fear of difference, reducing differences among faiths to the level of unessential trappings on a common core or subordinating those differences within a supposedly broader framework. In either case, difference is domesticated and commodified, with different religions and belief systems treated like products amongst which the sovereign consumer can choose.[3]

In contrast, Barth resisted any approach to religious and philosophical difference that would downgrade Christian claims about Jesus, insisting instead on advancing normative and exclusive claims about Jesus. "Jesus Christ is *the* light of life," he proclaimed. "To underline the 'the' is to say that He is the one and only light of life. Positively, this means that He is the light of life in all its fullness, in perfect adequacy; and negatively, it means that there is no other light of life outside or alongside His, outside or alongside the light which He is."[4]

Barth recognized that this claim is "a hard and offensive saying which provokes doubt and invites contradiction" (*CD* IV/3.1, 87). From a missiological perspective, the temptation is always great to reduce Jesus from *the* to *a* light of life, to acknowledge him as simply one prophet among others. Such a move can seemingly gain a hearing for Jesus in the synagogue, the mosque, and the corridors of Western idealism (*CD* IV/3.1, 87-88). The pluralist approaches sketched above succumb precisely to this temptation. They might shift the focus away from Jesus toward a mysterious God of which he is said to be but one manifestation, or they might deny that Jesus Christ is constitutive of salvation, but rather claim that he represents a possibility of salvation that might be had apart from him. Either way, they mitigate the provocation and the possible offense that Jesus Christ is *the* light of life.[5] What if, however, one did not avoid the provocation but in fact insisted on it? Can the "hard and offensive" insistence that Jesus Christ is *the* light of life leave room for receiving true words about God from non-Christians? In brief, the answer is yes. In fact, claims that Jesus Christ is *the* light of life should lead us to *expect* to receive such true words. To understand why, one must grasp the radicality of the confession that Jesus Christ is the light of life, the one Word of God.

Jesus Christ, the One Word of God

To say that Jesus Christ is the one Word of God leads to several conclusions. In the first place, it means that Jesus "is the total and complete declaration of God concerning Himself and the men whom He addresses in His Word." However, this claim is not reducible to an assertion that what Christians say about Jesus is identical to the one Word of God. Jesus Christ may be the complete and final revelation of God, but "our hearing of [His Word] is profoundly incomplete." While the Bible and the message, life, and activity of the church bear witness to the fact that Jesus Christ is the one Word of God, they are not themselves the Word of God, but are only lights that shine thanks to the light of Christ (*CD* IV/3.1, 99).

Second, that Jesus is the one Word of God means that his truth "is not exposed on any third side to any serious competition, any challenge to His truth, any threat to His authority" (*CD* IV/3.1, 100). Third, one may not make God's Word in Jesus Christ part of a supposedly broader system that encompasses that Word and other words. Such attempts at systematization "imply a control over Him to which none of us has any right, which can be only the work of religious arrogance" (*CD* IV/3.1, 101). Finally, to assert that Jesus Christ is the one Word of God implies a finality to this Word. One does not expect new and different words that will supersede what has been said and done in Jesus (*CD* IV/3.1, 102).

The proclamation that Jesus Christ is the one Word of God, we must stress, does not grant any special privilege or status to the proclaimer. The proclamation "looks away from the non-Christian and Christian alike to the One who sovereignly confronts and precedes both as *the* Prophet. As Jesus Christ is its content, the one who confesses it in no sense marks himself off from those who do not" (*CD* IV/3.1, 91). Furthermore, the fact that Christian proclamation points to Jesus Christ does not mean that the Christian *understands* that proclamation fully or well. The reality of Jesus Christ always transcends and evades the cognitive grasp of the Christian, and the Christian is thus in the position of always learning more about who Jesus is.

The Christological Basis of Parables of the Kingdom

The claim that Jesus is *the* light of life, that he is the one true Word of God, of necessity raises the question of the truth of all human words, for "can we think of any word actually spoken, or any conceivable word which might be spoken, that says what the life of Jesus Christ says?" (*CD* IV/3.1, 107). Do not, in fact, all human words fall short of expressing what this one Word says? Barth answered that whereas the kingdom of God *is* Jesus Christ, human words can, by God's grace, disclose the kingdom: such words are what Barth called "parables of the kingdom." "The one true Word of God makes these other words true," Barth explained. "Jesus Christ utters, or rather creates, these parables, speaking of the kingdom, of the life, and therefore of Himself, and doing so in stories which it might seem that others could tell, yet which they are unable to do, because His Word alone can equate the kingdom with such events" (*CD* IV/3.1, 112).

One type of parable of the kingdom is found in Scripture and the church's proclamation. Scripture, Barth argued, is true to the extent that it is directed and guided by the Word, while church proclamation is true insofar as it receives its shape from Scripture (*CD* IV/3.1, 114). The Bible and church proclamation in and of themselves are not fully equivalent to God's one true Word in Jesus Christ. Rather, they only *become* God's Word to the extent that they are taken up into Jesus Christ by God's free, gracious action.

But what of so-called "secular" parables of the kingdom, true words of God outside the walls of the church?[6] Do they exist? If so, how do Christians discern what is a true parable of the kingdom? In response to the first question, regarding the possibility of the existence of secular parables of the kingdom, Barth gave an unequivocal affirmation. If Scripture and church proclamation constitute an "inner sphere" of a circle with Christ as the center, then the secular world constitutes an "outer sphere": true words can be found in both (*CD* IV/3.1, 97). To deny this possibility is tantamount to trying to control God's free grace. "Does it not necessarily lead to ossification," Barth asked, "if the community rejects in advance the existence and word of these alien witnesses to the truth?" (*CD* IV/3.1, 115). There are no prima facie theological reasons

> not to accept the fact that such good words may also be spoken extra muros ecclesiae either through those who have not yet received any effective witness to Jesus Christ, and cannot therefore be reckoned with the believers who for their part attest Him, or through more or less admitted Christians who are not, however, engaged in direct confession, or direct activity as members of the Christian community, but in the discharge of a function in world society and its orders and tasks. (CD IV/3.1, 110)

To reject out of hand the possibility of secular parables of God's Word would be to dictate from a human standpoint what is and is not possible for God, to try to control the free workings of God's Spirit.

Not only can we not rule out a priori the possibility of secular parables of the kingdom because of God's freedom, but we should in fact *expect* these parables because of the universality of Christ's lordship and the objective and universal reconciliation effected in and through him. Barth reminded his readers that Scripture testifies to a God whose reign encompasses all of history and creation: "According to the witness of His prophets and apostles grounded in His resurrection, the sphere of His dominion and Word is in any case greater than that of their prophecy and apostolate"; so the appearance of parables of the kingdom attesting to God's reign outside the walls of the church should come as no surprise (*CD* IV/3.1, 116). God does not let the secular realm fend for itself in its illusions of self-sufficiency, but disturbs it with the inbreaking of his word in the form of secular parables. These parables constitute "the strange interruption of the secularism of life in the world" (*CD* IV/3.1, 117). No "Prometheanism can be effectively maintained against Jesus Christ," so there can be "no secular sphere abandoned by Him or withdrawn from His control," no realm of history or creation that God cannot take up as a testimony to God's Word (*CD* IV/3.1, 119).

Christians must not take any pride in themselves for proclaiming Jesus Christ. If all true human words about God are miraculous, fully dependent on God's gracious action, then God can raise up children for Abraham from stones, making those who do not know the name of Jesus Christ become his unwitting witnesses (*CD* IV/3.1, 118). The church may not complacently assume any position of privilege or presumed superiority over the world:

> If the Church is visible, this need not imply that we actually see it in its full compass, that the dimensions of its sphere might not be very different from what we think we know them to be. God may suddenly be pleased to have Abraham blessed by Melchizidek, or Israel blessed by Balaam or helped by Cyrus. Moreover, it could hardly be denied that God can speak His Word to man quite otherwise than through the talk about Himself that is to be found in the Church as known or as yet to be discovered, and therefore quite otherwise than through proclamation. He can establish the Church anew and directly when and where and how it pleases Him. (*CD* I/1, 54)

Not only should Christ's lordship over all of history and creation lead us to expect secular parables of the kingdom, but the objective and universal character of his salvific work should lead the Christian to the same expectation: "*De iure* all men and all creation derive from His cross, from the reconciliation accomplished in Him, and are ordained to be the theater of His glory and therefore the recipients and bearers of His Word" (*CD* IV/3.1, 117). One need not, then, have recourse to a natural theology to claim that true words can be found outside of church walls: secular parables can be grounded exclusively in revelation in Christ.

That parables of the kingdom have their basis in Christ's lordship and atoning work, and not in some generally available revelation, is underscored by the fact that they are spoken by people "quite apart from and even in the face of their own knowledge or volition," people who thus become "something which they could never be of themselves, namely, His witnesses" (*CD* IV/3.1, 118). Parables of the kingdom are grounded, not in the subjectivity of those who speak them, but in the objectivity of God's reconciling work in and through Jesus Christ. The "religions of heathendom" may "come about because man simply does not know or refuses to know the ground of divine immanence in Jesus Christ," but this does not mean that those religions cannot speak true words which are "in" Jesus Christ.[7]

How, one might ask, can the historical person of Jesus Christ encompass all true words throughout history? The Rahnerian option in favor of an "anonymous Christianity" was closed to Barth, for he refused to turn the name of Jesus Christ into a label for a supposedly more universal grace that can be had apart from him. To understand how Barth's argument holds together, one must understand that for Barth the reality of Jesus Christ is preexistent to the historical person called by that name. As George Hunsinger has observed, Barth's Jesus is not fully reducible to his historicity:

> He is not encapsulated in this historicity in an unqualified way. For his historicity is indissolubly connected with his eternality. It is therefore at once affirmed, negated, and reconstituted on a higher plane. Its mere historicity is transcended and overcome. Its distinctive particularity is at once preserved and yet overcome by being integrated into the perichoresis of eternity. It is made integral to the eternal life of Jesus Christ and therefore acquires a differentiated presence and distinctive power in relation to all other historical moments and beings.[8]

The key term here is perichoresis. Jesus Christ's humanity takes part in the trinitarian interplay and the communication of properties among the persons of the Trinity and thus shares in all of the qualities of the three persons of the Trinity. Jesus Christ is "the ground of divine immanence" (*CD* II/1, 319). Because Jesus Christ is this basis of the divine immanence throughout history and creation, "nothing is to be conceived in which Jesus Christ is not coinherent and which in turn is not somehow coinherent in him."[9]

Hunsinger proposes the image of a circle to grasp Barth's christology on this point. Christ forms not only the center but also the outer edge: "Center and periphery . . . are regarded as two forms of single truth."[10] All of history and creation is encompassed by this circle, so whatever truth can be found in history and creation can be said to be *in* Christ. It is thus *distinct* from Jesus Christ while not being outside or alongside of him.

John Howard Yoder, a student of Barth's whose theology of religions closely followed Barth's approach to non-Christian religions and ideologies, explained that Christians should expect "on purely logical grounds prior to any experience, that there may be groups calling themselves non-Christian which are more Christian than they know"—logical meaning here that it follows reasonably from the fact of God's revelation in Jesus Christ.[11] He contrasts the universalism of Karl Rahner and his concept of anonymous Christianity with what he calls Barth's incipient universalism. The Barthian kind of universalism

> is that of the confessing minority whose commitment to her Lord, despite its being against the stream, is so convinced of the majesty of his Lordship that she risks trusting that his power and goodness can reach beyond the number of those who know him by his right name. [A Rahnerian universalism] is a high view of the human; [a Barthian universalism,] a high view of Jesus.[12]

Christians thus have good reasons to expect to encounter Christ outside of the places where he is known by name, for his lordship covers all of history and creation.

Evaluating Parables of the Kingdom

Christians should thus expect to encounter parables of the kingdom outside of the church's walls. By what criteria should these secular, non-Christian words be evaluated in order to determine if they are true words of God, real parables of God's kingdom? Human words distinct from God's one Word of Jesus Christ are true insofar as they stand "in the closest material and substantial conformity and agreement with the one Word of God." Parables of the kingdom can share in the content and truth of God's Word in Christ "only to the extent that they declare nothing of their own, but in their utterance and emphasis are prepared to attest this one Word exactly as it is, without subtraction, addition or alteration" (*CD* IV/3.1, 111).

But how can any human word "ever succeed in attesting and corresponding to the one Word of God, or even try to do so?" (*CD* IV/3.1, 111). Human words—in Scripture, in the church, or outside the church—will never fully and comprehensively correspond to God's one true Word. Instead, they must be evaluated according to whether or not they point to Jesus Christ. As they point to Christ, they do not embody Christ's truth fully, but rather "express the one and total truth from a particular angle, and to that extent only implicitly and not explicitly in its unity and totality" (*CD* IV/3.1, 123). When the consummation of God's reign in Christ occurs, all words will fully reflect the light of Christ, but until then

> there can be no question of anything more than signs of His lordship or attestations of His prophecy, whether in Scripture, in the confession and message of the community, or in such true words as pierce the secularism of the worldly life surrounding it in closer or more distant proximity. (*CD* IV/3.1, 122).

While all human words thus can only attain to the truth of God's Word, one can still delineate several guidelines for evaluating whether or not a secular word is a parable of the kingdom. Foremost is the question of the "agreement [of these secular words] with the witness of Scripture" (*CD* IV/3.1, 126). No direct prefiguration is to be expected, but rather harmonization. True secular parables must not bring forth anything manifestly contradictory to Scripture. A true secular word "will not lead its hearers away from Scripture, but more deeply into it" (*CD* IV/3.1, 126). It will "materially say what [Scripture] says, although from a different source and in another tongue" (*CD* IV/3.1, 115). This does not mean that secular words must consist only in a straightforward repetition of Scripture in order to be true. As Hunsinger explains, "The issue is simply one of compatibility or logical consistency. Secular words are not expected flatly to repeat what is already known of the content of scripture, but rather to cast light on scripture by being compatible with it."[13]

A second criterion for evaluating the truth of secular words involves their compatibility with the dogmas and confessions of the church.

While secular parables should in general harmonize with these dogmas and confessions, in this sphere some newness is permissible. Secular parables can provoke new interpretations of Scripture, extend and fill in existing church dogmas, and might even provoke dogmatic revision (*CD* IV/3.1, 126). The revisions made because of the reception of these parables must, of course, be compatible with Scripture. They must harmonize with it.[14] But the encounter with parables of the kingdom can expose the church's interpretation of Scripture as deeply distorted, opening up new hermeneutical possibilities.

Secular parables can also be tested by the fruits they bear in the world at large. If they have a generally salutary effect, the chances are greater that they might be parables of the kingdom than if they have generally negative consequences (*CD* IV/3.1, 128). One should also consider the impact that these secular, non-Christian words have on the church. To be parables of the kingdom, they must be both comfort and correction for the church, challenging the church to repent for past sins, to live up to its mission, and to be confirmed in its calling to testify and submit to its Lord (*CD* IV/3.1, 128).

Receiving Parables of the Kingdom

What use are Christians to make of secular parables? Above all, they should serve to remind the church of its failure in its mission. Their existence should prompt the church to ask itself why it "has lagged behind when it ought to have been in the vanguard? Why has it not told itself what it must now learn from the children of the world?" (*CD* IV/3.1, 128). Barth thus contends that the reception of secular parables should not alter the church's fundamental mission, the proclamation of what God has done in Jesus Christ, but should instead make it more faithful to that duty, calling it as needed to reformation and even repentance.

As useful as secular parables may be for the church as corrective and comfort, they cannot become norms for the church, unlike the Bible, for "they lack the unity and compactness and therefore the constancy and universality of His self-revelation as it takes place and is to be sought in Holy Scripture" (*CD* IV/3.1, 131). Simply because true words appear in the secular sphere, Christians are not thereby obligated or authorized to canonize such free words of grace:

> God may speak to us through a pagan or an atheist, and thus give us to understand that the boundary between the Church and the secular world can still take at any time a different course

from that which we think we discern. Yet this does not mean, unless we are prophets, that we ourselves have to proclaim the pagan or atheistic thing which we have heard. (*CD* I/1, 55)

The church's use of these secular parables will always be provisional and done on an ad hoc basis. The free words from outside of the church's orbit are always context-specific, coming to the church in a specific time and situation. Furthermore, their reception by the church is never in practice an affair of the whole community. Because "the right use of these free communications of the Lord can never be regarded as other than extraordinary," secular parables "cannot be fixed and canonized as the Word of the Lord" (*CD* IV/3.1, 133). To canonize secular parables would mark a failure to exercise the cautious skepticism proper to the reception of such extraordinary words. Those in the church who hear true words from outside should "show themselves to be such as have heard a true word and been radically smitten by it. They should bring forth the appropriate fruits" (*CD* IV/3.1, 134).

Because the reception of secular parables should always occur on a provisional and ad hoc basis, there will be a prima facie case against engaging in dogmatic revision on their basis. One should be careful not to claim too much for secular parables, for "all such phenomena are doubtful and contestable." Conversely, one should not claim too little for the "almighty power [of Christ] to bring forth such true words even *extra muros ecclesiae* and to attest itself through them" (*CD* IV/3.1, 135). Determining which of the words and deeds the church encounters beyond its borders are parables of the kingdom will always be a contingent affair involving provisional, fallible judgments. In this sense they are no different from words spoken inside the church, words that are also subject to ongoing discernment.

Parables of the kingdom can also spur the church to enter into provisional coalitions with non-Christian groups and individuals to address pressing social, economic, and political concerns. The church might encounter non-Christians feeding the hungry and visiting prisoners, reminding the church of its task to minister to Jesus in the form of the stranger and the outcast and pushing Christians to join in such ministries. Or, to take examples from Palestine-Israel, when the church witnesses Israeli Jews joining with Palestinians to rebuild Palestinian homes destroyed by an Israeli military enforcing a discriminatory planning regime in the Occupied Territories, it can receive these actions as parables of God's reconciling work in Jesus Christ.

Persons of different religious convictions need not relinquish normative convictions and strong truth claims if any progress is to be made in tackling social ills and injustices. Rather, religious persons with a strong commitment to the universal normativity of their convictions can find resources within their own traditions for justifying cooperative action across confessional boundaries. When entering such coalitions, the church must remain free in a dual sense: free to receive parables of the kingdom from those with whom it works, and free from permanent alliances that would bind the church's witness to Christ to particular political movements. Just as the church's reception of parables of the kingdom always occurs on an ad hoc basis, so too must the coalitions into which the church enters always be provisional. But the provisional character of these coalitions does not obviate the importance and the urgency of the church's always being ready to receive parables of the kingdom from outside its walls and to discern and act accordingly.

Apostolic Weakness and Christian Witness

I have discussed in previous chapters how the church in exile is not only politically but also theologically not in charge. In the case of parables of the kingdom, this interrelationship between the exilic character of the church's political witness and the exilic manner of its theology is particularly tight. Because God's one true Word stands in judgment over all human words, any pretensions of superiority to which Christians might want to cling are shattered. With God's revelation negating all human strivings, all religious (including Christian) attempts to grasp at God, Christians know that the truth of human words, of human religion, depends solely on God. Thus, "the Christian religion is the true one only as we listen to the divine revelation."[15] However, since divine revelation continually exceeds our comprehension, because the one Word of Jesus Christ is united with the Father in the Spirit, Christians know that we can only properly attend to God's revelation by being open to encountering Jesus outside of the all-too-human walls erected by the church.

This stance of openness calls for a renunciation of any self-satisfied sense of privilege on the part of Christians toward non-Christians, demanding instead a spirit of humility that is at odds with all forms of Christian triumphalism. "Christian faith," Barth insisted, "does not live by the self-consciousness with which the Christian man can differentiate himself from the non-Christian," but instead lives by and through Jesus Christ alone (*CD* I/2, 331).

The church's witness is strongest when it depends solely on God instead of on its own resources, when with humility it is receptive to true words of God from beyond its orbit: "Strong human positions are only those which are fully abandoned to God." This relinquishing of theological control correlates with an exilic politics of not being in charge, for "the Church has to be weak in order to be strong" (*CD* I/2, 331, 334). Before the uniting of the church with empire, "Christianity had one great advantage," according to Barth. "As a *religio illicita* [outlawed religion], and *ecclesia pressa* [suffering church], it was, as it were, automatically forced into something like the apostolic position, i.e., the apostolic weakness." Without political power, it was less tempted to use apologetics to try to coerce assent to Christ (*CD* I/2, 333).[16] Instead, radically dependent upon God, it was receptive to the provocative and unsettling parables of the kingdom outside its walls.

The church that cultivates openness to these parables today, then, must rediscover the mission of exile, disavowing the Constantinian legacy and painstakingly disentangling its proclamation of Jesus Christ from Constantinianism and its colonialist analogues.[17] If the church is truly to embrace the challenge and the promise of life in exile, it must cultivate an exilic style of theology, ready to encounter Jesus in unexpected places.

Return

7

The End(s) of Return
Memory Against Forgetting

In his novel *The Book of Laughter and Forgetting*, Milan Kundera writes that "the struggle of people against power is the struggle of memory against forgetting." In contexts where the victors seek to erase the textual and material traces of the vanquished and to obscure the bloody means by which victory was obtained, acts of memory can become political acts, disturbing and challenging dominant narratives. Thus, when Palestinians make pilgrimages to the ruins of their ancestral homes in places such as Bir'im, Mujaydil, and Suhmata, walking around the remaining stones and narrating the life of the village and its destruction by the Israeli military, they re-create landscapes from which Palestinian presence has been removed, and they name as a *Nakba*, or catastrophe, what prevailing Israeli narratives call redemption. Or when communities of Palestinian refugees in Lebanon, Syria, Jordan, or elsewhere in the diaspora compile memory books for their villages, collecting the history and folklore of places like Ein Hawd, Beit 'Itab, or Lifta, they put the more than 500 destroyed Palestinian towns and villages back on the map, thus sustaining the hope that exile will not be forever, that the day of return will not be postponed indefinitely. These acts of memory are embodiments of what the German Jewish thinker Walter Benjamin termed the historian's task of brushing against the grain of history, of disturbing the tapestry of official accounts and state narratives in pursuit of silenced lives and voices. The historian's vocation is thus a political vocation: to be an agent of memory against forgetting.

Unfortunately, churches in the West have sometimes functioned as agents of forgetting regarding Palestinians, failing to grapple with the desire of Palestinian refugees, both Christian and Muslim, to return home. By maintaining a strange silence concerning Palestinian refugees and by refusing to undertake a theological engagement with and critique of Zionism, Western churches, I contend, have been complicit with those who would put an end to the Palestinian refugee issue, to the idea of Palestinian refugee return, by a simple denial of Palestinian rights of return and restitution. After examining the nature of and reasons for this silence, I will argue in this chapter that the church should be concerned about the end, as in the goal, of return.

Two Forms of Christian Zionism

In describing Western Christian approaches to the Palestinian-Israeli conflict, the simple thing to do would be to contrast two phenomena. On the one hand, one has Christian Zionism of the premillennial dispensationalist variety, with its luminaries, political action committees, and pop culture, all informed by a particular theology that reads the biblical story as pointing toward an apocalyptic end of history in which the founding of the State of Israel and the ingathering of the exiled Jewish people play decisive roles in precipitating the last battle of Armageddon with the decisive defeat of Satan. Not surprisingly, Palestinian aspirations and rights are at best irrelevant in such a theological vision. At worst, Palestinians are obstacles to apocalyptic triumph, obstacles to be removed.

To this form of Christian Zionism one could contrast efforts by various Christian bodies to explore selective divestment as a tool to pressure Israel to end its military occupation. These Western churches have ties to the Palestinian church and have been moved by their Palestinian co-religionists to work for justice. Or one could contrast this type of Christian Zionism with the advocacy efforts of progressive evangelical, mainline Protestant, and Catholic churches for a two-state resolution of the Palestinian-Israeli conflict. Whereas Christian Zionists of the Tim LaHaye and Pat Robertson variety insist that all of Palestine is the exclusive patrimony of the Jewish people, these churches press for an end to occupation and the creation of a Palestinian state next to Israel.[1]

This contrast, however, would fail to get at root questions that Western churches need to address. In comparison to the lurid and arguably heretical theology of the *Left Behind*-style of Christian Zionism, the activity of Christian churches and ecumenical advocacy groups against the occupation and for a two-state solution, and the tentative exploration by Christian churches of divestment initiatives, are of course preferable. What is glaringly absent from these initiatives, however, is any sustained discussion of Palestinian refugees. For churches captivated by dispensationalist theologies in which Zionism and the founding of the State of Israel represent key events in the unfolding of apocalyptic scenarios, Palestinian refugees do not represent a particular moral problem. Like all Palestinians, they are viewed as interlopers onto and usurpers of the territory rightly belonging to the Jewish people. For the so-called mainline churches, however, those churches that have been engaged over decades in various forms of peace advocacy related to the Palestinian-Israeli conflict, Palestinian refugees do represent a problem, for their very existence raises questions and issues that Western churches would rather avoid. One finds only limited mention of Palestinian refugees, let alone refugee rights of return and restitution, in the Middle East resolutions of mainline Protestant churches framed in terms of ending the occupation and support for a two-state solution. The primary reason for the scant attention paid to Palestinian refugees, I would suggest, is that facing the Palestinian refugee issue forces the church to determine what it thinks about Zionism and about Israel as a Jewish state.[2]

Support for a two-state solution is comfortable for many Western churches because it allows them to say: "We affirm Israel's right to exist. We affirm Israel's legitimacy as a Jewish state. We're simply against the occupation." Calls to end the occupation fit easily into this framework. Advocacy for refugee rights, however, complicates the picture, for it forces the difficult question of what the Zionist call for a *Jewish* state means. Rather than tackle this challenging conversation head-on, the churches allow Palestinian refugees, along with Palestinians inside Israel, to fade from their view.

This reticence on the subject of Palestinian refugees, stemming from a reluctance to engage in a theological assessment of Zionism, could, I argue, be considered a second type of Christian Zionism, one that implicitly grants the Zionist project theological legitimacy.[3] Two recent statements arising from Christian-Jewish dialogue initiatives exemplify this tacit embrace of Zionism. One comes from a Catholic-Jewish conference held in Buenos Aires in July 2004; the other is a May 2005 report emerging from a series of Jewish-Protestant conversations at the University of Chicago.[4] Both statements follow the same line of reasoning: to question Israel's military occupation, with its attendant human rights abuses, might be legitimate, but what falls beyond the pale of acceptable criticism are questions concerning the justice of the State of Israel's founding or about the Zionist project of establishing and maintaining a Jewish state. The Buenos Aires statement declares a "rejection of anti-Semitism in all its forms, including anti-Zionism as a more recent manifestation of anti-Semitism." The report emerging from the conversations at the University of Chicago cautions that "those who criticize Israeli policies should take care to ensure that such criticism not threaten Judaism, the Jewish people, or the legitimacy of the State of Israel." The Christian participants in the Chicago dialogue—whose liberal theological orientation is far removed from the fundamentalist orientation of dispensationalist Christian Zionism—affirm as an "act of justice the establishment of a Jewish state after two thousand years of Jewish exile, wandering, and homelessness." The document thus draws on biblical imagery concerning the pain and anguish of exile, affirming the "Jewish state" as the antidote to homelessness. Such an approach both mirrors the standard Zionist "negation of the diaspora" (*shelilat ha-galut*) and appears to assume without question that the only political alternative to "exile" is exclusivist, nationalist sovereignty.

Both statements thus warn that critiques of Zionism and of the "legitimacy of the State of Israel" are akin to anti-Semitism. While the meaning of anti-Zionism is left unclear, Zionism is implicitly defined by these statements as the movement to establish a Jewish state, so anti-Zionism must therefore be understood to be a theological or political position that at least questions, if not opposes, the justice of establishing and maintaining a Jewish state. Recognizing the State of Israel's legitimacy is bound up, from this perspective, with affirming it as a Jewish state. A reader of these documents is left with the understanding that Christians, while they might criticize particular Israeli policies or actions, should embrace Zionism and thus recognize the justice of "the establishment of a Jewish state."

What Jewish state means in these types of claims is often left undefined and ambiguous, the essential matter at stake unarticulated. The key issue that goes unstated in these claims is demography. In contemporary Israeli political discourse, the question of the Jewishness of the Israeli state is repeatedly tied to questions of demography. Proponents of the disengagement, or convergence plan and of the wall argue that separation from Palestinians is required in order to protect Israel's Jewish majority from the demographic threat represented by Palestinians in the Occupied Territories. Israeli officials, meanwhile, when arguing against Palestinian refugee return, routinely describe calls to allow refugee return as attacks on Israel's character as a Jewish state. Israel's identity as a Jewish state, on the terms of this political discourse, was and is tied to creating and maintaining a Jewish demographic majority within particular territorial boundaries.

This project, many Israeli demographers warn, is under threat. Haifa University demographer Arnon Soffer has been the most prominent of many Israeli voices warning of demographic disaster for Israeli Jews. The number of Palestinians between the Jordan River and the Mediterranean Sea (that is, in both Israel and the Occupied Territories, or within the boundaries of British Mandate Palestine), Soffer has warned, will equal the number of Jews in that land by 2010.[5] Israeli politicians from across the political spectrum view this demographic reality with alarm. Public-opinion researchers Ephraim Yaar and Tamar Hermann have found that "the strong desire for a separation, even a unilateral one, is connected to a fear among the overwhelming majority of the Jewish public regarding the emergence of a *de facto* binational state."[6] The fear of an emerging binational reality has been put most pointedly by Israeli Labor politician Avraham Burg. "I am not afraid of weapons and terrorism," Burg notes. "I am afraid of the day that all of them [Palestinians] will put their weapons down and say 'One man, one vote.'"[7]

Demographic fears, coupled with a commitment to Zionism understood in terms of a linkage of demographic hegemony and territorial control, explain why nearly all Israeli Jewish politicians concur in rejecting any significant return of Palestinian refugees to homes and properties inside Israel, arguing that this would threaten the *Jewish* character of Israel. That the Palestine Liberation Organization (PLO) has continued to call (at least on paper) for Palestinian refugees to be allowed to return to their homes and properties if they so choose has been taken as a sign that the Palestinians reject Israel as a state. It is not sufficient, the argument goes, to recognize Israel (as the PLO did in the Oslo accords)—one must recognize Israel as a *Jewish* state, that is, its right to maintain a Jewish majority.

If a Jewish state and Zionism are understood as projects to create and maintain demographic and political hegemony over a particular territory, then the following conclusions would flow from the Chicago and Buenos Aires critiques of anti-Zionism and their affirmations of the justice of Israel as a Jewish state. First, the expulsion of hundreds of thousands of Palestinians (Christians and Muslims) from their homes and villages in 1948 was, if tragic, also necessary. If Zionism meant creating a state with a Jewish majority in historical Palestine, and if one affirms Zionism as a just vision, then one must view some form of uprooting of Palestinians from their homes as imperative, even just. Israeli historian Benny Morris unapologetically advances precisely this argument with a logic that should cause Euro-American Christians to pause in critical self-reflection: "The need to establish this state [Israel] in this place overcomes the injustice that was done to the Palestinians by uprooting them. . . . Even the great American democracy could not have been created without the annihilation of the Indians. There are cases in which the overall, final good justifies harsh and cruel acts that are committed in the course of history."[8]

Second, it follows that any return of these Palestinian refugees that would undermine this Jewish majority must be prevented. The logic of the Chicago and Buenos Aires documents thus falls in line with the Israeli characterization of calls for refugee return as anti-Semitic threats to Israel's Jewish identity. Both statements can thus be aptly characterized as implicitly Christian Zionist, albeit in a markedly different way from the apocalyptic theology normally bearing that name.

Refugees, Return, and Reconciliation

Western churches, I contend, need to question the logic that links the Jewishness of Israel to exclusivist discourses of demographic and territorial control. Part of breaking this logic would mean for the churches to become much more vocal than they have been regarding support for the rights of Palestinian refugees.

However, even if Western churches continue to ignore Palestinian refugees, realities on the ground will make a critical examination of Zionism more difficult to avoid. Championing the two-state solution has, one could argue, allowed mainline churches to avoid a serious evaluation of Zionism as an ideology and a practice. The two-state solution appeals to liberalism's sense of fairness: there are two peoples, so there should be two states. It also appeals to the Christian concern for reconciliation. When the two peoples each have their own states, the logic goes, enmity will be transformed, first into good neighborliness and then into friendship. Israel's unilateral separation, or convergence plan, however, writes the epitaph for a two-state solution based on the 1949 Armistice Line and shows how the State of Israel has effectively hijacked the rhetoric of the two-state solution in order to solidify its permanent control over the Occupied Territories. When Israeli politicians like Ariel Sharon, who over their careers had adamantly rejected talk of a Palestinian state and who had insisted that Israel's control over the West Bank, East Jerusalem, and the Gaza Strip did not constitute occupation, began calling for an end to the occupation and indicating that they would accept the creation of a

Palestinian state, this did not reflect a change of heart or policy; it was instead a skillful manipulation of language.

"Ending the occupation," in this language regime, becomes code for the withdrawal of the Israeli military from Palestinian population centers while maintaining firm control over movement between Palestinian cities and villages and advancing the de facto, albeit not de jure, annexation of large settlement blocs, the Jordan Valley, and areas over West Bank aquifers. The fate of the Gaza Strip is instructive: when Israel dismantled its settlements inside the Strip and withdrew its forces, it declared that the occupation of Gaza was over, even as it maintained firm control over the passage of persons and goods into and out of the Strip, turning Gaza into a large, open-air prison for its nearly 1.5 million Palestinian inhabitants.

"Accepting Palestinian statehood," in turn, comes to mean an Israeli willingness to allow Palestinians to call the discontiguous parcels of land to which they are now confined a state if they so wish. In short, the language of Palestinian statehood and the rhetoric of ending the occupation, once fervently rejected by Israel, has been co-opted in order to gain legitimacy for the longtime Israeli attempt to control all of the Occupied Territories while divesting itself of the responsibilities for the Palestinian population that international law places on occupying powers.

Western churches have been slow to recognize how seriously distorted the discourse of statehood has become. In the conference halls and seminar rooms of Washington and Tel Aviv, road maps to a Palestinian state have become exercises in trying to find a Palestinian leadership willing to accept the fragmented reservations created by Israel's walls, fences, and checkpoints as a state and as the basis for an end to the conflict. However, the advocacy of Western churches for a two-state solution continues to operate as if Israel, with the United States' blessing, is not actively engaged in obliterating the territorial basis for such a solution. Palestinians have increasingly begun to question the feasibility and the desirability of the two-state vision. As the walls, fences, and checkpoint regimes throughout the Occupied Territories are finalized and as the success of Israel's colonial enterprise becomes apparent, Christians serious about working for long-term landed security for Palestinians and Israelis alike, for a resolution of the conflict rather than the protracted containment of it through militarized fortifications, will have to move beyond advocacy for two states toward advocacy for the dismantling of discriminatory laws and institutions throughout Palestine-Israel, including the dismantling of the legal and political structures that prevent refugees from returning home.

For Christians, rights are not ultimately ends in themselves. Rather, they make sense within a teleological framework, within, that is, a vision of the broader political good to be nurtured and developed through the securing and implementation of those rights. The political telos toward which Christian action should be directed is a holistic vision of reconciliation in the context of landed security. This vision is captured well by two portions of Scripture: first, the prophet Micah's vision of a day in which God's people will live secure under vine and fig tree, with no one to make them afraid (Mic 4:4); and second, the proclamation by the writer of Ephesians that in Christ Jesus the dividing wall of hostility between Jew and Gentile has been broken down (Eph 2:15). Christian concern about refugee rights is not about retribution and not even solely about restitution—rather, Christian support for Palestinian refugee rights is driven by a concern for future Palestinian-Israeli reconciliation.

After the horrors of the Shoah, it is understandable that the idea of Israel as a safe haven with a Jewish majority would resonate with many Jews. But must such a safe haven be tied to a project of maintaining and protecting a Jewish majority by any and all means? Might not a binational future in one state be one in which both Palestinians and Israelis alike sit securely under vine and fig tree? The current reality in Palestine-Israel is, after all, already a binational reality of two peoples within one sovereign state from the Jordan River to the Mediterranean Sea, a warped binationalism of ethnocratic domination.[9] Remembering Palestinian refugees opens up the possibility of moving beyond the distorted binational reality of the present toward a binational future in which the presence of the other is viewed not as a threat but as an opportunity for reconciliation. Such reconciliation, however, will not emerge from the practices and ideologies of historial amnesia. For the church to be an agent of reconciliation, it must be an agent of memory, not of forgetting.

8

The Ephesian Vision Against
the Iron Wall

"For he is our peace; in his flesh he has made both groups into one and has broken down the dividing wall, that is, the hostility between us" (Eph 2:14). In this christological proclamation to the church at Ephesus we have one of the great peacemaking texts of Scripture, describing a vision and present reality of reconciliation between two peoples, Jews and Gentiles, with the stories and histories of those once divided by hostility now reconciled in one body. The difference between the two is not erased by this reconciliation: peace is not here about homogenizing or obliterating difference, but rather about breaking down walls of antagonism and about the formation of bridges and bonds between those who remain different.[1] The Ephesian vision is incarnated whenever the dividing walls of injustice, oppression, and violence that fuel enmity are brought down and opportunities for a shared existence of mutuality are made possible. For those of us who confess Christ as Lord, it is impossible to find a more compelling image for the peace and reconciliation toward which nonviolent action should be directed.[2]

The Ephesian vision of two peoples reconciled, the dividing wall of hostility between them broken down, stands in sharp contrast to the current reality of Palestine-Israel, to a spatial-political regime in which legal, planning, and military barriers are erected to guarantee demographic hegemony and control over water and land resources.[3] In order to understand more fully this contrast of visions, a consideration of the political program outlined by Ze'ev Jabotinsky, the leader of Revisionist Zionism in the early decades of the twentieth century and the spiritual ancestor of the Israeli Likud party, proves useful. In a 1923 article entitled "The Iron Wall," Jabotinsky wrote: "We must either suspend our settlement efforts or continue them without paying attention to the mood of the natives. Settlement can thus develop under the protection of a force that is not dependent on the local population, behind an iron wall which they will be powerless to break down."[4] The colonization of Palestine, Jabotinsky understood, was a unilateral action, one that would have to be imposed on the indigenous population. Until the native Palestinian Arab population accepted the Zionist goal of creating a state with a Jewish demographic majority in most or all of Mandate Palestine, the Zionist movement would have to depend on unilateral actions. Revisionist Zionists like Jabotinsky acknowledged more forthrightly than Labor Zionists that the success of this settler-colonial project to achieve territorial-demographic hegemony would depend on force and dispossession.

The construction of the so-called security fence, or separation wall, in the Occupied Territories, Ariel Sharon's disengagement plan, and Ehud Olmert's convergence plan should all be understood as late developments in a Jabotinsky-style iron wall strategy, a strategy that Israel has been implementing for six decades. The nine-meter concrete walls and militarized zones of patrol roads, razor wire, and electrified fences did not simply emerge from nowhere. Rather, they function as a blunt continuation of a long line of legal and physical walls that Israel has erected against the Palestinian population. Consider, for example, the legal barriers erected by Israel to prevent the return of, and property restitution to, Palestinian refugees and internally displaced persons (or present absentees).[5] Or consider the legal and planning barriers Israel erects to deny Palestinian citizens of Israel land for urban expansion.[6]

Following its conquest of the West Bank, East Jerusalem, and the Gaza Strip in 1967, Israel has been erecting legal and physical walls aimed at trying to solve its dilemma of wanting control over all of the Occupied Territories while simultaneously excluding Palestinians in those territories from political life, a dilemma of wanting territorial control without jeopardizing demographic control. The left and the right of the Israeli political spectrum (not counting the far left) have favored Israeli control over all of the "land of Israel," with the religious right viewing Judea and Samaria as the biblical heartland, and the secular left and right considering the Jordan Valley, the aquifers of the northern West Bank, and large areas around Jerusalem and the western edge of the West Bank to be nonnegotiable strategic and military assets. Outright annexation of the West Bank (not to mention the Gaza Strip) has not been an option for the major Israeli parties, however, since annexation would mean that the

Palestinians in the conquered territories would become Israeli citizens, endangering the Jewish demographic majority in the state.

The Israeli dilemma since 1967, then, can be understood as a struggle about how to maximize control over all of Mandate Palestine while minimizing the number of Palestinians under its direct control. Israeli military and political leaders have forwarded various plans that would minimize Israeli responsibility for Palestinians in the Occupied Territories by granting some form of autonomy to those Palestinians in specific enclaves: the Allon Plan, which would have created northern and southern enclaves in the West Bank, separated by Israeli-annexed territory from Jerusalem to Jericho and up and down the Jordan Valley; the Village Leagues plan of the late 1970s that would have granted semi-autonomous status to Palestinian cities in the West Bank; and, most recently, the Oslo Accords, in which the newly created Palestinian Authority was given semi-autonomous control over portions of the West Bank and the Gaza Strip.

To repeat: the separation wall now being built throughout the Occupied Territories, and the accompanying disengagement plan, are best understood in this historical perspective. The wall will allow Israel to maximize its control over the Occupied Territories while avoiding any responsibility for the Palestinian population from which it separates itself by walls and fences: enjoying the fruits of occupation without any of occupation's responsibilities. The wall will function as a means of demographic control.[7] Israeli Prime Minister Ehud Olmert outlined the goals of this "unilateral solution" with characteristic bluntness: "To maximize the number of Jews; to minimize the number of Palestinians; not to withdraw to the 1967 border and not to divide Jerusalem."[8] This formula, portions of which have received explicit approval from the United States, means the de facto annexation of large settlement blocs around Jerusalem and Bethlehem (the Gush Etzion block, Maale Adumim, Givat Ze'ev), in the northern West Bank (the Ariel block), and in the Jordan Valley. Palestinians are left with discontiguous cantons, cut off from key water resources, cut off from Jerusalem, cut off from each other.

That Israeli and U.S. leaders can talk about these pieces of land being a future Palestinian state should underscore that statehood is not an end in itself, that a Palestinian state in and of itself does not equal a solution to the conflict. The fundamental question should not be whether or not one is for or against a Palestinian state, or for or against an Israeli state, but rather should be to ask what makes for a politics of justice, peace, and reconciliation in which Palestinian and Israeli alike might sit under their own fig trees, real and metaphorical, without fear (Mic 4:4). For many years now, a majority of the proponents of peace—Palestinian, Israeli, and international—have assumed that a two-state solution, with a Palestinian state in all of the West Bank, East Jerusalem, and the Gaza Strip, could meet the demands of justice, laying the groundwork for peace and reconciliation. But what if it becomes increasingly clear, in the face of the walls being erected and in the face of official U.S. approval of the de facto (if not de jure) annexation of settlement blocks, that a two-state solution is being or has been eclipsed?

The Ephesian vision versus the iron wall or, as the late Pope John Paul II phrased it, bridges instead of walls: that is the stark alternative facing the Holy Land today. The iron wall has, strangely enough, produced a distorted version of the Ephesian vision. The walls and fences meant to divide Israeli from Palestinian are, by solidifying Israeli territorial control over all of Mandate Palestine, binding Palestinians and Israelis more tightly into one body. There is, after all, only one sovereign power between the Jordan River and the Mediterranean Sea: Israel, a sovereign power that denies rights of citizenship and other basic human rights to 3.7 million Palestinians. There is one sovereign state, Israel, but it is not a state of its citizens, and state power is marshaled to exclude and restrict Palestinian access (both in Israel and in the Occupied Territories) to land and water. This one sovereign state erects dividing walls that will generate hostility for years to come. One political body, then, but with walls and fences of enmity dissecting it. One political body, without reciprocity and reconciliation between equals. The Ephesian vision points in the opposite direction: one political body for two peoples, but instead of the current binationalism of exclusion and dispossession, a binationalism of equality and mutuality.

What concrete hope, however, can the Ephesian vision offer in the face of the triumphant project of the iron wall? Ariel Sharon boasted, "The Palestinians understand that [the disengagement] plan is, to a great extent, the end of their dreams, a very heavy blow to them."[9] The separation walls and fences, along with the imprisonment of the Gaza Strip and the solidification of the regime of checkpoints and settlement roads inside the West Bank, have dismembered the Occupied Territories and have buried hope for a two-state solution based on the 1949 Armistice Line. Talk of a two-state resolution to the conflict limps along but has come practically to mean the attempt of the United States and Israel to force the Palestinian leadership to accept geographically fragmented, economically subservient territories as a state and as the basis for an end to the conflict.

With the geographical fragmentation of the Palestinian territories not surprisingly leading to political fragmentation (such as the ongoing struggle between the Islamist Hamas movement and the PLO's Fatah) and with unemployment and poverty figures chronically high, despair permeates the Palestinian political field.[10] For Palestinians who refuse to quit dreaming and for those Israelis who dream with Palestinians of a future in which Palestinians and Israelis will live in justice and equality in the land, the question amidst these grim circumstances is how best to counter the ideology and practice of the iron wall.

Over the past four decades of occupation, some Palestinians have answered that nonviolence offers the best hope for achieving justice, equality, and reconciliation. The Palestinian Center for Rapprochement between Peoples, the Sabeel Ecumenical Liberation Theology Center, and the Wi'am Palestinian Conflict Resolution Center are but some of the groups that have sought to show through word and deed that nonviolence offers practical hope for the future. Palestinian nonviolent activists, to be sure, have faced numerous challenges over the years. They have had to dispel stereotypes of nonviolence as passive acceptance of military domination. In more recent years, Palestinian activists have faced attempts by donor governments to bureaucratize nonviolence, as the United States and the European Union have funded training courses in nonviolence that ultimately had less to do with empowering communities to resist ongoing dispossession and more to do with acquiescing to the iron wall regime. Can nonviolent action, Palestinians today wonder, challenge the walls and fences of division and enmity?

Ayid Murar, from the village of Budrus near Ramallah, a village that has been at the forefront of nonviolent protest against the separation wall, perceptively observes that nonviolent action can empower a broader segment of the population than can violence. "We have to bring the entire Palestinian people into the struggle against the occupation," says Murar, "women, children, the aged—and they cannot take part in a violent struggle. But they can take part in this kind of struggle, which also contributes to the unity of our nation. We also know that a nonviolent struggle puts more pressure on the Israelis," he continues, noting that, while soldiers know how to respond to armed attacks, they are sometimes caught off guard by nonviolent protest.[11]

The daily protests in Biddu, Budrus, Beit Surik, and Bil'in against the construction of the wall have been inspiring and galvanizing, even as the predictable Israeli stigmatizing of nonviolent protest as terrorism has been depressing. That after years of roadblocks, curfews, economic siege, and daily violence, Palestinian communities are finding the resources to organize to try to stop bulldozers from uprooting trees and clearing the path for the wall is truly a testament to God's Spirit at work to bring blessing and hope in the midst of destruction, apathy, and hopelessness.

When speaking about nonviolent direct action in Palestine, it is important not to minimize the challenges before those communities who gather to face the bulldozers. In the summer of 2002, residents of villages such as Jayyous and Falamiyeh in the Qalqilyah district were organizing to try to stop the uprooting of their trees and the construction of the separation wall on their lands. The next summer the walls and fences cutting these villages off from their farmland and aquifers were complete. In October 2003, the Israeli civil administration of the military government announced that non-Israelis would require a permit, issued by the civil administration, in order to enter the "seam area" between the wall and the 1949 Armistice Line (the Green Line). This meant, for example, that villagers in Jayyous would have to obtain a permit if they wanted to work land on the other side of the wall.

Vigorous discussions ensued within communities whose lands had been segregated by the wall. Should people try to negotiate the hostile, Kafkaesque bureaucracy of the civil administration in order to try to get a permit to pass through the gates in the wall? Or should they refuse on principle? The idea of refusing to apply for a permit in order to access one's own land has a moral purity and power about it that is undeniably attractive. But one must certainly hesitate before criticizing farmers whose livelihoods depend on accessing their land for applying for permits. As it is, only a small percentage of farmers in Jayyous and other affected communities managed to obtain the required permits, and most fear that it is only a matter of time before Israel begins confiscating land behind the wall on the pretext that it is not cultivated.

Were the nonviolent protests in Jayyous six years ago then for naught? Will the protests in villages around Ramallah and Jerusalem prove futile? Aziz Armani, from Khirbata, one village near Ramallah where the wall is going up now, suggests not: "The main thing," he says, "is that we feel we are doing something—if not for ourselves, then for the coming generations. Even if we are able to get the fence moved two meters and save a few meters of our land, that will be something."[12]

Armani's words might seem to provide little comfort and hope, measuring success in the nonviolent struggle in getting the walls and fences moved a couple of meters, saving a little bit of one's land from the bulldozer's teeth. In addition to the construction delays and the adjustments in the wall's path that nonviolent action has managed to effect, however, there is a longer-term reason for hope, even if this hope might at times appear faint. Israelis, at the invitation of Palestinian communities, have joined with Palestinians in nonviolent attempts to stop the uprooting of trees, to halt the wall's seemingly inexorable path of destruction. In addition to whatever short-term successes these Israelis and Palestinians chalk up, in their shared work for justice they offer signs of hope for the future (signs that Israel seeks to obliterate, as it criminalizes the entry of Israelis into Palestinian cities in the West Bank in an attempt to squelch such nonviolent solidarity).

Perhaps Israel's iron separation wall will be soon be dismantled and a two-state solution based on a withdrawal to the Green Line will yet materialize. However, the United States' blessing of the disengagement plan, with its de facto annexation of Israeli settlement blocks in the West Bank, makes this exceedingly unlikely. Determined not to resolve the conflict, Israel looks to manage it through iron walls. With its military might and backing from the United States, the iron wall strategy would seem to be successful, at least for the medium term. However, the walls and fences will not last forever, and the dismembered geographic and political body they circumscribe will prove neither sustainable nor the stable foundation for a resolution of the conflict. The question then becomes, what will replace them?

The shared struggle of Palestinians and Israeli Jews against injustice and dispossession in the present embodies the Ephesian vision of the breaking down of the dividing walls of hostility and thus offers a sign of hope for a shared, binational future in the land. Those who seek the peace of Haifa and Tel Aviv, Gaza and Nablus, Dimona and Khan Younis, and Al-Quds/Yerushalayim (Jerusalem) look beyond the ideologies and practices of iron walls toward a future of interdependence and mutuality.

The Palestinian Muslim theologian Mustafa Abu Sway captures this politics of interdependence with his concept of *dar al-hiwar*. Distinct from the traditional categories of *dar al-islam* (the house of submission) and *dar al-harb* (the house of war), *dar al-hiwar*, or the house of conversation, presents a political vision in which distinct identities are maintained but in which one's identity is shaped through conversation with others.[13] This notion of *dar al-hiwar*, furthermore, intersects with the Pauline understanding of the body. Paul, in his letter to the Corinthians, articulates a political theology in which the distinct members of Christ's body participate in each other, joining in one another's joys and tribulations. "If one member suffers, all suffer together with it; if one member is honored, all rejoice together with it" (1 Cor 12:26).[14] In a Pauline body politics, as in binational visions, particular identities are not fixed and static, but rather are fluid and interactive. A binational approach to the Palestinian-Israeli conflict undermines exclusive correlations between nation and territory and opens the door to Palestinian and Israeli Jewish identity being shaped through *hiwar* (conversation) with the other.[15] True security, secure identity, will not be found behind the fortifications of the iron wall, but finally, through participation with the other, in seeking the well-being, the *shalom* and the *salaam*, of all the people in the land.

9

Thinking About Terrorism
The Case of Palestine-Israel

What counts as terrorism? A young Palestinian man enters a pizzeria on Jaffa Road in West Jerusalem, explosives strapped around his waist, and blows himself up, killing with him twenty Israelis: this horrific act is routinely named terrorism by media outlets and government officials. But how about the following: five boys from Khan Younis are walking home from school when one of them kicks a metal object by the side of the road. The object turns out to be a bomb planted by the Israeli military. It explodes, and all five children die. Was the Israeli decision to plant an explosive device in an area frequented by civilians an act of terror? Or consider the case of three-month-old Iman Hijo, also of Khan Younis, who, prior to the Israeli government's evacuation of the Gaza Strip's settlements in 2005, was killed by a stray bullet from indiscriminate fire from Israeli military outposts built around those settlements: terror victim or collateral damage? And what about pregnant Palestinian women trying to reach a hospital but turned back at gunpoint by Israeli soldiers at a checkpoint? When the baby dies, is she a victim of terror?

Terrorism, as a particular form of violence, is notoriously difficult to define. The word is bandied about in popular culture and political discourse as if its meaning were clear, but its ubiquity often functions as a short-circuit to critical thought. For a pacifist to enter into the debate about what constitutes terrorism is a particularly challenging task, since it requires the pacifist to differentiate between species of a genus, violence, that must be categorically rejected as wrong, as sinful.

In this chapter I undertake two interrelated tasks. First, examining the case of the Palestinian *intifada* (uprising, or shaking off) against Israeli occupation, I describe how the discourse of terrorism as produced by government institutions, think tanks, and the media serves ideological interests by delegitimizing the violence of one group as terrorism while justifying the violence of another group as counter-terrorism. Second, rejecting the easy moral equivalence suggested by the phrase, "One person's terrorist is another's freedom fighter," I suggest that pacifist Christians, as exiled witnesses amidst the violent empires of the world, can make moral distinctions among types of violence while simultaneously maintaining our conviction that *all* violence is a rebellious turning away from God, a failure to worship God properly. Making such distinctions, I suggest, is part of the pacifist Christian's responsibility to use "middle axioms"—a distinctive form of communication for Christians in exile—as we encourage states and revolutionary groups that aspire to statehood to place limitations on the sin-laden enterprise of war and violent revolution. Even as we make these distinctions, however, and even as we promote practical alternatives to the politics of violence, the case of Palestine-Israel should prove a healthy reminder that our witness on behalf of the nonviolent politics of the Lamb will often appear foolish when measured against the ruling wisdom.

The Deceptive Discourse of Terrorism

The Palestinian-Israeli conflict offers a clear example of how the discourse of terrorism can be employed to serve ideological interests. Israeli academics and military officers make up a significant percentage of the world's self-proclaimed experts on terrorism, pundits who present their purportedly objective and scholarly analyses over talk-show airwaves and in the pages of newsweeklies. Foremost in this group is former Israeli Prime Minister Binyamin Netanyahu. A self-made terror expert, Netanyahu regularly expounds the view that terrorism presents a unique threat directed against the West from fanatical stateless groups or from so-called rogue states. The notion that Western democratic states might be purveyors of terror does not fit into Netanyahu's conceptual scheme.[1] For Netanyahu, Israeli government officials, and pro-Israel apologetes generally, all violence directed against Israel qualifies as terrorism. Not only, then, is the indiscriminate killing of Israeli civilians inside Israel proper by a suicide bomber terrorism, but so are attacks on settler-colonists and against Israeli military personnel in the Occupied Territories.

While the delegitimizing of all Palestinian resistance to the military occupation has been a standard trope of Israeli discourse for decades, it gained new vigor after the attacks on the United States on September 11, 2001, with the Israeli government not-so-subtly seeking to use the U.S.-led "war on terror" for its own ends, namely, to tar all Palestinian resistance with the brush of terrorism. Now perhaps Americans will understand the daily reality of Israelis, several pundits opined. Then-Israeli Prime Minister Ariel Sharon repeatedly described the late Palestinian leader Yasser Arafat as "our Bin Laden," with the implication that it would be hypocritical for the United States and its allies to criticize Israel for its actions in the Occupied Territories, since Israel was simply engaged in a form of counter-terrorism similar to that of the United States in its battle against al-Qa'ida and the Taliban. Gideon Samet observed that the Arafat-equals-Bin Laden equation dominated the Israeli security establishment and noted that this rhetorical move had some effect in Washington. For example, at an Israeli conference on security in December 2001 in Herzilya, former CIA director James Woolsey described Israel as a greater victim of terrorism than the United States, calculating Israeli casualties since the beginning of the *intifada* as at least three times that of the Twin Towers disaster (when measured by percentage of victims relative to the overall population of each country).[2] Not surprisingly, Woolsey passed over in silence the Palestinian casualties of the *intifada*, which at the time were well over ten times the casualties of the New York attacks, again when calculated relative to the percentage of the overall population.

I will return later in this chapter to discuss what this discourse omits: specifically, (1) any acknowledgment of the indiscriminate, punitive, and retributive character of Israeli violence in the Occupied Territories and the human toll this has exacted on Palestinians; and (2) any nuanced appraisal of the forms of violence used against Israel. For now, I will limit myself to two observations. First, the Israeli discourse of terrorism is flexible enough to stigmatize *all* Palestinian resistance, even unarmed civilian (i.e., nonviolent) resistance. Dov Tamari, a former brigadier general in the Israeli Defense Forces, observed that while serving in Lebanon in 1982, he found that the term "terrorist infrastructure" was so vague that it essentially meant the entire people: "To 'dismantle' [that infrastructure] you have to start killing people *en masse*, and if you don't want to do that you should just give up the idea."[3] If entire political movements are labeled as terrorist—say, for example, the political factions with the PLO—because of actions carried out by the military wings associated with those movements, then all activities conducted by those movements become terrorist activities. Thus, for example, a health clinic operated by a non-governmental organization whose board members are predominantly affiliated with the Popular Front for the Liberation of Palestine (PFLP) becomes a terrorist institution because of attacks by the PFLP's military wing deemed to be "terrorist" attacks. When the quasi-autonomous Palestinian Authority does not succeed in securing absolute calm in the Occupied Territories, then it too becomes a terrorist organization, or at least an entity that "harbors" terrorists. This rhetorical move of guilt-by-association can be taken to comical lengths. Uzi Landau, a former Israeli Internal Security Minister, defended his decision to ban a reception in Jerusalem for foreign diplomats to mark Eid al-Fitr, the feast at the end of the Muslim month of Ramadan, on the grounds that it was organized by Sari Nusseibeh, then the holder of the Jerusalem file for the PLO and a prominent Palestinian academic, and was thus, from the perspective of the Israeli government, a "terror-related" activity.[4]

The second initial point to make is that the case of Palestine-Israel confirms the broader thesis, articulated most pointedly by Edward Herman, that the news media manufacture consent to state policy, particularly military policy, by presenting only certain forms of violence as terrorism. Violent resistance by stateless groups is stigmatized as terrorism, while violence carried out by states, regardless of the extent of "collateral damage" to civilians, is justified as a legitimate attempt to secure order and justice.[5]

The Difficulties of Defining Terrorism

The ability of the discourse of terrorism to legitimize certain forms of violence while stigmatizing others depends, Herman suggests, on a specific definitional move, namely, that of excluding states from the possibility of engaging in terrorism. Once one questions the givenness of this definitional move, then it becomes clear that states often engage in violent acts similar in nature and scope to those classified as terrorism, save for the fact that the actors are the state and its representatives rather than non-state actors. As the similarity between the violence perpetrated by state and the violence carried out by non-state actors becomes apparent, the temptation for the pacifist to pronounce a pox on all houses and dismiss all talk of terrorism as ideological attempts to justify one form of violence over another becomes great. The cynicism with which particular governments (say, the United States and Israel) use the discourse of terrorism increases this temptation.

While understanding the appeal of this temptation, I suggest that, despite the ideological distortions to which the discourse of terrorism is prone, the word terrorism can minimally suggest to us that certain forms of violence, regardless of the actor, are worse than others. Perhaps the word "terrorism" itself is too emotive and prone to ideological distortion. John Rempel, former director of Mennonite Central Committee's liaison office to the United Nations in New York, argues that "'terrorism' is not a neutral concept. One person's terrorist," he continues, "is another's freedom fighter."[6] Rempel certainly captures an important truth. I would nevertheless suggest that Christian pacifists should learn from an engagement with the discourse of terrorism to be nuanced about the forms in which violence can manifest itself. All violence certainly embodies a sinful turning away from God, but not all violence is thereby of the same scope and quality.

But to jump into the question of whether or not the word terrorism can be used with integrity is to get ahead of ourselves. Let us begin, rather, by noting some standard definitions of terrorism and the forms of violence that these definitions exclude. The U.S. State Department defines terrorism as "premeditated, politically motivated violence perpetrated against noncombatant targets by subnational groups or clandestine agents, usually intended to influence an audience."[7] Three elements in this definition are particularly noteworthy. First, terrorism is violence that targets civilians, or noncombatants. Second, the definition does not include acts committed by a state's military forces (although a state's "clandestine agents" could, apparently, implicate a state in terror). Third, terrorism is designed to "influence an audience," presumably by generating enough fear to motivate a change of policy. The U.S. Defense Department's definition sounds the same three notes: "Terrorism is the unlawful use or threatened use of force or violence by a revolutionary organization against individuals or property, with the intention of coercing or intimidating governments or societies, often for political or ideological purposes."[8] More clearly than the State Department definition, the Defense Department's construal of terrorism excludes states from the ranks of those who perpetrate terror. The potential victims of terrorism in the Defense Department's definition, however, form a broader group than in the State Department's definition. Not only noncombatants, but individuals generally (presumably, this could include soldiers), along with property, can be terror victims.

What is significant in these two definitions for our purposes is the way in which both view terrorism as predominantly, if not exclusively, as an activity carried out by stateless, revolutionary groups: states are thus not terror agents. That states would have a vested interest in such a definition should be obvious. After all, states routinely engage in activities that meet all of the other criteria of the two definitions: carrying out violence or threatening violence against individuals (including noncombatants) for political and ideological purposes. Not only do these limited definitions of terrorism betray states' self-interest, but they also reflect outmoded social scientific analyses of war. Dov Tamari notes that wars between "a state and non-state entity" have not been properly analyzed in standard social science research, since they do not "fit the idealized criteria of Clausewitz." Anything that does not fit the model of two states at war is then often lumped "under the simple-minded label of 'terrorism.'"[9]

At the international level, no consensus exists on what constitutes terrorism. Eyal Gross, expert on international law at Tel Aviv University, insists that no obvious reason exists for excluding states from the purveyors of terror: "When a bomb explodes in a school and 20 children are killed—that is terror, but when a plane bombs the same school and the same children are killed—it is referred to as a military action. These things should be said," he continues. "According to the various international conventions, there is no legal differentiation between the attacks on the Twin Towers and the bombing of a school in Kabul. Why is an attack in Ma'alot [a town in northern Israel] considered terror, while an attack on Lebanese soil not terror? Why are the acts now being committed by the Palestinians called terror, while Israel's actions in the territories are not? There is terror committed by organizations and then there is state terror," he concludes.[10]

Gideon Levy, echoing Gross, pointed in November 2001 to the planting of an explosive charge along the roadside in Khan Younis as an example of Israeli state terror: "A state places explosive charges where children are likely to pass and then claims that only the other side practices terrorism?" Levy asked indignantly. "We have to admit that an act of this kind can be considered an act of terrorism because it strikes at the innocent and doesn't discriminate between the victims, even if the intention was not to kill and even if the goal was the war on terrorism. . . . Israel must direct the demand for a cease-fire and for a cessation of terrorism not only at the Palestinians but, to a certain degree, to itself, too."[11] Two months later, following the destruction of more than fifty homes in Rafah by Israeli military bulldozers, Levy returned to this theme: "A country that opposes terrorism against civilians cannot demolish homes of innocent civilians and then claim that what it did is not an act of terrorism."[12]

In his condemnation of Israeli military actions, Levy did not present a formal definition of terrorism, but his implicit definition is clear: terrorism is violence against civilians, violence that does not discriminate between the innocent and others. While Levy does not spell it out, it appears that his understanding of innocence involves nonparticipation in military confrontations or in other attacks against Israel. In other words, terrorism is violence motivated by ideological purposes that does not discriminate between combatants and noncombatants. Both states and revolutionary groups practice terrorism under this definition.

This understanding of terrorism forms the foundation of the mainstream Palestinian consensus that while attacks on civilians should be avoided, attacks on Israeli targets in the Occupied Territories are legitimate. Thus, the shooting of an Israeli soldier near Nablus would not be a terrorist act under Levy's working definition, while a gunman opening fire at a bat mitzvah in Herzilya would be. Or to take another example, when Hezbollah (repeatedly cited by the United States and Israel as a terrorist organization but viewed throughout the Arab world as a liberation movement) attacked Israeli military targets during Israel's occupation of southern Lebanon, this did not constitute terrorism, whereas the firing of a Katyusha rocket at Kiryat Shmona could be viewed as a terrorist act.[13]

If one must continue to use the word terrorism, then Levy's working definition has, I believe, much to recommend it. It captures our moral repugnance for attacks on civilians while not masking the fact that states routinely engage in such objectionable acts. Before accepting this working definition, however, let us consider some objections. A first objection would hold that there is a significant moral difference between the killing of thousands of civilians in the Twin Towers and the killing of thousands of civilians in Afghanistan as part of the so-called war against terror. Binyamin Netanyahu, the former Israeli prime minister, has articulated this position, lauding the United States for firmly establishing "a moral differentiation between terrorism and self-defense through military action that could inadvertently affect civilians." Netanyahu goes on to stress "the importance of victory, namely . . . the end justifies the means."[14] If the end justifies the means in this war against terror, however, if unlimited collateral damage is acceptable, then it becomes very difficult to see how Netanyahu proposes to establish his firm "moral differentiation" between terrorism and counter-terrorism. Both aim for particular visions of peace, that is, of world order; and both, if they accept that the end justifies the means, are willing to sacrifice noncombatants to secure those visions.

A second challenge to Levy's working definition of terrorism would involve the observation that both states and revolutionary groups maintain that distinguishing between combatants and others poses a difficult-to-impossible challenge. The Israeli government, for example, staunchly defended the demolition of the fifty-plus homes along the Philadelphi corridor in Rafah next to the the Egyptian border on the grounds that gunmen shot from between the homes and that Palestinians had dug tunnels underneath the homes to smuggle weapons. Regardless of the validity of those claims (and there were undeniably some tunnels and armed activity near the border), the massive demolitions functioned as collective punishment for the killing of four Israeli soldiers the day before, collective punishment that blurred the distinction between combatant and noncombatant. If some civilians are killed and injured and their property damaged, that simply constitutes collateral damage, an incidental, perhaps even regrettable effect of a military action against military targets. The Palestinian death toll during the second uprising against the occupation shows that the level of collateral damage has been quite high. Of the 686 Palestinians killed from September 29, 2000 to September 29, 2001, 59 percent died when no Palestinian-Israeli clashes were underway, 36 percent died in unarmed (i.e., stones, not guns) clashes, while only 5 percent of the dead were participating in armed clashes.[15]

Stanley Hauerwas, meanwhile, has observed that "terrorist" organizations offer strikingly similar justifications for attacks that indiscriminately affect civilians. "From the 'terrorist' point of view," he notes, "distinctions between combatants and noncombatants are not easily maintained."[16] A crowd of people along Jaffa Road in West Jerusalem will consist mostly of unarmed people, but how many of these men and women contribute to the successful functioning of the violent military occupation of the West Bank, East Jerusalem, and the Gaza Strip, serving as military officers, paying taxes, and so forth? Hauerwas continues by acknowledging that "those called terrorist" do not necessarily attack noncombatants, "but if they do," he suggests, "they are not without some moral response. Such an attack may be an attempt to make clear the kind of war they understand they are forced to wage—namely, a war of the desperate that must use selective targeting in non-selective ways." A bus bombing "may be tied to policy objectives that may even make such a bombing analogous to the defense of civilian deaths on just war grounds of indirect effect; for alleged terrorist strategies are meant—like war itself—to make people prefer peace, or at least order, rather than continue the conflict."[17] Israeli military personnel who demolish homes and carry out various types of attacks (shelling from tanks and helicopters, sniper fire, shooting into a crowd, assassinations) can claim (often cynically) a just intention—the apprehension or killing of a gunman, for example, or creating the conditions in which Palestinians will accept the "peace" of permanent Israeli control over the Occupied Territories—even as its actions have the indirect effect of significant civilian casualties. A Palestinian "terrorist," meanwhile, even a bus bomber, could claim that his actions are framed by a just intent, one that aims for a different form of peace.[18]

The justifiable war tradition, of course, claims that constraints can and should be placed on the waging of war so that, for example, civilians are not targeted. Acts traditionally labeled terrorism, meanwhile, disregard such constraints. The unspoken assumption in efforts to distinguish between the violence of stateless groups and the violence of state armies would hold that states can (and do) place more effective constraints on the use of violence. Any distinction between terrorism and war, observes Hauerwas, "gains its moral warrant from the assumption based in just war theory that there is continuity between the police function of the state and its war-making potential." This assumption, Hauerwas continues, is unwarranted, for "war lacks exactly the prior institutions and practices that limit the violence intrinsic to the police function of the state and, at least to some extent, make such violence less arbitrary."[19] States may claim that they limit violence and wage just wars, but, Hauerwas poignantly suggests, the constraints of the justifiable war tradition regularly break down during wartime, proving ineffective at placing controls and limits on the military.

Pacifist Responses Amidst the "Terror" of Palestine-Israel

Defining "terrorism" is clearly an ambiguous enterprise. Definitionally excluding states from being terrorists appears purely arbitrary, given the fact that both state and non-state actors engage in similar types of violent actions, in quality and in scope. Even a bare-bones definition of terrorism as violence against noncombatants proves challenging to sustain, since both states and revolutionary groups often blur the distinctions between combatant and noncombatant. Finally, if we cannot offer a definition of terrorism that will gain universal affirmation, we must nevertheless grapple with the question of how to respond as Christian pacifists in the midst of a conflict that has seen its fair share of horrific violence, whether or not one calls that violence terrorism. In what follows I propose five tasks for Christian pacifists living and working in the midst of the Palestinian-Israeli conflict, with its varied forms of violence and its charges and counter-charges of terrorism.[20]

Unmasking Deceptive Language

Christians must not fall prey to the deceptive use of language that stig-matizes certain forms of violence while legitimizing others. As I suggested above, the discourse of terrorism routinely functions in this deceptive man-ner, both generally and particularly in the case of Palestine-Israel. We must exercise healthy suspicion of claims by states that they act for the sake of justice (especially when they claim as did U.S. President George W. Bush, to pursue "infinite justice"). Ya'ir Hilu, an Israeli conscientious objector, succinctly pointed to the similarities shared by Palestinian and Israeli vio-lence when he declared his refusal to serve "in the Israeli army or in any other terrorist organization."[21] A critical reading of history, meanwhile, will remind us that, in the case of Israel, yesterday's successful terrorists are today's statespersons. The retired U.S. diplomat Phil Wilcox, former head of the State Department's section on terrorism, observed after reading an article on events in Mandate Palestine between 1946 and 1948 that he was "struck by how much the role of the Jewish terrorists, principally from the Irgun (Etzel) and Stern Gang (Lehi), sounded like Islamic Jihad and the PFLP, and how much the Zionist leadership sounded like Arafat, in its unwillingness to cooperate with the British in apprehending them."[22] Cultivating a historical perspective thus renders problematic any easy demonizing of one group's violence as terrorist.

Naming Forms of Violence

Suicide bombings, gunmen opening fire in a pedestrian mall—these are the dramatic forms of violence in Palestine-Israel routinely covered in the Western media, acts of violence typically designated as "terrorism." Christians must unquestionably deplore such violence and lament its vic-tims. At the same time, however, we must also lament the many and var-ied forms in which people exercise violent power in Palestine-Israel. Thousands of Palestinians have been killed since the start of the *intifada* in September 2000—most of them, as noted above, civilians, and many of them children—and tens of thousands of Palestinians have sustained injuries, many permanently disabling. In addition to this violence, one must add many other manifestations of violence, acts rarely captured on radio and television newscasts. "Aren't massive land expropriations, sys-tematic house destruction, the uprooting of orchards and groves, also a form of violence?" asks Israeli journalist Gideon Levy. "Isn't cutting off entire towns and villages from their source of water a type of violence?

Isn't limitation on freedom of movement by slicing whole areas of the population off from each other and denying medical attention to the residents—even when it's a matter of life and death, as painful as highway shootings? The humiliations and beating, and the settlers' own violence against Palestinians—what should that be called?"[23]

Christians from the United States, for that matter, should remember their complicity in violence as the U.S. government provides billions of dollars per year to Israel in military assistance. Referring to the unseen violence on which Israel's occupation of the West Bank and the Gaza Strip depends and to U.S. aid to Israel, Mennonite Central Committee worker Ed Nyce cautioned that "the violence which we see will not cease until the violence which we do not see ceases. In the meantime, telling Palestinians to stop their actions, given our own military might, is presumption enough. Selling and giving Israel weapons and technology and providing training assistance simply adds to the audacity."[24]

Appealing for Limits to Violence

At one level, all violence shares notable characteristics. Lee Griffith is correct to note that at the spiritual level terrorism and counter-terrorism are strikingly similar phenomena, both partaking in the assumption that striking fear in one's opponent can generate significant change.[25] All violence, one could argue, is a form of terror, aimed to instill fear, to disrupt the status quo. Theologically put, all violence represents a rebellious turning away from God, a failure to worship God properly.

Recognition of these similarities, however, should not prevent us from acknowledging the impulse behind the emotive and ideologically fraught discourse of terrorism to declare certain violent practices unacceptable. Establishing universal consensus on which practices these are would probably prove elusive. Judgments on what constitutes unacceptable violence in a wartime or revolutionary situation will vary from context to context. Nevertheless, that different peoples routinely make such contextual judgments provides pacifists with a point of appeal to warring parties to limit their violence. These appeals to standards recognized by parties engaged in armed conflict are what the late John Howard Yoder called "middle axioms," the form of discursive reasoning and appeals through which God's exiled people speak with their rulers and neighbors.[26] Appealing to Israelis and Palestinians, for example, to refrain from attacks on noncombatants would use Palestinian and Israeli leaders' own self-proclaimed standards for the basis for that appeal.

Using the world's (admittedly ambiguous and context-relative) standards for what constitutes unacceptable violence would push us to protest and lament not only suicide bombings but also indiscriminate Israeli fire, extra-judicial killings (assassinations), house demolitions, and sieges on Palestinian population centers. Within the Israeli peace camp one hears vocal protests against Israeli military actions in the Occupied Territories, protests that these actions go beyond the acceptable use of force. Adi Ophir of Tel Aviv University declared at a symposium organized by the Israeli Peace Bloc (Gush Shalom) that "the army in the Occupied Territories is involved in war crimes. . . . The problem is to find tribunals where those responsible can be tried."[27]

Former Israeli Minister of Education Shulamit Aloni echoed Ophir's assessment, urging fellow peace activists: "We have to call a spade a spade. We have to say out loud that our government is committing war crimes, to say it clearly and explicitly and repeat it again and again. And yes, the time has come to start compiling dossiers on the war criminals!"[28] Insisting that Israel respect the provisions of the Fourth Geneva Convention to regulate its behavior in the Occupied Territories would be a concrete example of appealing to the world's self-proclaimed limits on violence (limits that Israel has officially acknowledged but that it denies apply to the Occupied Territories) in an effort to curb death and destruction.

Promoting Nonviolent Alternatives

The myth that violence can bring security grips too many Israelis. The myth that violence can secure liberation captivates too many Palestinians. These myths of violence exercise a powerful hold on people's imaginations, constricting the sense of the possible and blinding people to the ultimate impotence of violence. Christian pacifists must expand the sense of the possible, both raising questions about the effectiveness of violence and encouraging alternatives to violent struggle.

In both instances, Western Christians would not speak in a vacuum but would join their voices to those of Israeli Jews and Palestinian Christians and Muslims. Even as the military-security mentality reigns supreme within Israel, many question it, recognizing that no military solution exists to Palestinian "terror." "All of the anti-terror measures which we've implemented during the past year can be compared figuratively to trying to empty the sea by using a spoon," said a senior Israeli security officer. An internal Israeli Defense Forces study admits that the siege network of roadblocks and checkpoints that severely constrict Palestinian movement do not enhance Israeli security. Ami Ayalon, former chief of the Shin Bet, Israel's internal security services, acknowledges, "You cannot kill ideologies by killing leaders. It's easy to prove that under circumstances of negotiations and political hope and expectation, selective killing of a terrorist will lead some away from the terror side, and bring them to the discussion sphere. But when there is no political expectation [of a peace agreement], assassinations do the opposite."[29] When even those within Israel's security establishment acknowledge the ineffectiveness of the occupation's violence at suppressing terror attacks, it comes as no surprise that a growing number of Israelis assert that real security will only come from justice, from a real end to the occupation, from a real withdrawal from all of the Occupied Territories.

Palestinians, for their part, while unwilling to accept imposed solutions that would perpetuate Israeli control over the Occupied Territories, dismembering the Palestinian body politic, increasingly question the militarized character of the current *intifada* against the occupation. The Palestinian Center for Rapprochement between Peoples in Beit Sahour, the Sabeel Ecumenical Liberation Theology Center, and the Palestinian Non-Governmental Organization network (PNGO) all in different ways promote nonviolent resistance against the occupation as not only the most moral but also the most promising path of struggle. Palestinian Christian lawyer Jonathan Kuttab underlines the ineffectiveness of violence in a confrontation with Israel. During the first *intifada* against Israel, Kuttab observes, "the nonviolent struggle highlighted the justice of our cause, which rests on morality, international solidarity, and international law rather than on brute force and overwhelming military superiority. To insist on waging the struggle only in the military sphere," he continues, is "doubly foolish because it deprives us of our natural advantages and allows the conflict to play out in an arena of military violence where our enemies are vastly superior."[30]

Embracing the Foolishness of the Cross

Mennonites have in recent years developed a professional identity as peacebuilders. Establishing graduate programs in conflict transformation, cultivating expertise in mediation and conciliation, organizing activists to intervene in Haiti and Hebron—no longer the quiet in the land, Mennonites are ready to offer the world solutions. The laudable commitment to peace that drives such activities, however, can easily be deformed into a prideful conviction that, armed with adequate training (and a diploma), we can manage tensions, defuse conflicts, make history come out right. As much as we are called to cry for justice, transform conflicts, "build" peace, we must not become peace technocrats, promoters of one more technique by which to regulate and manage the world. We must rather confess that ultimately it is not we but God who builds peace, who has built and builds the kingdom, and that God's way of peacebuilding goes through the cross. Sometimes, at a *kairos* moment, our critiques of the politics of violence will resonate with our neighbors and our suggestions for nonviolent alternatives will strike a chord. But other times, perhaps most times, our colleagues and neighbors will find our witness to a politics of nonviolence jarring, foolish, even infuriating. We must be ready to sound foolish to our neighbors; this is a difficult discipline, for few among us wish to appear foolish.

In the whirlwind of occupation and resistance in Palestine-Israel, witness to a nonviolent politics, be it by Palestinian, Israeli, or expatriate, is often drowned out by the deafening storm of voices clamoring for retribution. We can maintain this witness only if our lives are grounded in the seemingly foolish history of God's work in the world, joined to God's life through prayer and sacrament. The discourse of "terrorism" is one of the forms that worldly wisdom has taken in our present age, obfuscating clear thought and marshalling forces against those persons demonized as terrorists. May God grant us the courage to embrace the foolishness of the cross and the wisdom to deconstruct the world's violent knowledge.

10

Remembering the *Nakba* in Hebrew
Return Visits as the Performance of a Binational Future

Let us begin with moments of erasure. In July 2006, bulldozers hired by the Israel Land Administration approached two structures near an orchard in what is today central Israel and proceeded to destroy them. One doubts that the bulldozer operators knew what the buildings were: the two structures looked old, but they also showed evidence of recent renovation. It did not take long for the machines to reduce the two buildings to piles of stone. After the rubble had been cleared, other workers came to plant trees. Most who would now pass by the site would have no idea that buildings once stood here.[1]

Six decades ago the two demolished buildings in question served as the boys' schoolhouse for Miskeh, a village in the Tulkarm district of Palestine. The 1945 census placed Miskeh's population at 1,060; the 1931 census counted 123 houses. Other village structures included the elementary school for local boys and a mosque. Historians believe that Miskeh's name comes from the name of the Arab tribe, the Miskain, which settled in Palestine's coastal plain during the early years of the Islamic conquest in the seventh century CE.[2]

Miskeh was also—depending on what one counts as a separate town or village—one of the between 413 and 531 Palestinian population centers destroyed by the Israeli military in 1948 and 1949.[3] Israeli forces entered Miskeh on April 20, 1948, and expelled the remaining inhabitants. These new refugees were some of the at least 750,000 Palestinians who became refugees between 1948 and 1950. Most of the Miskawis were expelled to the West Bank, which came under Jordanian control. One extended clan, the Shbeita family, was allowed to stay inside Israel, thanks to connections with an Israeli military officer. The Shbeita family ended up in the nearby town of Tira. Over the coming months they sought to return to their village but were prevented from doing so. The Israeli military destroyed some of Miskeh's buildings in 1948, but much of the village was left standing. In 1952 Israeli authorities destroyed all of the village's remaining buildings. Only the schoolhouse's two buildings and the village mosque remained. Shortly after Miskeh's destruction, Israeli authorities planted trees over much of its land.

For most Israeli Jews, the events of 1948 bear the name "the War of Independence" and conjure up memories of heroic sacrifice. Palestinians, however, name this period as the *Nakba*, an Arabic word meaning catastrophe. Little wonder, for the war of 1948 was indeed catastrophic for Palestinians, tearing apart their society's fabric, dispossessing many of their land and transforming well over half of the Palestinian population into refugees. Some refugees had left their homes to escape from the fighting. Israeli military units forcibly expelled others. For all, the reality after 1948 was the same: they were now the dispossessed, refugees.

In this chapter I examine different ways that Palestinians and Israelis have remembered the events of 1948, paying attention to what Laleh Khalili calls "the polysemic nature of commemorative practices that arise out of relations of power."[4] In particular, I focus on the memory practices of the Zochrot Association, an Israeli organization committed, in its words, to "remembering the *Nakba* in Hebrew." Over the past few years Zochrot has organized multiple events at the ruins of Miskeh, often in conjunction with groups of internally displaced Palestinians. The actions at Miskeh are representative of the ways in which Zochrot performs and provokes memory. Ahmad Sa'di has noted the polyvalent character of *Nakba*-memory for Palestinians, "its ability to reclaim new terrains, to acquire new meanings and representations, and to maintain its powerful presence."[5] Zochrot's practices of performative memory show how the *Nakba* can also acquire "new meanings and representations" within an Israeli Jewish society in which traces of the catastrophe, like the ruins of Miskeh, are actively erased or are, in the words of Lena Jayyusi, "tucked away, under and within the folds of history, a lesion within memory."[6] Specifically, I claim that Zochrot's acts of memory *perform* in the present an embodied hope for a binational future.

In order to paint the backdrop against which Zochrot's memory performances unfold, I first place the recent demolition of the Miskeh schoolhouse in the historical and contemporary context of a larger

Zionist project of spatial obliteration and active historical amnesia, a project that works to erase Palestinian presence from the land and to construct Palestinians as "absentees." I then turn to a discussion of different modalities of Palestinian refugee memory work in order to better situate and explain the significance of Zochrot's acts of performative memory. I next explore some of the multifaceted ways in which Zochrot seeks to provoke memories in Hebrew about the *Nakba*, to make present what had been rendered absent through embodied performances. I conclude by arguing that a consideration of Zochrot's memory work sheds light on an often-obscured dimension of Palestinian refugee acts of memory. Not simply nostalgic attempts to reclaim a pristine past or a steadfast obduracy in insisting on one's rights, acts of memory of the *Nakba*, be they in Arabic or, as in the case with Zochrot, in Hebrew, can be sacramental acts. These sacramental acts of memory enact in the present a hoped-for future of reconciliation, creating a binational space that disrupts the violence and dispossession of nationalist and colonialist ideology and practice.

Spatial Obliteration and the Present Absentees

The majority of Palestinian refugees displaced by the *Nakba* ended up in United Nations–administered camps outside what at the end of the war had become the new State of Israel, beyond the 1949 Armistice Line. Many, along with their descendants, continue to live in the refugee camps of the West Bank, the Gaza Strip, Lebanon, Syria, and Jordan. Others, however, remained in Israel, so international humanitarian law classifies them not as refugees but as "internally displaced persons." They became citizens of the new State of Israel (albeit not citizens entitled to the same rights and benefits as Jewish citizens).[7]

Like the officially recognized refugees, these internally displaced Palestinians also lost their homes and properties. As in Miskeh, Israeli forces leveled the buildings in most of the villages they had depopulated. In 1950 the Israeli Knesset passed the Absentee Property Law, which handed over refugee property to a new state agency, the Custodian of Absentee Property. Much of this land, in turn, was sold to *Keren Kayemeth L'Yisrael,* the Jewish National Fund (JNF), to hold in perpetuity for the Jewish people. Until recently, the JNF also enjoyed an intimate relationship with the Israel Land Administration (ILA), which administered state-seized land under JNF guidelines limiting property transactions of administered land to Jews only.[8]

As noted above, the Shbeita family from Miskeh managed to remain in the State of Israel, in Tira, one of the main towns in the so-called Arab Triangle. Physically, they were not far from Miskeh: it was only a matter of a few kilometers. In terms of legally constructed space, however, the distance was great and remains so. Under the Absentee Property Law, internally displaced persons like members of the Shbeita clan received the Orwellian Hebrew classification *nifkadim nochachim*, or in English, present absentees. They were "present" in the country, but the law constituted them as "absent" for the purpose of property confiscation.[9]

The destruction of Miskeh, along with the demolition of hundreds more Palestinian villages, did not take place in a vacuum. It occurred within a particular ideological framework. Specifically, it unfolded in the context of one dominant form of Zionist ideology, which sought to link spatial and demographic control and which understood the Zionist mandate to be the establishment of a Jewish state in which an indispensable part of the Jewishness of the state would be demographic control over a circumscribed territory.[10]

To understand this ideological context, one may consider the writings and career of Yosef Weitz, who served both before and after 1948 as an official of the JNF. Miskeh's destruction was ordered by Weitz, a longtime advocate of what was (and is) euphemistically called the "transfer" of Arabs outside of *eretz yisrael*. Transfer did not suddenly emerge as an ideology during 1948 but had been widely discussed among Zionists of the left and the right for decades. For Weitz, transfer was a means to a territorial end, an end framed by the religious language of redemption appropriated from Scripture and rabbinic tradition.

During a meeting with the Transfer Committee on November 15, 1937, Weitz linked the demographic dimension of transfer with its territorial objective: the "transfer of Arab population from the area of the Jewish state," he underscored, "does not serve only one aim—to diminish the Arab population. It also serves a second, no less important aim," namely, to "redeem" land "presently held and cultivated by the Arabs and thus to release it for Jewish inhabitants."[11] From Weitz's perspective, any form of binational accommodation was doomed to failure. The Zionist movement simply required more space, and the way to create that space was through the expulsion of the Palestinians. In his diary, Weitz wrote on December 20, 1940:

> It must be clear that there is no room in the country for both peoples. . . . If the Arabs leave it, the country will become wide and

spacious for us. . . . The only solution is a Land of Israel, at least
a western land of Israel, without Arabs. There is no room here
for compromises. . . . There is no way but to transfer the Arabs
from here to the neighboring countries, to transfer all of them,
save perhaps for Bethlehem, Nazareth, and the old Jerusalem.
Not one village must be left, not one tribe. The transfer must be
directed at Iraq, Syria, and even Transjordan. For this goal funds
will be found. . . . And only after this transfer will the country be
able to absorb millions of our brothers and the Jewish problem
will cease to exist. There is no other solution.[12]

Weitz's June 26, 1941, diary entry presents the hoped-for "transfer"
in explicitly religious, even messianic, terms:

Only through population transfer will redemption come. . . .
There is no room for us with our neighbours . . . development is
a very slow process. . . . They are too many and too much rooted
. . . the only way is to cut and eradicate them from the roots. I feel
that this is the truth. . . . I am beginning to understand the essence
of the *MIRACLE* which should happen with the arrival of the
Messiah; *MIRACLE* does not happen in evolution, but all of a
sudden, in one moment.[13]

There has been much debate among historians of the war of 1948 as to
whether the expulsions and demolitions during the war were the implementation phase of a plan devised prior to the war or if instead they occurred
on a spontaneous and haphazard basis during the course of hostilities.[14] As
intriguing as the debate is, the writings of Weitz and other proponents of
transfer (and they were numerous) point to a more fundamental problem.
Namely, if Zionism is understood in spatial-demographic terms as the creation of a state with a Jewish majority within specific borders, then some
form of transfer of Palestinians was inevitable, be it voluntary (as some
Zionists deluded themselves it might be) or involuntary. No part of Palestine
could be carved out that would hold a Jewish majority—Palestinians were
simply too many and too widespread.[15]

The process of erasing Palestinian villages and historical presence
from the new Israeli landscape did not end in 1948 but continues into the
present in a process that sociologist Sari Hanafi has called "spacio-cide"
and geographer Ghazi Falah terms "spatial obliteration." This "spatial
obliteration of village landscapes," Falah argues, "was an integral component of Israeli military strategy during the 1948 war," a strategy that

"persisted into the post-war period. . . . Israel's current cultural landscape . . . is one that has been established by the obliteration of another via designification."[16] The Zionist slogan of "making the desert bloom" both advanced a claim—that the Zionist project unfolded on an empty space, a "land without a people for a people without a land"—and shaped the Zionist project of covering up the Palestinian landscape while creating a new Israeli landscape. The JNF did its part to "redeem" the land by planting forests over the remains of many destroyed villages.[17]

The few buildings that remained standing—like Miskeh's schoolhouse and mosque or the cemeteries and ruined buildings of other villages—lost their historical specificity as part of communities that had only recently been destroyed and dispersed, merging into the background of a seemingly timeless past.[18] The Society for the Protection of Nature in Israel posted signs that obscured or misrepresented the origins of the remaining ruins—or simply ignored them. As Meron Benvenisti observes, "The changes to the landscape wrought by the war have been disregarded and a convenient 'time-out' created in the historical-geographical continuum."[19] In the Israeli school system, meanwhile, youth were taught to "erase" the Arab landscape "from their mental map."[20] The Israeli Jewish community, Benvenisti correctly claims, has thus been "raised on denial of the embarrassing past and of the Palestinians' ability to feel emotional ties to the homeland."[21]

Performative Memory: Oral History, Memory Books, and Return Visits

The refugees from 1948, whether they remained in Israel like those Miskawis who ended up in Tira or made their way to refugee camps beyond Israel's new de facto borders, did of course have emotional ties to their former homes; and they fostered memories of home while living in *al-ghurba*, the estrangement of exile, and dreamt dreams and made plans for *al-awdah*, return. They clung to Ottoman- and British-issued land deeds and to the large metal keys for the doors of homes wiped from the map.[22] This memory, or "refrain," of home has sustained Palestinians through the uncertainties, disruptions, and violence of exile.[23] As Susan Slyomovics observes, Palestinian refugees have developed numerous "performative" means by which they "have refused to relinquish their allegiance to the land."[24] These acts of memory, or refrains of home, include the recording of oral histories of the *Nakba*, the compilation of memory books, organizing formal and informal return visits to the sites of destroyed villages, and setting up Website databases like PalestineRemembered.com dedicated to the *Nakba*.

Many Palestinian activists and academic historians have turned to oral history for help in representing the obliterated past. A sense of urgency animates the work of historian-activists like Mahmoud Issa and Salah Mansour as the generations that lived through the *Nakba* as children and young adults age and approach death. The stories and memories these people carry are vital, they argue, for achieving a fuller picture of the events of 1948. The Israeli government, United Nations agencies, and, to a much lesser degree, the Palestine Liberation Organization (PLO) and the Palestinian Authority, have the institutional resources to disseminate and authorize official memories, while the stories of refugees themselves mostly go undocumented: "Most of our modern documents are in the Zionist archives, in UNRWA, in the UNCCP," Issa notes, and as a result, the stories of Palestinian refugees have been narrated only indirectly.[25] Given the sheer number of refugees whose stories have gone untold, oral history becomes, according to Mansour, *"the only tool* left to solve" the problem of inadequate documentation.[26]

At times writers like Issa and Mansour appear to operate with an objectivist understanding of the historian's craft, with oral history primarily viewed as an effective way for expanding the archive, increasing the number of raw "facts" with which the historian can work.[27] Other researchers engaged in oral history writing, however, have tackled the interpretive complexities and ambiguities involved in oral history. Diana Allan, for example, correctly highlights the political context in which the new interest in oral histories has emerged, a context in which Palestinian refugees fear that the PLO leadership might bargain away their right of return. She explains that "this renewed interest in oral testimony—at the very moment when 'Palestine' as a historical signifier at times appears in danger of losing its signified—thus appears to be both retroactive and prospective in that it looks back to the catastrophe of 1948, and forward to the possibility of further erasure."[28] Contemporary narrations of the *Nakba*, she insists, are less about the past and more about giving "shape to an imminently uncertain present and future."[29]

Against understandings of oral history as the simple uncovering of additional facts, Allan urges a more complex understanding of memory-work, a "re-examination of the view that" Palestinian refugees are "actively engaged in the transmission of local, oral histories that are restoring Palestine palimpsestically."[30] At least two dangers need to be avoided. First, historians operating from objectivist assumptions can fail to see how their own presuppositions shape their reception and interpretation of refugee memories: "Searching for certain kinds of national truths" can "effect the structural forgetting of others: in this context, the diversity of historical experience is sometimes elided in favor of codified nationalist narrative."[31] The ambiguities and personal dimensions of refugee memories are ironed out in the service of nationalist narratives of collective dispossession and heroic struggle. Lori Allen stresses the importance of exploring "the gap between nationalist form and the content of popular desire, where political potentials are suspended between surface slogans and the depth of people's recognition of catchphrase vacuity." One must, she insists, acknowledge "the tension between the meaningful nature of nationalist action and sentiment, on the one hand, and feelings of cynicism and ennui on the other, which exist simultaneously and in every aspect of Palestinian life."[32]

A second danger oral historians must avoid is failing to recognize "the fact that different generations should, and do, have distinct relations to the past." New media, for example, create novel ways of relating to the past, fostering "the emergence of a more synchronic and associative form of consciousness. Internet, television and other visual media are not simply new modes of 'transmitting' history and memory but seem actually to be reshaping them completely."[33] Memory is not the static, straightforward retrieval of information, but is instead a dynamic process that takes a variety of forms over time. Being respectful of refugee memory means being respectful of its multiplicity.

Palestinian refugee memory acts are not simply about creating an archive but have also shaped refugee identity. For example, the compilation of *dhakirat* ("memory books") that commemorate villages of origin does not merely serve antiquarian purposes but also shapes identities as *a'idun* (returnees), rather than as *laj'iun* (refugees).[34] As Slyomovics observes, the "recording of historical memory" in memory books "sanctifies the lost land not only as it was in the past but also, most emphatically, as it is in its present reality."[35] These *dhakirat* aim "to represent a destroyed, common national past for future generations, but also represent a hoped-for return."[36] By remembering the past, refugees look "to breathe life into a name, to give body to a statistic, to render to these vanished villages a sense of their distinctiveness."[37] Many memory books include photos of elderly Palestinian women and men standing on the site of a destroyed village and pointing to where they remember their former homes having once stood. "The pointing finger" of a refugee pictured standing on the remains of her village, as Slyomovics notes, "is a morally accusatory gesture" that "simultaneously demands mourning and seeks justice."[38]

For the refugees who ended up in Syria, Lebanon, and Jordan, international borders and continuing hostilities have kept them from making return visits. After Israel's conquest of East Jerusalem, the West Bank, and the Gaza Strip in 1967, refugees in those areas were able to make the journey, often of only a few kilometers, to their former homes. Some eagerly grasped the opportunity, while for others the prospect of a temporary return proved too painful. However, given Israel's current separationist policies of walls, fences, checkpoints, and a permit system inside the Occupied Territories, trips by refugees in the West Bank and Gaza to villages of origin inside Israel have become difficult at best, often impossible.

Return visits have often been and continue to be undertaken by families and individuals of internally displaced Palestinians inside Israel. After Israeli authorities killed six Palestinians peacefully protesting land confiscations in the Galilee on March 30, 1976, Palestinians inside Israel began annual observances of *Yawm al-Ard*, or Land Day, and some of these internally displaced Palestinians have observed Land Day by making return visits. More recently, similar return visits have been organized to commemorate *Yawm an-Nakba*, the Day of the Nakba, held every year on May 15, the day after *Yom Hatzma'ut*, the Israeli Day of Independence. These return visits embody multiple meanings. They sometimes become opportunities for community celebration, a celebration of persistence as a distinct community living in conditions of exile and an affirmation of the hope for return. However, celebration stands alongside mourning. Wakim Wakim, the director of the Association for the Defense of the Rights of the Internally Displaced (ADRID), explains that "the day when Israel celebrates is the day when we mourn."[39] To make the trip from Tira to Miskeh, from Jish to Bir'im, from al-Nasreh (Nazareth) to al-Mujaydil, is to make a pilgrimage of lament. But the act of lamentation also functions as an implicit, and sometimes explicit, call for justice. Return by the internally displaced to the sites of their original villages raises questions about why the state prevents their return and about discriminatory land practices inside Israel.

Return visits by refugees to the sites of their destroyed villages exemplify what Carol Baderstein has called "the *active* nature of the construction of memory." These visits are performative "acts of memory" located "at or around points of perceived and experienced breaks, ruptures, and loss."[40] The remains of destroyed Palestinian villages like Miskeh become for refugees what Pierre Nora has termed *lieux de mémoire* (sites of memory), sites that "originate with the sense that there is no spontaneous memory, that we must deliberately create archives, maintain anniversaries, organize celebrations, pronounce eulogies, and notarize bills because such activities no longer occur naturally."[41]

Nora's contention that "the most fundamental purpose of the *lieu de mémoire* is to stop time, to block the work of forgetting, to establish a state of things, to immortalize death, to materialize the immaterial" is appropriated by Ahmad Sa'di, who describes the *Nakba* as "a Palestinian event and a site of Palestinian collective memory; it connects all Palestinians to a specific point in time that has become for them an 'eternal present.'"[42] Elias Sanbar takes up this understanding of memory-work as focused on ruptured temporality when he describes Palestinian memory as concerned with the restoration of time: with the present "forbidden to them," Palestinian refugees, according to Sanbar, "occupy a temporal space made up of both a past preserved by a memory afflicted by madness and a dreamt-of future which aspired to restore time."[43]

The claim that Palestinian refugee memory aspires to a future of restored time would, one imagines, worry a critic like Kerwin Lee Klein, who bemoans the "religious" character of much memory discourse, with its attempt "to re-enchant our relation to the world and pour presence back into the past."[44] Are Palestinian acts of memory related to the *Nakba* like return visits by members of the Shbeita family to the ruins of Miskeh attempts to reclaim or recreate a pristine version of an imagined past? Or are these acts of memory less about recapturing a lost past and more about the demands for and possibilities of justice and reconciliation in the present and the future?

Through a consideration of the Israeli Zochrot Association and its activities, I contend that Palestinian refugee memory-work around the *Nakba* is fundamentally misunderstood if it is viewed reductionistically as the desire to reclaim a pure past for the present. Klein, who does not write about Palestinian refugees but worries about the atavistic, reactionary potentials of memory discourse in general, potentials he associates with memory's religious character, fails to recognize that memory as a religious practice can be progressive and empancipatory. Specifically, I argue that the return visits organized by Zochrot and internally displaced Palestinians inside Israel are marked by what one might call a *sacramental* character— sacramental in that performed memories of the past physically make present a hope and a vision for the future.

Zochrot: Remembering the Nakba in Hebrew

If Palestinians have, over the past decades, created multiple ways to remember the destruction of homes and villages in 1948, Israeli Jewish public memory rarely has given voice to the *Nakba*. If one goes to the Baram National Park in the northern Galilee, for example, one finds scant mention of the Palestinian village of Bir'im that once stood there. The Israeli general Moshe Dayan was the exception, not the rule, of Israeli public memory when in 1969 he bluntly observed that "there is not one place built in this country that did not have a former Arab population."[45]

Maurice Halbwachs has contended that "every group develops the memory of its own past that highlights its unique identity vis-à-vis other groups."[46] In 2002, however, a group of Israeli Jewish peace educators implicitly challenged Halbwachs' dictum, founding the Zochrot Association, an organization dedicated to "remembering the *Nakba* in Hebrew." Zochrot operates from the premise that the *Nakba* needs to be confronted and owned as an integral part of Israeli Jewish identity.[47] The name Zochrot describes the objective: the feminine plural participle from the Hebrew verb *zachar*, "to remember," Zochrot encodes an attempt to subvert the "masculine" erasure of the other, to open up possibilities for different forms of memory. "The hegemonic Zionist discourse," argues Eitan Bronstein, director of Zochrot, "conjures up images of a violent memory, invariably exclusive and masculine, and leaves no room for the (Palestinian) 'other.' Zochrot seeks to promote an alternative discourse on memory, one that strives towards true reconciliation and is openly inclusive and compassionate towards the Palestinian side."[48]

Zochrot, I would argue, seeks through its practices to establish what Tessa Morris-Suzuki has called a "political economy of historical truthfulness." By directing public attention to the remains of Palestinian villages, Zochrot displays what Morris-Suzuki describes as *an attentiveness to the presence of the past within and around* us." This attentiveness, she explains, stems from the "recognition that we ourselves are shaped by the past and that knowing the past is therefore essential to knowing ourselves and others."[49] Historical truthfulness requires us to "think about our position in the present, and how it influences our interpretations and choices."[50] Zochrot works to push the Israeli public to confront the Palestinian refugee question, not as a matter of the distant historical past, but as a question of contemporary acts and ideologies of exclusion and erasure.

Zochrot's main strategy is simple. Several times a year it organizes trips open to all Israelis, be they Jewish or Palestinian, to the sites of destroyed Palestinian villages. At the village site internally displaced Palestinian refugees share their memories of the village and offer testimonies regarding its depopulation and destruction. Sometimes they speak in Hebrew, sometimes in Arabic with Hebrew translation provided. Zochrot distributes memory books telling the story of the village, with both Arabic and Hebrew text. Finally, Israeli Jews and Palestinians together erect signs in both Hebrew and Arabic, naming ruined buildings (identifying them as churches, mosques, schoolhouses, private residences, etc.) and, in places where Israeli cities now stand, like Ashkelon (Arabic al-Majdal) or Beersheva (Arabic Bir al-Saba'), posting street signs with the pre-1948 names. So, for example, under the contemporary street sign in Ashkelon for Rehov Herzl (Herzl Street), one Zochrot group placed a sign in Hebrew and Arabic reading Shari' al-Ustaaz (the Teacher's Street).[51]

Posting these signs, as Bronstein notes, works to reconstruct "the 'space' in which Jews and Arabs operate."[52] Through posting these bilingual signs, "Zochrot seeks to add to the space a reminder of what had been taken away, and the people who take down the signs seek to maintain the illusion of transparency, the purely Jewish-Israeli nature of the space."[53] The signs "represent a challenge to written history inscribed on the landscape" and work, through aesthetic-political means, to reshape the geography. "Posting signs at villages integrates the past, present, and future" and operates simultaneously in "ethical, aesthetic, and political" registers. "This is taking action upon the landscape in the hope of rediscovering and remodeling it, creating a renewed landscape that will reveal the traces of what has refused to be wiped out."[54]

The signs, Bronstein contends, name that which is unnamable in Zionist discourse, explaining that "the *Nakba* represents for the Zionist subject an event that cannot possibly have occurred and—at the same time—had to occur."[55] It could not have occurred because the forcible expulsion of Palestinians gives the lie to the Zionist claim of settling a "land without people for a people without a land," yet it of course had to occur in order for the Zionist vision to be implemented. "Looking away from the *Nakba*," according to Bronstein, "enables this society to continue holding on to the fantasy of the whole, pure body, of the collective that climbed out of the concentration camps and the persecutions of exile and became its own master in its mythological homeland."[56] Through its public acts of memory, Zochrot seeks "to bring about conciliation between the [Israeli Jewish] society and the ghost of the *Nakba*, which haunts it and stirs up uncomfortable emotions and fears."[57]

The status of the *Nakba* as a taboo topic within Israeli Jewish society has, not surprisingly, resulted in Zochrot attracting steadily increasing attention from the mainstream Israeli media—more attention than Israeli Jewish organizations on the far-left of the political spectrum typically receive— including significant coverage in leading newspapers such as *Maariv* and *Ha'aretz*, in smaller periodicals like *Hakibbutz*, on Internet portals such as Walla, and on a nationwide radio channel like Reshet Aleph.[58] Some of the reaction in the press is bemused and curious. Other media reaction is decidedly hostile. For example, Yoav Keren, on the op-ed pages of *Maariv*, described Zochrot activists as "Hamas propagandists in our midst."[59]

Zochrot's signposting activities are also routinely met with hostility "on the ground" as they are conducted, especially when staged in cities such as Ashkelon (al-Majdal), Haifa, and Ramle, instead of at the sites of village remains in national parks and in the countryside. Posted signs are torn down, and bystanders become agitated and shout at Zochrot volunteers.[60] During a December 11, 2004, tour organized by Zochrot of Ramle, Israeli police questioned Bronstein and then issued an order forbidding him from returning to the city for eight days.[61] Two years later, during another larger Zochrot signposting event in Ramle, police intervened, took down one of the posted street signs, confiscated the others, and declared the city off-limits for five days to two of the participants.[62] For Ramle's mayor, Zochrot's signposting raised the specter of an Arab takeover, and he responded vehemently: "If he [an Arab] doesn't like it [Ramle's Israeli Jewish identity], he can go live in Jaljulya. That's an Arab name. Just because some Jamal wants to change the name, or because some Mohammad wants to change the name? . . . They can go f— themselves."[63] Zochrot then organized a follow-up "signing" activity of a different sort on January 6, 2007, this time with participants wearing the signs as T-shirts instead of posting them. Thus in a bodily way Zochrot, at least temporarily, rendered the traces of the *Nakba* in Ramle present.[64]

This hostility, Bronstein recognizes, stems from the fact that "the acknowledgment of the *Nakba* and Palestinian suffering, and of a sense of responsibility towards the refugees, appears in Jewish eyes to be turning over the wheel of history." It springs from a fear that "the outcome of acknowledging the Palestinian *Nakba* would be an exile of the Jews from the land."[65] Bronstein suggests that the feeling of threat generated by Zochrot's activity "can be understood through the Hebrew word *shelet*, 'sign,' which is similar to the Hebrew word *shlita*, 'control.' The sign makes a statement, and through it gains control over that space."[66] Dominant Zionisms norm space in an exclusivist fashion, so not surprisingly alternative attempts at norming space are experienced as threats. However, what if Zochrot's acts of remembering the *Nakba* in

Hebrew temporarily create and point toward the possibility, not of an exclusivist, homogeneous land, but of a "heterogeneous space"?[67]

Remembering Miskeh Together

To see what such heterogeneous space might look like, let us return to Miskeh. Miskawis, like other internally displaced Palestinians, have routinely returned to their village sites, sometimes as families, sometimes in larger groups. For the past several months, Zochrot has joined with Miskawis to organize a variety of events at the ruins of Miskeh. Zochrot volunteers assisted former residents of Miskeh in renovating the school buildings, which they in turn used for a variety of cultural events. In mid-June 2006, however, the ILA fenced off the school and posted its own sign, indicating that the land was private property and entry onto the land constituted trespass.[68] In response, Zochrot gathered with Miskawis at the school. Standing around the buildings, the group proceeded to drape the enclosing fence with 50 meters of white cloth, Christo-style. Everyone in attendance—Israeli Jew and Palestinian, man and woman, young and old—then had the opportunity to place their own pieces of art on the cloth. Some painted drawings and murals; others posted their own original artwork. To replace the ILA's sign, now covered over, the group hung a new sign reading, "Miskeh School house—the land belongs to the Miskeh uprooted people and the entrance is permitted to all with love."[69]

Only a few days later the demolition crews arrived, tore down the school, and planted saplings in a renewed bid to bury the village's past. On August 19, 2006, members of Zochrot and Miskawis made a pilgrimage to the site of the destroyed schoolhouse. They looked around for bits of rubble that remained from the demolished building and used those stones to mark the outlines of the school. They then posted signs with the names of children who had once attended the school.[70]

Envisioning New Futures: Opening Possibilities for Reconciliation

Through the acts of memory organized by Zochrot in partnership with groups of internally displaced Palestinians, new possibilities for future Palestinian-Israeli reconciliation are opened. In describing *lieux de mémoire*, Nora noted "their capacity for metamorphosis, an endless recycling of their meaning and an unpredictable proliferation of their ramifications."[71] Through its return visits and signposting activities, Zochrot stages acts of performative memory in which destroyed Palestinian villages acquire new sets of meanings—while they remain sites of rupture, dislocation, erasure, and mourning, they also become places where new possibilities of justice and reconciliation are envisioned and embodied.

These performances of memory, be they enacted by internally displaced Palestinians or by the mixed groups of Palestinians and Israeli Jews organized by Zochrot, have a sacramental quality in which a binational future is embodied in the present through the remembering of the past. My identification of these memory performances as sacramental is deliberately provocative, meant to counter critiques of memory discourse as bound up with a religious primitivism, nationalism, and essentialism. The acts of memory staged by Zochrot and internally displaced Palestinians might seem to these critics to be religious insofar as they are marked by the sacramental character I have identified above, but they cannot be easily dismissed as reactionary. Instead, these memory performances disrupt nationalist essentialisms by creating binational spaces in which, for a fleeting moment, the violent conjoining of demographic hegemony and territorial control no longer holds sway, in turn animating hopes for a binational Palestinian-Israeli future.[72]

Zochrot's return visits do not establish justice, if by justice one understands refugees being free to choose whether or not to return home.[73] They do, however, set the stage for a future reconciliation based on a welcome embrace of the other, of the refugee. The very repetitiveness of Zochrot's signposting actions, Bronstein argues, "creates opportunities for the forming of a new pattern; denial is not the determined pattern, and it can be changed." Zochrot carries out its work in the hope and the trust that "there is always the potential that this time, when signs are posted and refugees return, they will be warmly greeted."[74] Furthermore, by bringing together Israeli Jews and displaced Palestinians in shared acts of memory, Zochrot's activities serve as signs of a possible future reconciliation between the two peoples.

The late Edward Said stressed the need for Palestinians and Israelis to envision a binational future, to view life with the other as a promise, not a threat. Said observed that "the problem of the Other remains, for Zionism, for Palestinian nationalism, for Arab and/or Islamic nationalism. There is, to put it simply, an irreducible, heterogeneous presence always to be taken account of which, since and because of 1948, has become intractable, unwishable away, *there*."[75] By creating a heterogeneous space through the enacted memories of a heterogeneous public, Zochrot's memory performances embody the promise of justice, the promise of forgiveness, the promise of reconciliation in a shared, binational future.

Epilogue
Breaches in the Walls

In *Mourning Becomes the Law*, her last major work before her untimely death, the philosopher Gillian Rose called attention to the gaps and exclusions in our political philosophies and structures. "The 'city,' like the 'nation-state,'" she wrote, "implies the bounded political entity, but especially the breaches in its walls."[1] Rose did not have any illusions about the possibility (or even the desirability) of an anarchic and utopian abolition of all walls, all boundaries, all divisions. The establishment of a *polis* does imply the drawing of some boundaries. However, Rose insisted, a political philosophy that properly addresses the complexity of social and political existence must be more attentive to the exclusions created by these boundaries and to the disruptive possibilities at those liminal spaces than with the policing and fortification of those frontiers.

Throughout the essays in this book I have sought to join Rose in dwelling on the significance of the breaches in the walls—the walls erected by nation-states and the boundaries delimited by the church's practices. A theology of exile, I have contended, is shaped by "not being in charge," nurtured by the practice of being receptive to provocations from God's word from outside its orbit. A church that confesses faith in a Lord whose reign extends from the creation to the apocalypse should expect to meet that Lord in strange places, to encounter that Lord in those spaces where God's word has ruptured the church's self-satisfied defenses, piercing any illusions the church might harbor of superiority or self-sufficiency. The church faithfully witnesses to Christ when it is prepared to relinquish control of theological conversations, to be a servant in its encounters with its neighbors, co-workers, and fellow citizens in the cities of its exile, ready not simply to testify to Christ's lordship, but to receive God's word anew.

If a theology *of* exile nurtures a receptive spirituality of not being in charge, a theology *in* exile, one that joyfully accepts diaspora as the *site* of the church's mission, will, through its very existence as a minority community, stand opposed to all totalizing political projects that attempt to draw political boundaries so rigidly as to exclude difference. Such an exilic theology, by reflecting on the breaches in the walls—legal and physical—that nation-states construct, will find common cause with political theorist William Connolly in disputing that "the boundaries of a state must correspond to those of a nation, both of these to a final site of citizen political allegiance, and all three of those to the parameters of a democratic ethos."[2] It will join anthropologist Talal Asad in affirming that "the sovereign state cannot (never could) contain all the practices, relations, and loyalties of its citizens," recognizing that the church's own ultimate loyalties are higher than state and nation and expecting to live and work alongside persons of differing practices and loyalties.[3] A theology in exile will, in brief, not only accept the state of exile for the church, but will also embrace *exilic states*— what Daniel Boyarin calls "diasporized" states—as positive goods.

These exilic, or diasporized states will not fall prey to nationalist projects of erecting legal and physical walls in order to shore up exclusivist connections between people and territory but will instead welcome difference and complexity within the polity. Drawing on the work of theologian John Milbank, Asad argues that we must think beyond the homogeneous "simple" spaces of modern nation-states by denaturalizing them, exposing their artificiality, and instead rediscovering an understanding of the "complex" spaces of human political and social existence. Milbank explains that "complex space has a certain natural, ontological priority," whereas "simple space remains by comparison merely an abstracting, idealizing project. . . . [N]o action can be perfectly self-contained, but always impinges upon other people, so that spaces will always in some degree 'complexly' overlap, jurisdictions always in some measure be competing, loyalties remain (perhaps benignly) divided."[4]

Nationalisms are prime examples of such "abstracting, idealizing" projects since they claim and strive for one-to-one correlations between nation and state. Creating such simple spaces, Asad suggests, is an illusory project, although plenty of real suffering and hostility can be generated by the dividing walls constructed in the service of such projects. A political theology in exile will stand against such illusory, destructive projects, championing instead a recognition of and a striving toward complex spaces of a "multiplicity of overlapping bonds and identities," spaces marked by "the intersecting boundaries and heterogeneous activities of individuals as well as groups related to traditions."[5]

The Ephesian proclamation of reconciled (not erased) difference within one body, the reality experienced by the church in its corporate life, animates the vision of an exilic, diasporized state. Boyarin's plea for a complex understanding of political identity, one "in which there are only slaves but no masters,"[6] is echoed by Asad, who presses the question of "What kind of conditions can be developed . . . in which *everyone* may live as a minority among minorities?"[7] The church in exile, as a minority community amidst the Babylons of the world, should not expect Babylon to be a homogeneous space, but should expect it to be a polity marked by deep difference and plurality. Political pluralism, Connolly insists, must be re-envisioned, conceptualized not in terms of "a majority nation presiding over numerous minorities in a democratic state," but rather in terms of "a democratic state of multiple minorities contending and collaborating with a general ethos of forbearance and critical responsiveness."[8] A theology in exile, when it dreams of and works for "return," strives for this exilic state, one in which the presence of difference is welcomed as opportunity rather than simply and solely as threat. The political theology of an exilic state is thus one for which the breaches in the walls, the constant inbreaking of the other, the irreducible complexity and diversity of human existence, are central.

The Improbable Slipping In

Israel's walls and militarized fences in the Occupied Territories, in contrast, aim at creating "simple space," seeking, in the words of Israeli architectural theorist Eyal Weizman, "to create a defensible and homogeneous Israeli political space that will guarantee, if not protection from Palestinian attacks, a space of Jewish demographic majority and control."[9] The consequences for Palestinians have been various and devastating. Territorial fragmentation, not surprisingly, has contributed to social unrest, political infighting, and economic disintegration. The barriers around the Gaza Strip have transformed it into a massive, open-air prison for 1.5 million people. Throughout the West Bank the wall cuts Palestinians off from farmland, from wells, from family, from educational and medical services. Palestinians holding Jerusalem identity cards who had moved to the West Bank cities of Ramallah or Bethlehem (only a few kilometers to the north or south) in order to be closer to work or school, or in search of cheaper rents, must move back to East Jerusalem's increasingly crowded neighborhoods, areas prevented from significant expansion or development by Israeli zoning regulations, or else face confiscation of their IDs, depriving them of the right to live in the city of their birth. Families with Jerusalemites married to West Bankers have been torn apart, with one spouse staying in Jerusalem to preserve residency status. Palestinian Christians and Muslims from the West Bank find it difficult-to-impossible to make pilgrimages to pray at the Church of the Holy Sepulcher or at *Haram al-Sharif* (the Noble Sanctuary). Palestinian medical, social, educational, and cultural institutions in Jerusalem that once served the entire West Bank and depend on West Bank Palestinian staff members now struggle to survive. The imposing concrete barrier has truly become a dividing wall, dividing not only Palestinian from Israeli but Palestinian from Palestinian, generating daily humiliation and economic desperation, and fostering hostility, not reconciliation.

The wall is built on a premise of the possibility of hermetic closure, with passage through the wall and between the fragmented territories created by the barrier to be possible only for those holding Israeli-issued permits (and in many cases, only those with permits and Israeli-issued magnetic cards containing biometric data about the cardholder). Complete control, of course, has proven elusive, and the walls and barriers of what Israeli sociologist Jeff Halper calls Israel's "matrix of control" are breached.[10] Regimes of domination might develop a pervasive reach, but as Siegfried Kracauer claims with regards to the disruptive work of memory in the face of historical erasure, "There are always holes in the wall for us to evade and the improbable to slip in."[11]

Some of the breaches in the wall have the military connotations associated with the word: one thinks, for example, of the tunnels dug under the border wall separating the Gaza Strip from Egypt through which guns, cigarettes, and persons (but also desperately needed medications or other hard-to-acquire commodities in besieged Gaza) are smuggled. Most of the breachings, however, have a more mundane character. As the wall went up in the East Jerusalem neighborhood of Abu Dis, for example, Palestinian students on their way to university or day laborers on their way to jobs squeezed through gaps in concrete slabs that had not yet been closed. Meanwhile, Palestinians visiting family or going to school, work, or hospital have daily found new ways to evade the ever-expanding and always-shifting regime of roadblocks and checkpoints controlling everyday life, with shared taxis driving through olive groves and commuters walking or riding donkeys over mountains to meet up with other shared taxis when the makeshift roads become impassable.

Other breaches are more virtual. The British graffiti artist Banksy "hacks" public spaces within different urban centers, spray-painting images and murals that bring to attention what legal, educational, and psychological walls attempt to block out from public consciousness. In the summer of 2005 he traveled to the Occupied Territories to paint on the nine-meter-high concrete walls around Jerusalem. As he hacked the wall, Banksy created several arresting images: a rat (a common Banksy character) with a shovel poised to start digging under the concrete slabs; two overstuffed armchairs on either side of a *trompe l'oiel* window looking out onto open skies; a boy painting a rope ladder with which he might scale the wall; and a girl holding onto balloons as she ascends, ready to float over the barrier.

The images of escape that Banksy presents highlight and challenge the brute artificiality of the wall, pointing to the way the concrete barrier imprisons, and offer a tentative hope for a future dismantling of these dividing walls of hostility. However, one should be cautious about attributing too much emancipatory potential to these virtual breaches. As Banksy painted, an elderly Palestinian man approached him. "You paint the wall, you make it look beautiful," he said. The artist thanked him, but the old man continued, "We don't want it to be beautiful, we hate this wall, go home."[12]

Some walls simply must come down as part of the exilic task of seeking the peace of the city. We can work and hope in faith that eventually the physical and legal barriers in Palestine-Israel that are generating dispossession, violence, and suffering, and are exiling people from their homes and their land will come down, like they have in other contexts throughout history. In the meantime, however, the walls appear strong and forbidding, the regime of separation triumphant. We are therefore driven to pay heed to the tentative breaches in the walls, to those places where Palestinians and Israelis return from exile to a home far richer and complex than defensive fortifications can ever create.

These returns, examples of what Ilan Pappé calls "a cautious emanation of desegregated spaces of coexistence, on a parity basis," embody today a hope for a binational future (be it a future of one state or a federation of two).[13] These returns happen when Jewish Israeli and Palestinian activists from Ta'ayush gather in Bil'in to try to stop the encroaching bulldozers.[14] These returns happen at the ruins of villages like Miskeh as Zochrot workers join internally displaced Palestinians in remembering the land's binational past and commiting themselves to a binational present and future of mutuality and care. These returns happen when Israelis accompany Palestinians in the predominantly Christian town of Beit Sahour on the annual Christmas Eve candlelight vigil against the military occupation and for a just peace. The breaches in the walls might seem increasingly narrow, the land and its peoples ever more captive to violence and ideologies of separation, but even now the improbable slips in, and the promise of a return shaped by the mission of exile beckons.

Notes

Introduction

1. Edward Said, *Out of Place: A Memoir* (New York: Vintage, 2000).
2. Naim Ateek, *Justice, and Only Justice: A Palestinian Theology of Liberation* (Maryknoll, NY: Orbis Books, 1989), 9.
3. Munib Younan, *Witnessing for Peace: In Jerusalem and the World* (Minneapolis: Fortress Press, 2003), 23-26.
4. Riah Abu El-Assal, *Caught in Between: The Extraordinary Story of an Arab Palestinian Christian Israeli* (London: SPCK, 1999), 2-4.
5. Elias Chacour, with David Hazard, *Blood Brothers* (Grand Rapids, MI: Chosen Books, 2003).
6. Ella Shohat, *Taboo Memories, Diasporic Voices* (Durham, NC and London: Duke University Press, 2006), 331.
7. Quoted in Ilan Pappé, *The Ethnic Cleansing of Palestine* (Oxford: Oneworld, 2006), xi.
8. Jacqueline Rose, *The Last Resistance* (London and New York: Verso, 2007), 13. See also Jacqueline Rose, *The Question of Zion* (Princeton and Oxford: Princeton University Press, 2005).
9. Ella Shohat also rightly insists that Zionist "return" ended up tied to the exile of Sephardic/Mizrahi Jews from Iraq, Egypt, Yemen, and elsewhere. See Shohat, *Taboo Memories, Diasporic Voices*.
10. Throughout this book I take, and build on, the idea of exile as a state of being both politically and theologically "not in charge" from Yoder's essay, "On Not Being in Charge," now chapter 9 of John Howard Yoder, *The Jewish-Christian Schism Revisited*, ed. Michael G. Cartwright and Peter Ochs (Grand Rapids, MI: Eerdmans, 2003).
11. While I do not directly engage Romand Coles's work, my understanding of Yoder's theology as a "not in charge" form of discourse has been shaped in part by his description of Yoder's theology as marked by "wild patience." See Coles, "The Wild Patience of John Howard Yoder: 'Outsiders' and the 'Otherness of the Church,'" *Modern Theology* 18/3 (July 2002): 305-31.
12. For essays questioning the continued relevance of two-state

approaches, see the essays in *Where Now for Palestine? The Demise of the Two-State Solution*, ed. Jamil Hilal (London and New York: Zed Books, 2007).

13. I have quoted from the English translation of Darwish's poem that was included in the "Made in Palestine" exhibit held in 2003 at the Station Museum of Contemporary Art in Houston, Texas. Available at www.stationmuseum.com/Made_in_palestine-Mahmoud_Darwish

Chapter 1
On Not Being in Charge

1. The phrase, "not being in charge," comes from the title of Yoder's essay, "On Not Being in Charge," included as chapter 9 in the posthumously published compilation, *The Jewish-Christian Schism Revisited*, ed. Michael Cartwright and Peter Ochs (London: SCM Press, 2003 and Grand Rapids, MI: Eerdmans, 2003), hereafter *JCSR*. Parenthetic references in the text are from this work. From the 1970s to the 1990s, Yoder delivered a series of lectures in Jerusalem (at the Tantur Ecumenical Institute), Bethel College in North Newton, Kansas, and Earlham College in Indiana, assessing Jewish history and Christianity's relationship to Judaism from a "free church" perspective. In the mid-1990s Yoder gathered these lectures together and distributed them as a Shalom Desktop Packet under the title, *The Jewish-Christian Schism Revisited*. Michael Cartwright, a student of Yoder's thought and a Methodist theologian at the University of Indianapolis, and Peter Ochs, a prominent Jewish scholar actively involved in the Society for Scriptural Reasoning, edited this material for publication after Yoder's death under the same title. This published version, which adheres closely to the text of the original essays, includes critical introductions by the editors, an afterword by Cartwright in which he engages and critiques Yoder's positions, responses to individual chapters by Ochs, and an overview by Cartwright of Mennonite mission and peacemaking efforts in Palestine-Israel. Cartwright's portion of the editor's introduction is particularly valuable for tracing the relationship of the essays to the work of Yoder's longtime friend Rabbi Steven Schwarzschild. Ochs and Cartwright's critical responses also help carry forward a conversation for which Yoder clearly had much passion. The posthumous nature of the volume, unfortunately, prevents the reader from knowing how Yoder might have responded to the criticisms of his position leveled by Cartwright and Ochs. The best interpretation one can give to the decision to bracket Yoder's work with so much critical material is that the editors have tried to embody textually a polyphonic discourse, with Cartwright and Ochs offering midrash-style commentaries on Yoder's work. One worries, however, that the effect of boxing in Yoder's text with commentary that is at points sharply critical of his work will not be the presumably intended effect of embodying a critical, multivocal conversation in print, but instead will erect a *cordon*

sanitaire around Yoder's work, warning the reader of the alleged theological contaminants within.

2. Roy Kreider, *Judaism Meets Christ: Guiding Principles for the Christian-Jewish Encounter* (Scottdale, PA: Herald Press, 1960), 34.

3. Yoder noted that "both in doctrine and in sociology the king is relativized. He is at best the servant of divine righteousness, not its origin" (*JCSR*, 73). For Yoder, the Israelite temptation to kingship prefigures the Christian temptation of Constantinianism. Cartwright observes that for Yoder the "Davidic Project" of constituting "a monarchy in Jerusalem was prototypical of Christian forms of faithlessness."—Cartwright, "Editors' Introduction," in *JCSR*, 20.

4. Or also: "To be scattered is not a hiatus, after which normality will resume. From Jeremiah's time on . . . dispersion shall be the calling of the Jewish faith community" (183).

5. For Yoder, Jeremiah's call to the exiles in Jeremiah 29:7 was a call to embrace "Galut as vocation" (*JCSR*, 190).

6. Yoder argued that "the reorientation of identity by the Jeremianic shift even comes back to give a new quality to the part of the story which returns to *Eretz* Israel [*sic*]" (*JCSR*, 188), observing that with "Ezra and Nehemiah the return to live and worship in Judea was brought about without political independence or a king" (71). At points Yoder went beyond this nuanced observation to an attack (unnecessary, to my mind) on Ezra and Nehemiah as relapses into unfaithfulness. See, for example, Yoder's claim that Ezra and Nehemiah "need to be seen as inappropriate deviations from the Jeremiah line, since each of them reconstituted a cult and a polity as a branch of the pagan imperial government" (194). For a helpful approach to Ezra and Nehemiah that stands in general accordance with Yoder's approach even while extending it, see "'Purity' as Nonconformity: Communal Solidarity as Diaspora Ethics," in Daniel L. Smith-Christopher, *A Biblical Theology of Exile* (Minneapolis: Fortress Press, 2002), especially the portrayal of Ezra as an "Amish elder."

7. While pacifist Christians may often be tempted by Marcionite-style theologies, I trust that my discussion makes it clear that Yoder was not. A. James Reimer and John W. Miller have repeatedly suggested that Yoder has a Marcionite approach to the Old Testament. A cursory reading of Yoder's writings should suffice to dispel this charge. Reimer and Miller's charge of "Marcionitism" does little to advance the critical conversation about how Christians should read the multiple Old Testament narratives. See Reimer, "'I Came Not to Abolish the Law but to Fulfill It': A Positive Theology of Law and Civil Institutions," in *A Mind Patient and Untamed: Assessing John Howard Yoder's Contributions to Theology, Ethics, and Peacemaking*, ed. Ben C. Ollenburger and Gayle Gerber Koontz (Telford, PA: Cascadia

Publishing House, 2004): 245-73 and John W. Miller, "In the Footsteps of Marcion: Notes toward an Understanding of John Yoder's Theology," *Conrad Grebel Review* 16 (Spring 1988): 82-92.

8. "Paul is thus not the pioneer of mission to the Gentiles. Mission to Gentiles had been going on for generations" (*JCSR*, 95).

9. Yoder correctly identified the source of one debate being over whether or not Jesus was the *Meschiach*, the Anointed One, rather than over a sense that claims for Jesus as the "Son of God" threatened monotheism. The title "Son of God," Yoder explained, "was an offence to anyone who did not want Jesus to be King; but not because it was either metaphysical nonsense or blasphemy" (*JCSR*, 48-49).

10. In a more guarded version of this claim, Yoder spoke of an "original, tense but tolerable, overlapping of Jewish and Christian identities" (*JCSR*, 54).

11. Key works include the essays collected in *The Ways that Never Parted: Jews and Christians in Late Antiquity and the Early Middle Ages*, ed. Adam H. Becker and Annette Yoshiko Reed (Tübingen: Mohr Siebeck, 2003); Daniel Boyarin, *Border Lines: The Partition of Judaeo-Christianity* (Philadelphia: University of Pennsylvania Press, 2004); and Daniel Boyarin, *Dying for God: Martyrdom and the Making of Christianity and Judaism* (Stanford: Stanford University Press, 1999). The "conversations" charted by Boyarin and others were, of course, often contentious arguments, but, as Yoder reminded us, "The fact that people argue against one another does not prove that they are in incompatible movements: it may prove just the opposite" (*JCSR*, 56).

12. See also *JCSR*, 31 for a nearly identical claim.

13. Or similarly: "Doubting that things had to go as they did way back when correlates logically with doubting the rightness of how they continued to go later" (*JCSR*, 45).

14. The Eerdmans edition of *JCSR* retains the British spellings of the SCM edition.

15. Yoder insisted that it is an "erroneous" assumption to view "Judaism" or "Christianity" as "stable and autonomous" entities, identical with themselves throughout history (*JCSR*, 150). On the one hand, Yoder was making a perfectly valid historical point: "Christianity" has taken a variety of shapes over time. On the other, Yoder's claim is puzzling. Yes, one agrees, there are a multitude of groups claiming the mantle of "Christian," but this descriptive point need not lead to the claim that there are not ways of being Christian that are more faithful than others: surely this is the thrust of Yoder's decades-long argument with Constantinian Christianity. Similarly, Jews of varying theological dispositions will all want to argue that some ways of appropriating the Torah are more faithful than others.

16. Most "diaspora Jews," Yoder claimed, "kept on living the life set up by the generation of Jeremiah, which Jesus said he had come to 'fulfil' (i.e. confirm), without ever being faced with a chance to accept or reject that claimed fulfillment" (*JCSR*, 77).

17. A complementary list can be found at *JCSR*, 82-84.

18. The theology of diaspora existence, Yoder insisted, was "not, as some would have us believe, developed as a merely pragmatic expedient, out of the collapse of Jewish nationhood after the year 70 or 135. Those vital tragedies only settled and restated what had already existed in the messages of Jeremiah and Ezekiel, and in the ministries of Ezra and Nehemiah" (*JCSR*. 79).

19. A similar list includes the church's "capacity for decentralized congregationalism" (102).

20. For a historical study comparing the status of Jewish and Anabaptist communities in early modern Europe, see Michael Driedger, "Crossing Max Weber's 'Great Divide': Comparing Early Modern Jewish and Anabaptist Histories," in *Radical Reformation Studies: Essays Presented to James M. Stayer*, ed. Werner O. Packull and Geoffrey L. Dipple (Aldershot: Ashgate, 1999), 157-74.

21. It is instructive to compare Yoder's understanding of the "non-sacerdotal, non-hierarchical" character of rabbinic Judaism with the notion of "priesthood" developed in *The Fullness of Christ: Paul's Revolutionary Vision of Universal Ministry* (Elgin, IL: Brethren Press, 1987) and the notion of "sacrament as social process" in the essay by that name in *The Royal Priesthood: Essays Ecclesiological and Ecumenical*, ed. Michael G. Cartwright (Grand Rapids, MI: Eerdmans, 1994), 359-73. The polemic against "ritualism" also appears in a characteristically Yoderian opposition of "history" and "religion" (*JCSR*, 108), an opposition that is most likely influenced by the Barthian contrast between "faith" and "religion." What one misses from Yoder's critiques of hierarchy and "episcopal politics" is an acknowledgment that in the real lives of churches the distance from being "non-hierarchical" to a rejection of any binding authority in the name of individual autonomy proves perilously short.

22. Douglas Harink makes a persuasive case that Yoder's theology, if it is to cohere, relies on an implicit understanding of God's election of a people. See Harink, *Paul among the Postliberals: Pauline Theology beyond Christendom and Modernity* (Grand Rapids, MI: Brazos Press, 2003) and "The Anabaptist and the Apostle: John Howard Yoder as a Pauline Theologian," in *A Mind Patient and Untamed: Assessing John Howard Yoder's Contribution to Theology, Ethics, and Peacemaking* (Telford, PA: Cascadia Publishing House, 2004), 274-87. As Harink writes, "Yoder . . . shows almost no interest in the doctrine of Israel's non-superseded election,

even as he at the same time also seems to assume it."—Harink, "The Anabaptist and the Apostle," 283-84. A radical, Yoderian ecclesiology, I would argue, requires a doctrine of election if it is to withstand the forces of commodification and compartmentalization generated by liberalism and capitalism. As Scott Bader-Saye observes, "election challenges the universalizing epistemologies of modernity as well as the political priority of individual autonomy."—Scott Bader-Saye, *Church and Israel after Christendom: The Politics of Election* (Boulder, CO: Westview Press, 1999), 28.

23. Also: "The culmination of the Christianization of Judaism is the development of Zionism" (154). Compare this to Daniel Boyarin's more strongly-worded claim that "Zionism leads to the ruination of rabbinic Judaism."—Boyarin, *A Radical Jew: Paul and the Politics of Identity* (Berkeley: University of California Press, 1994), 256.

24. "A tiny but growing number of Jews with strong roots in the theology of Jewish existence before Auschwitz," Yoder observed, "have since the beginnings of Zionism seen Israeli statehood in the same terms in which Jotham (Judg 9) and Samuel (1 Sam 8) saw Canaanite kingship: not as an absolute evil which it should be possible to reject completely, but as an accommodation, regrettable, to the ways of the Gentiles, an innovation which will disappoint, which will not deliver on its promises" (84-85).

25. Ochs, "Commentary" on Chapter 2, in *JCSR*, 90.

26. Ibid.

27. Ochs, "Commentary" on Chapter 9, in *JCSR*, 180. Cartwright agrees with Ochs that Yoder's linking of rabbinic Judaism's "nonviolence" with the "pacifism of the messianic community" does "not aptly characterize the deviance of the 'pacifism of rabbinical nonviolence.'"—Cartwright, "Editors' Introduction," 23-24.

28. Ochs, "Commentary" on Chapter 2, 92. Ochs's linking of this point to his larger critique of what he views as Yoder's "binary thinking" displays, to my mind, a misreading of Yoder's account of Christian pacifism. Ochs appears to believe that for Yoder Christian pacifism is primarily about rule-following: either one adheres to the categorical imperative of pacifism or one does not. For Yoder, however, Christian pacifism is not so much to be understood in terms of rule-following as a doxological response to and participation in the cruciform work of the triune God in the world.

29. Ochs, "Commentary" to Chapter 4, in *JCSR*, 119.

30. Ibid. Yoder, Ochs argues, froze a historical insight about the emergence of parts of the Mishna "into the strongly overstated dogma that 'Mishnaic Judaism' allowed itself to be defined by its rejection of missionizing religion."—Ochs, "Commentary" on Chapter 3, in *JCSR*, 102.

31. Cartwright, "Afterword: 'If Abraham is Our Father': The Problem of Christian Supersessionism *after* Yoder," in *JCSR*, 217.

32. Yoder's mourning for the loss of missionary spirit within diaspora Jewry and his assessment of the role of parts of the Mishna in that loss should not be equated with a whole-sale dismissal of the Mishna as theologically valuable: the Mishna discourages intervisitation between messianic and non-messianic-Jews, but "in the total bulk of that literature it is not an important topic." Yoder, *JCSR*, 106. See also the following: "The Judaism of the *Mishna*, being post-schism, is committed (in some but in fact very few of its parts) to being non- or anti-messianic" (60).

33. Cartwright, "Afterword," 217.

34. Ochs, "Editors' Introduction," in *JCSR*, 39. Yoder, according to Ochs, "appears to reason or argue in such a way that divides the world of thought and of belief into radically opposing positions" (6). This approach, Ochs continues, creates "purisms" that "retain too much of the conceptualism that marked the colonialist philosophies of western civilization, even if they are offered beautifully and virtuously on behalf of God's gracious compassion for human suffering" (4).

35. Ibid., 6; Cartwright, "Afterword," 217. Ochs contrasts Yoder's supposed "logic of twos" with the "logic of threes" he sees operating in the work of various Christian theologians, including Stanley Hauerwas. If there is a case to be made that Yoder and Hauerwas differ in any appreciable way on the question of how the multiple strands of the Old Testament are to be read by Christians, or on how pacifist Christians are to read the multiple voices in Scripture on the question of violence, Ochs does not make it.

36. Ochs, "Commentary" on Preface, in *JCSR*, 40.

37. I take the image of "borderlines" from Boyarin's book of the same name.

38. Cartwright, "Editors' Introduction," 11. Ochs accuses Yoder of "a modern tendency to mistrust all inherited traditions, which means, in Cartesian or Lockean fashion, to place an excessive trust in immediate or direct disclosures of knowledge."—Ochs, "Commentary" on Preface, 39. This characterization, I believe, fails to capture the nuances of Yoder's approach to tradition. Yoder believed that new truth can always break forth from Scripture as the community gathers to read it. These new insights must then be tested against Scripture and against the community's received knowledge. The conviction that God's people can be radically renewed through communal readings of the Scripture does not, contra Ochs, mean "an indifference to history and tradition."—Ochs, "Commentary" on Chapter 6, 143. Yoder is quite clear that "the event of 'restitution' is not a new start 'from scratch,' going 'back to GO.'"—Yoder, *JCSR*, 138. Heirs of the radical reformation do, admittedly, always stand in danger of displaying indifference to or repudiation of tradition, and such dangers are compounded by modernity's "excessive trust in immediate or direct disclosures of knowledge." Yoder's theology of

history, I believe, is more complex than suggested by Cartwright or Ochs. See, for example, Yoder's treatment of history in "The Ambiguity of the Appeal to the Fathers," in *Practiced in the Presence: Essays in Honor of T. Canby Jones*, ed. Neil Snarr and Daniel Smith-Christopher (Richmond, IN: Friends United Press, 1994), 245-55; "Primitivism in the Radical Reformation," in *The Primitive Church in the Modern World*, ed. Richard T. Hughes (Chicago: University of Illinois Press, 1995), 74-97; and "The Burden and the Discipline of Evangelical Revisionism," in *Nonviolent America: History through the Eyes of Peace*, ed. Louise Hawkley and James C. Juhnke (North Newton, KS: Bethel College, 1993), 21-37. That said, Yoder's failure to discuss the positive theological significance of how rabbinic tradition in its diverse textual manifestations shapes Jewish identity opens him up to this misunderstanding.

39. Ochs, "Commentary" on Chapter 7, in *JCSR*, 158.

40. Cartwright, "Editors' Introduction," 23-24, 19.

41. Cartwright, "Afterword," 218.

42. Ochs, "Commentary" on Chapter 1, in *JCSR*, 68. Ochs believes that at points in his reading of Scripture Yoder ceases drawing "new and unpredictable conclusions" and begins "drawing Jews and non-Anabaptist Christians into a sphere of already completed interpretive conclusions."—Ochs, "Commentary" on Chapter 7, in *JCSR*, 159.

43. Cartwright, "Afterword," 226.

44. Cartwright and Ochs's critiques of Yoder on this score have helped me to see that Yoder's writings, insofar as they do not explicitly address the question of election, can produce "neo-neo-supersessionist" effects, i.e., can contribute to the assumption that Israel's peoplehood is valuable only insofar as it mirrors free church Christianity. In my initial writings on Yoder and Judaism I failed to see this gap in Yoder's work and so overstated the case for Yoder being a theologian who escapes "supersessionism." Despite my critiques of Cartwright and Ochs throughout this chapter I readily acknowledge that they have identified problematic holes in Yoder's theology of Judaism, and I am indebted to their gracious, although certainly sometimes critical, responses to my work. I first examined Yoder's theology of Judaism in my paper, *Constantinianism, Zionism, Diaspora: Toward a Political Theology of Exile and Return*, MCC Occasional Paper #28 (Akron, PA: Mennonite Central Committee, 2001). For Cartwright's critique of my discussion of Yoder, see his "Afterword," 213-14.

45. Daniel Boyarin, "Judaism as a Free Church: Footnotes to John Howard Yoder's *The Jewish-Christian Schism Revisited*," *CrossCurrents* 56/4 (January 2007), 19.

46. Ibid.

47. Scott Bader-Saye, *Church and Israel after Christendom*, 97.

48. Cartwright, "Afterword," 230.

49. R. Kendall Soulen, *The God of Israel and Christian Theology* (Minneapolis: Fortress Press, 1996), 170.

Chapter 2
An Exilic Politics of Land and Return

1. Mahmoud Darwish, "We Travel Like Other People," included in Larry Towell, *Then Palestine* (New York: Aperture, 1998), 32.

2. For Yoder on "methodologism," see his article, "Walk and Word: The Alternatives to Methodologism," in *Theology without Foundations: Religious Practice and the Future of Theological Truth*, ed. Stanley Hauerwas, Nancey Murphy, and Mark Nation (Nashville, TN: Abingdon Press, 1994): 77–90.

3. John Howard Yoder, "Exodus and Exile: Two Faces of Liberation," *CrossCurrents* (Fall 1973): 279–309.

4. Yoder, *For the Nations: Essays Public and Evangelical* (Grand Rapids, MI: Eerdmans, 1997), 82.

5. The difference that the exilic perspective makes for an assessment of the Palestinian-Israeli conflict is developed briefly at the end of this chapter and is addressed more thoroughly in the book's final section.

6. The religious-secular opposition will surface several times in the following section. Rather than attempting to parse the different, and to my mind ultimately incoherent, ways in which Said uses this opposition, I will only note that I find the opposition to lack critical persuasiveness. For a helpful critique of Said on "religious" and "secular" criticism, see William D. Hart, *Edward Said and the Religious Effects of Culture* (Cambridge: Cambridge University Press, 2000).

7. Said's defense of "amateurism" as an intellectual stance that revels "in making connections across lines and barriers, in refusing to be tied down to a specialty, in caring for ideas and values despite the restrictions of a profession" brings to mind Yoder's wide-ranging intellect and his fruitful bringing together of scholarship in biblical studies, church history, ethics, theology, and beyond. See Said, *Representations of the Intellectual* (London: Vintage, 1994), 57.

8. For a discussion of Barth's treatment of "secular parables of the Kingdom," see chapter 6.

9. Edward Said, *After the Last Sky: Palestinian Lives* (London: Vintage, 1986), 5.

10. A comprehensive source of information on Palestinian refugee history, their legal status, and their present living conditions is *A Survey of Palestinian Refugees and Internally Displaced Persons, 2004-2005* (Bethlehem: BADIL Resource Center, 2006). For treatments of the war of 1948 and the Palestinian *Nakba*, see *The War for Palestine: Rewriting the History of 1948*, ed. Eugene L. Rogan and Avi Shlaim (Cambridge: Cambridge University Press, 2001); Ilan Pappé, *The Making of the Arab-Israeli Conflict, 1947–1951* (London: I.B.

Tauris, 1992); Benny Morris, *The Birth of the Palestinian Refugee Problem, 1947–1949* (Cambridge: Cambridge University Press, 1987); Avi Shlaim, *Collusion Across the Jordan: King Abdullah, the Zionist Movement, and the Partition of Palestine* (Oxford: Clarendon Press, 1988); Nur Masalha, *Expulsion of the Palestinians: The Concept of "Transfer" in Zionist Political Thought, 1882–1948* (Washington, DC: Institute for Palestine Studies, 1992); Walid Khalidi, ed., *All That Remains: The Palestinian Villages Occupied and Depopulated by Israel in 1948* (Washington, DC: Institute for Palestine Studies, 1992); and Meron Benvenisti, *Sacred Landscape: The Buried History of the Holy Land since 1948* (Berkeley: University of California Press, 2000).

11. For more on internally displaced Palestinians inside Israel, see *Catastrophe Remembered: Palestine, Israel, and the Internal Refugees*, ed. Nur Masalha (London: Zed Books, 2005).

12. Critical descriptions of the Israeli matrix of control in the Occupied Territories include Eyal Weizman, *Hollow Land: Israel's Architecture of Occupation* (London: Verso, 2007) and Jeff Halper, *Obstacles to Peace: A Re-Framing of the Palestinian-Israeli Conflict* (Jerusalem: The Israeli Committee against House Demolitions, 2004).

13. Said, *After the Last Sky*, 130.

14. Ibid., 12.

15. Ibid., 20–21.

16. Ibid., 164.

17. Ibid., 20–21.

18. Ibid., 68.

19. Said, *Representations of the Intellectual*, 35.

20. Said, *After the Last Sky*, 51.

21. Said, *Reflections on Exile and Other Essays* (Cambridge: Harvard University Press, 2000), 178.

22. Ibid., 183.

23. Ibid., 175.

24. Ibid., 174. "Secular" in this context appears to mean for Said that exile cannot be placed into a larger transcendental, theological context of meaning. It is an agonizingly concrete situation with no hope for amelioration (other than what the exile herself can produce).

25. Said, *Power, Politics, and Culture: Interviews with Edward Said*, ed. Gauri Viswanathan (New York: Pantheon Books 2001), 56.

26. Said, *Representations of the Intellectual*, 39. Said insisted that intellectuals should not become yea-sayers for their communities, and he served as a vociferous critic of the PLO and its often misguided handling of the Palestinian struggle. Yoder too was no "yea-sayer," or apologist, for the Mennonite community, but rather reserved his most polemical barbs for critiques of the Mennonite churches. See, e.g., "Anabaptist Vision and Mennonite Reality," in

Consultation on Anabaptist-Mennonite Theology: Papers Read at the 1969 Aspen Conference, ed. A. J. Klassen (Fresno: Council of Mennonite Seminaries, 1970): 1–46.

27. Said, *Representations of the Intellectual*, 39.

28. Ibid., 46.

29. Ibid., 45.

30. Theodor Adorno, *Minima Moralia: Reflections from Damaged Life* (London: New Left Books, 1951), 38-39. Quoted in Said, *Reflections on Exile*, 564–65.

31. Adorno, *Minima Moralia*, 87. Quoted in Said, *Reflections on Exile*, 568.

32. Said, *Reflections on Exile*, 568.

33. For a persuasive discussion of *pathos* in theology and the role of *poeisis* within that *pathos*, see Reinhard Hütter, *Suffering Divine Things: Theology as Church Practice* (Grand Rapids, MI: Eerdmans, 2000).

34. Said, "Introduction: The Right of Return at Last," in *Palestinian Refugees: The Right of Return*, ed. Naseer Aruri (London: Pluto Press, 2001), 6.

35. Said, *After the Last Sky*, 33.

36. Said, *Power, Politics, and Culture*, 429.

37. Said, *Reflections on Exile*, 179.

38. Said, *After the Last Sky*, 150.

39. Ibid., 150. Note once more Said's rather wooden use of the religious-secular opposition. What Said cannot imagine is a religious criticism that prizes the "open" character of exile precisely because it confesses God's redeeming defeat of the powers of sin.

40. Gerald Schlabach, "Deuteronomic or Constantinian: What Is the Most Basic Problem for Christian Social Ethics?" in *The Wisdom of the Cross: Essays in Honor of John Howard Yoder*, ed. Stanley Hauerwas, Chris K. Huebner, Harry Huebner, and Mark Thiessen Nation (Grand Rapids, MI: Eerdmans, 2002), 463.

41. See, for example, Amnon Raz-Krakotzkin, "Peace without Arabs: The Discourse of Peace and the Limits of Israeli Consciousness," in *After Oslo: New Realities, Old Problems*, ed. George Giacaman and D. J. Loenning (London: Pluto Press, 1998), 59-76, and, by the same author, "A National Colonial Theology: Religion, Orientalism and the Construction of the Secular in Zionist Discourse," *Tel Aviver Jahrbuch für deutsche Geschichte* 30 (2002): 312-26, and "Exile, History and the Nationalization of Jewish Memory: Some Reflections on the Zionist Notion of History and Return," Annual Meyerhoff Lecture at the University of Pennsylvania, February 1, 2006. I do not mean, through this analysis of the ways in which Zionist discourse and practice have worked historically to dispossess

Palestinians, to deny the possibility that other forms of Zionism, Zionisms not dependent on the dispossession of others, might be possible. The "cultural Zionism," for example, of an Ahad Haam or a Judah Magnes, would be cases in point. In his interview with Ari Shavit, Said rejects any talk of de-Zionization or a simple dismissal of Zionism as a valid term. Jews should be able to be Zionists, Said believes, and "assert their Jewish identity and their connection to the land, so long as it doesn't keep the others out so manifestly." See Said, *Power, Politics, and Culture,* 451.

42. Schlabach, "Deuteronomic or Constantinian," 470.

43. Laurence Silberstein, *The Postzionism Debates: Knowledge and Power in Israeli Culture* (New York and London: Routledge, 1999), 20, 22-23.

44. For discussions of the Zionist negation of the diaspora beyond those of Silberstein and Raz-Krakotzkin, see Shalom Ratzaby, "The Polemic about the Negation of the Diaspora in the 1930s and Its Roots," *Journal of Israeli History* 16 (Spring 1995): 19-38, and Eliezer Don-Yehiya, "The Negation of Galut in Religious Zionism," *Modern Judaism* 12 (May 1992): 129-55.

45. Silberstein, *Postzionism Debates,* 20.

46. Quoted and translated in Silberstein, Postzionism Debates, 179. For the original Hebrew, see Amnon Raz-Krakotzkin, "Exile in the Midst of Sovereignty: A Critique of 'Shelilat HaGalut' in Israeli Culture," *Theory and Criticism (Theoria ve-Bikoret)* 4 (Fall 1993): 44. See also Raz-Krakotzkin, *Exil et Souveraineté: Judaïsme, Sionisme, et Pensée Binationale* (Paris: La Fabrique, 2007).

47. See Raz-Krakotzkin, "Exile, History and the Nationalization of Jewish Memory." This conclusion bears remarkable similarities to Yoder's critique of Zionism, noted above, as a Jewish assimilation to Christendom.

48. Quoted and translated in Silberstein, *Postzionism Debates,* 178–79; Raz-Krakotzkin, "Exile in the Midst of Sovereignty," 44.

49. Quoted and translated in Silberstein, *Postzionism Debates,* 181; Raz-Krakotzkin, "Exile in the Midst of Sovereignty," 39.

50. Silberstein, *Postzionism Debates,* 181, citing Raz-Krakotzkin, "Exile in the Midst of Sovereignty," 49.

51. Said, *Power, Politics, and Culture,* 425.

52. Commentators of various political persuasions increasingly describe the reality in the occupied Palestinian territories as one of apartheid. For an exemplary analysis, see Oren Yiftachel and Haim Yacobi, "Barriers, Walls, and Dialectics: The Shaping of 'Creeping Apartheid' in Israel/Palestine," in *Against the Wall: Israel's Barrier to Peace,* ed. Michael Sorkin (New York: New Press, 2005), 138-57.

53. Said, *Power, Politics, and Culture,* 457–58. Some Israeli writers share aspects of Said's binational vision. Raz-Krakotzin, for one, believes that *galut* as a critical concept makes possible "a Jewish identity based on the recogni-

tion of the potential embodied in the bi-nationality of the land" Quoted and translated in Silberstein, *Postzionism Debates*, 181; Raz-Krakotzkin, "Exile in the Midst of Sovereignty," 49. See also Raz-Krakotzkin, "Binationalism and Jewish Identity: Hannah Arendt and the Question of Palestine," in *Hannah Arendt in Jerusalem*, ed. Steven E. Aschheim (Berkeley: University of California Press, 2001): 165-80.

54. Quoted and translated in Silberstein, *Postzionism Debates*, 182; Emile Habiby, *Ehtayeh*, translated from Arabic into Hebrew by Anton Shammas (Tel Aviv: Am Oved, 1988), 9.

55. Quoted and translated in Silberstein, *Postzionism Debates*, 182; Raz-Krakotzkin, "Exile in the Midst of Sovereignty," 52.

56. See, for example, Yoder, *The Christian Witness to the State* (Newton, KS: Faith and Life Press, 1964, and Scottdale, PA: Herald Press, 2002), 77. I discuss Yoder's understanding of the ad hoc character of Christian political engagement in chapter 4.

Chapter 3
Zionism, Separation, and Diaspora Consciousness in the Land

1. Michael Cartwright summarizes Yoder's position thus: "Jews and Christians [according to Yoder] can exercise their choice to live as an alternative to the Constantinianism of both Christendom and Zionism." See Cartwright, "Appendix B," in Yoder, *The Jewish-Christian Schism Revisited* (Grand Rapids, MI: Eerdmans, 2003), 257; hereafter *JCSR*.

2. Cartwright, "Afterword: 'If Abraham Is Our Father,'" in Yoder, *JCSR*, 219.

3. Ochs, "Commentary" on chapter 10, in Yoder, *JCSR*, 203.

4. Carwright, "Afterword," 218. Italics in the original.

5. Ibid., 219.

6. Ochs, "Commentary" on chapter 9, in Yoder, *JCSR*, 179.

7. Ochs, "Commentary" on chapter 10, 203.

8. Ochs insists that "to be burdened with the land of Israel is not simply to apply a very modernist notion of national-political-ethnic sovereignty to the land." Jews, Ochs argues, "cannot be encouraged by Yoder's failure to think of the question of Israel beyond the stark either/or that stands between 'anti-Zionism' and the particular Zionism of Israel's right-wing nationalists" ("Commentary" on chapter 9, in *JCSR*, 180). All well and good: blanket condemnations of "Zionism," when proponents of binationalism such as Judah Magnes and Martin Buber could be called Zionists, are not necessarily productive. Ochs, however, does not acknowledge that in the real history of its thought and practice, Zionism—and not only in its Revisionist/Herut/Likud streams—has been about applying modernist notions of national-political-ethnic sovereignty onto Mandate Palestine, about ideologies of "transfer" shared by the left and right pre-1948, about discriminatory legislation and practices

regarding access to land and natural resources, about discourses and practices designed to counter a perceived "demographic threat" posed by the non-Jewish Palestinian Arab population both inside Israel and in the Occupied Territories. Could Jewish responsibility for the burden of the land of Israel be exercised in the future in the context of one binational state shared by Palestinians and Israeli Jews alike? If yes, then I would suggest that fundamentally no disagreement exists between Yoder and Ochs (or Ochs and myself). If no, however, then I would suggest that Ochs's Zionism, his political conception about what it means to be "burdened with the land of Israel," has not escaped the "very modernist notion of national-political sovereignty."

9. "*Dabru Emet*: A Jewish Statement on Christians and Christianity," in *Jews and Christians: People of God*, ed. Carl E. Braaten and Robert W. Jenson (Grand Rapids, MI: Eerdmans, 2003), 179-82. For a fuller discussion of *Dabru Emet*, see my article, "Speaking the Truth in Jewish-Christian Dialogue," *The Mennonite*, 31 October 2000, 6-7.

10. *Dabru Emet*, 180.

11. David B. Burrell, CSC, in "A Symposium on *Dabru Emet*," in *Jews and Christians: People of God*, 191.

12. Oren Yiftachel, *Ethnocracy: Land and Identity Politics in Israel/Palestine* (Philadelphia: University of Pennsylvania Press, 2006), 295. Yiftachel places the state of Israel in comparative perspective alongside other contemporary ethnocracies like Sri Lanka, Malaysia, and Serbia and in the company of settler societies like Australia, South Africa, and the United States, countries whose ethnocratic regimes have facilitated the domination of a particular territory by one particular group at the expense of others. It is important to stress that as an ethnocracy Israel is not unique, nor is Israel by any means unique in terms of having been built on the dispossession of another people—inhabitants of Canada and the United States should of course be acutely aware of this fact.

13. David Landau, "Maximum Jews, Minimum Arabs: Interview with Ehud Olmert," *Ha'aretz*, 15 November 2003.

14. Rashid Khalid, *The Iron Cage: The Story of the Palestinian Struggle for Statehood* (Boston: Beacon Press, 2006).

15. Ari Shavit, "The Big Freeze: Interview with Dov Weisglass," *Ha'aretz*, 6 October 2004. Negotiations may well resume after the construction of the walls and fences even under the banner of "peace talks" (see, for example, the talks inaugurated at the Annapolis conference in late November 2007) but the purpose of the wall is to render Israel's control of the Occupied Territories permanent and irreversible, thus threatening to reduce any future Palestinian-Israeli negotiations to the level of discussions over the details of Palestinian subsistence in the ghetto-like enclaves to which Israeli barriers and checkpoints have confined them.

16. The late Palestinian-American critic Edward Said framed the matter well: "Show me a scheme for separation that isn't based on abridged memory, continued injustice, unmitigated conflict, apartheid." See Edward Said, "Afterword: The Consequences of 1948," in *The War for Palestine: Rewriting the History of 1948*, ed. Eugene L. Rogan and Avi Shlaim (Cambridge: Cambridge University Press, 2001), 219.

17. Meron Benvenisti, "Founding a Binational State," *Ha'aretz*, 22 April 2004. See also Benvenisti, *Son of the Cypresses: Memories, Reflections, and Regrets from a Political Life* (Berkeley: University of California Press, 2007), esp. chaps. 6 and 7.

18. For two recent arguments in favor of binationalism, the first by a historian and the second by a political scientist, see Tony Judt, "Israel: The Alternative," *New York Review of Books*, 23 October 2003, and Virginia Tilley, *The One-State Solution: A Breakthrough for Peace in the Israeli-Palestinian Deadlock* (Ann Arbor: University of Michigan Press, 2005).

19. Daniel Boyarin, *A Radical Jew: Paul and the Politics of Identity* (Berkeley: University of California Press, 1994), 248-49.

20. Ibid., 255.

21. Daniel Boyarin and Jonathan Boyarin, *Powers of Diaspora: Two Essays on the Relevance of Jewish Culture* (Minneapolis: University of Minnesota Press, 2002), 53. See also Daniel Boyarin, *Unheroic Conduct: The Rise of Heterosexuality and the Invention of the Jewish Man* (Berkeley: University of California Press, 1997).

22. Boyarin, *A Radical Jew*, 335 n. 41.

23. Ibid., 245.

24. Ibid., 335 n. 41.

25. Boyarin and Boyarin, *Powers of Diaspora*, 5.

26. See Amnon Raz-Krakotzkin, "The Zionist Return to the History of Redemption: Or What Is the 'History' to which the 'Return' in the Phrase 'the Zionist Return to History' Refers?" (Hebrew) in *Zionism and the Return to History: A Reevaluation*, ed. S. N. Eisentadt and M. Lyssak (Jerusalem: Ben-Zvi Institute, 1999), 249-79.

27. Boyarin, *A Radical Jew*, 259.

28. Boyarin and Boyarin, *Powers of Diaspora*, 9.

29. Boyarin, *A Radical Jew*, 250.

30. Ibid., 334 n. 40.

31. Yoder, *Jewish-Christian Schism Revisited*, 164. Ochs acknowledges that here Yoder was proposing an alternative to an apolitical, "otherworldly" notion of diaspora and "oppressive landedness" ("Commentary" on chapter 8, in *JCSR*, 167).

32. Boyarin, *A Radical Jew*, 259.

33. Ibid., 260.

34. Ibid., 337 n. 46.

35. Boyarin, *Border Lines: The Partition of Judaeo-Christianity* (Philadelphia: University of Pennsylvania Press, 2004), xiv.

36. See Martin Buber, *A Land of Two Peoples: Martin Buber on Jews and Arabs*, ed. Paul Mendes-Flohr (Chicago: University of Chicago Press, 2005), and Hannah Arendt, *The Jewish Writings*, ed. Jerome Kohn and Ron H. Feldman (New York: Schocken Books, 2007). For an important treatment of Arendt on Zionism and binationalism, see Amnon Raz-Krakotzkin, "Binationalism and Jewish Identity: Hannah Arendt and the Question of Palestine," in *Hannah Arendt in Jerusalem*, ed. Steven E. Aschheim (Berkley: University of California Press, 2001), 181-93.

Chapter 4
Missionary Christology as Subversive Proclamation

1. See especially J. Denny Weaver, "Nicaea, Womanist Theology, and Anabaptist Particularity," in *Anabaptists and Postmodernity*, ed. Gerald Biesecker-Mast and Sue Biesecker-Mast (Telford, PA: Pandora Press US, 2000), 251-79, and "The United States Shape of Mennonite Theologizing: Some Preliminary Observations," *Mennonite Quarterly Review* 73/3 (July 1999): 631-44.

2. Articles by A. James Reimer exemplify this critique, especially "Trinitarian Orthodoxy, Constantinianism, and Theology from a Radical Protestant Perspective," in *Faith to Creed: Ecumenical Perspectives on the Affirmation of the Apostolic Faith in the Fourth Century*, ed. S. Mark Heim (Grand Rapids, MI: Eerdmans, 1991), 129-61, and "Towards a Theocentric Christology: Christ for the World," in *The Limits of Perfection: A Conversation with J. Lawrence Burkholder*, ed. Scott Holland and Ronald J. Sawatsky (Waterloo and Kitchener, ON: Institute of Anabaptist and Mennonite Studies and Pandora Press, 1993), 95-109.

3. See Craig A. Carter, *The Politics of the Cross: The Theology and Social Ethics of John Howard Yoder* (Grand Rapids, MI: Brazos Press, 2001), 113-36.

4. Yoder served with both Mennonite Central Committee and Mennonite Board of Missions, wrote extensively on mission matters, and maintained an active interest in the church's worldwide ministries. For a recent discussion of Yoder on mission, see Joon-Sik Park, "'As You Go': John Howard Yoder as a Mission Theologian," *Mennonite Quarterly Review* 78/3 (July 2004): 363-84.

5. Gerald Schlabach has helpfully characterized Yoder's writings as anthological rather than systematic in his "Anthology in Lieu of a System: John H. Yoder's Ecumenical Conversations as Systematic Theology," *Conrad Grebel Review* 16 (Spring 1988): 15-38.

6. Yoder described his approach "to the development of early Christian

dogma" as "narrative and relativizing" in "That Household We Are," unpublished paper presented at a conference, Is There a Believers' Church Christology? at Bluffton College, Bluffton, Ohio, October 1980, 9.

7. Yoder, *The Politics of Jesus: Vicit Agnus Noster*, rev. ed. (Grand Rapids, MI: Eerdmans, 1994), 102.

8. Ibid., 10.

9. Yoder, *Preface to Theology: Christology and Theological Method* (Grand Rapids, MI: Brazos Press, 2002), 220. The original versions of the course lectures, edited for publication after Yoder's death by Stanley Hauerwas and Alex Sider, were first circulated under the same title by Goshen Biblical Seminary, Elkhart, Indiana.

10. Yoder, *He Came Preaching Peace* (Scottdale, PA: Herald Press, 1985), 85.

11. Yoder, "Confessing Jesus in Mission," 2. Unpublished paper available at http://theology.nd.edu/people/research/yoder-john/documents/CONFESS-INGJESUSINMISSION.pdf. Originally written in English, this paper appeared in published form in Dutch translation as "Jezus belijden in de Zending," *Wereld in Zending* no. 24 (1996).

12. Ibid.

13. John Howard Yoder, *For the Nations: Essays Public and Evangelical* (Grand Rapids, MI: Eerdmans, 1997), 242.

14. Yoder, "Confessing Jesus in Mission," 4.

15. Yoder, *Preface to Theology*, 202.

16. Yoder, *Politics of Jesus*, 99.

17. Yoder, "How H. Richard Niebuhr Reasoned: A Critique of *Christ and Culture*," in *Authentic Transformation: A New Vision of Christ and Culture*, ed. Glen Stassen, D. M. Yeager, and John Howard Yoder (Nashville, TN: Abingdon Press, 1996), 62. Harry Huebner follows Yoder's lead in his critique of James Gustafson's appeal to creation as a way to subordinate the claims of Jesus. A properly trinitarian theology proclaims "the moral unity within the Trinity" and thus expects "moral continuity between creater/sustainer/culminator God and Jesus, the Christ." See Harry J. Huebner, "Moral Agency as Embodiment: How the Church Acts," in *The Wisdom of the Cross: Essays in Honor of John Howard Yoder*, ed. Stanley Hauerwas, Chris K. Huebner, Harry J. Huebner, and Mark Thiessen Nation (Grand Rapids, MI: Eerdmans, 1999), 202.

18. Arne Rasmusson, "Historicizing the Historicst: Ernest Troeltsch and Recent Mennonite Theology," in *Wisdom of the Cross*, 241-42.

19. Yoder, *Preface to Theology*, 222-223.

20. John Howard Yoder, *The Royal Priesthood: Essays Ecclesiological and Ecumenical*, ed. Michael Cartwright (Grand Rapids, MI: Eerdmans, 1994), 191.

21. Yoder, *Preface to Theology*, 204.

22. Yoder, "Confessing Jesus in Mission," 6 n. 17.

23. Yoder, *Preface to Theology*, 205.

24. Yoder, "Confessing Jesus in Mission," 4. Yoder approvingly cited Martin Hengel's attempt in *The Son of God: The Origins of Christology and the History of Jewish-Hellenistic Relations* (Philadelphia: Fortress Press, 1976) to show the essentially Jewish character of the gospel designation of Jesus as the Son of God. While Yoder recognized that trinitarian theology could be understood by Jews and Muslims as an abandonment of monotheism, he clearly did not believe the doctrine of the Trinity to be incompatible with monotheistic faith. Yoder asked if Jews and Muslims who equated the Trinity with polytheism were "conversing with the most careful theologians, who argued most carefully to distinguish trinitarian monotheism and tritheism?" See Yoder, *The Jewish-Christian Schism Revisited*, ed. Michael Cartwright and Peter Ochs (Grand Rapids, MI: Eerdmans, 2003), 55-56.

25. Yoder, *Royal Priesthood*, 185.

26. John Howard Yoder, *Priestly Kingdom: Social Ethics as Gospel* (Notre Dame, IN: University of Notre Dame Press, 1984), 54.

27. Yoder, "That Household We Are," 7.

28. Yoder, *Jewish-Christian Schism Revisited*, 143.

29. Ibid., chap. 1.

30. Yoder's full account of this six-part missionary christology can be found in his *Priestly Kingdom*, 53. He also developed this approach in his lecture "That Household We Are." Unless otherwise noted, the citations in this paragraph and the next are from *Priestly Kingdom*, 53.

31. Yoder, "That Household We Are," 8.

32. Ibid., 7.

33. Yoder, *Preface to Theology*, 205.

34. Yoder developed the image of Christ as the "light of the world" versus the "other lights" of reason, nature, etc. in his essay, "Christ, The Light of the World," first published in *The Original Revolution* (Scottdale, PA: 1971), 132-47; the essay was reprinted in *The Royal Priesthood*, 181-91.

35. Yoder, "That Household We Are," 7.

36. The accusation that Yoder's theology "buys into modern historicism" has been advanced most insistently by A. James Reimer. See, for example, Reimer, "Theological Orthodoxy and Jewish Christianity," in *Wisdom of the Cross*, 435.

37. Yoder, *Politics of Jesus*, 246-47.

38. For a discussion of Yoder's "apocalyptic politics," see David Toole, *Waiting for Godot in Sarajevo: Theological Reflections on Nihilism, Tragedy, and Apocalypse* (Boulder, CO: Westview Press, 1998), esp. chaps 7-8.

39. "That Household We Are," 7.

40. Yoder, *Preface to Theology*, 223.

Chapter 5
The Body Politics of the Church in Exile

1. The term *body politics* is taken from Yoder's short study, *Body Politics: Five Practices of the Christian Community before the Watching World* (Nashville, TN: Discipleship Resources, 1992; and Scottdale, PA: Herald Press, 2001). The complexities of Mennonite thought on politics, peace, and war in the twentieth century cannot be entered into here. For the best treatment of the subject, see Perry Bush, *Two Kingdoms, Two Loyalties: Mennonite Pacifism in Modern America* (Baltimore: Johns Hopkins University Press, 1998).

2. Thomas Heilke, "On Being Ethical without Moral Sadism: Two Readings of Augustine and the Beginnings of the Anabaptist Revolution," *Political Thought* 24/3 (August 1996): 494-95.

3. Yoder did not claim originality for his treatment of the political character of church practices but viewed himself as building on and developing models formulated by H. Richard Niebuhr in his "The Social Gospel and the Mind of Jesus" and by Karl Barth in his essay "Christengemeinde und Bürgergemeinde." Niebuhr's article was posthumously published in the *Journal of Religious Ethics* 16/1 (Spring 1988): 109ff. Yoder discussed that article in *For the Nations: Essays Public and Evangelical* (Grand Rapids, MI: Eerdmans, 1997), 21-23. Barth's essay, "The Christian Community and the Civil Community," appears in *Karl Barth: Theologian of Freedom*, ed. Clifford Green (Minneapolis: Fortress Press, 1989), 265-95. For Yoder on Barth, see *The Royal Priesthood: Essays Ecclesiological and Ecumenical*, ed. Michael G. Cartwright (Grand Rapids, MI: Eerdmans, 1994; and Herald Press, 1998), 102-26.

4. Yoder, *Body Politics*, ix.

5. John Howard Yoder, *The Christian Witness to the State* (Newton, KS: Faith and Life Press, 1964; and Scottdale, PA: Herald Press, 2002), 17.

6. Ibid., 18.

7. Yoder, *Body Politics*, ix.

8. In *Christian Witness to the State* Yoder discussed only the first three practices (18-19). He expanded the list to five, including baptism and communion, in *Body Politics*.

9. Yoder, *Body Politics*, 72-73.

10. Ibid., 72.

11. John Howard Yoder, *The Priestly Kingdom: Social Ethics as Gospel* (Notre Dame, IN: University of Notre Dame Press, 1984), 5.

12. Yoder, *Christian Witness to the State*, 19. In this type of experimental activity the church lives as a "pioneer." See Yoder, *Royal Priesthood*, 205-6.

13. Yoder, *Christian Witness to the State*, 20.

14. John Howard Yoder, "The Anabaptist Dissent: The Logic of the Place of the Disciple in Society," *Concern: A Pamphlet Series for Questions of Christian Renewal* 1 (June 1954): 46.

15. John Howard Yoder, "Withdrawal and Diaspora: The Two Faces of Liberation," in *Freedom and Discipleship: Liberation Theology in Anabaptist Perspective*, ed. Daniel S. Schipani (Maryknoll, NY: Orbis Books, 1989), 76-84. See also Yoder, "Exodus and Exile: Two Faces of Liberation," *CrossCurrents* (Fall 1973), 297-309.

16. Yoder, *Royal Priesthood*, 198.

17. Oliver O'Donovan, *The Desire of the Nations: Rediscovering the Roots of Political Theology* (Cambridge: Cambridge University Press, 1996), 224. For a perceptive comparison of Yoder and O'Donovan, see P. Travis Kroeker, "Why O'Donovan's Christendom Is Not Constantinian and Yoder's Voluntareity Is Not Hobbesian: A Debate in Theological Politics Redefined," *Annual of the Society of Christian Ethics* 20 (2000): 41-64.

18. Hauerwas discusses O'Donovan's critique of Yoder in *Wilderness Wanderings: Probing Twentieth-Century Theology and Philosophy* (Boulder, CO: Westview Press, 1997), 224 n. 15. For Hauerwas on the nonvoluntary nature of the church, see chapter 9 of *Sanctify Them in the Truth: Holiness Exemplified* (Nashville, TN: Abingdon Press, 1998). One might be tempted to locate the tension between the voluntary and nonvoluntary character of the church in the debate between pedobaptist and antipedobaptist positions. However, Yoder clearly emphasized that what was at stake for him in adult baptism was the distinctness of the church from the world, and he imagined ecumenical proposals that would bridge the differences between adult and infant baptism arguments. See Yoder, "Adjusting to the Changing Shape of the Debate on Infant Baptism," in *Oecumennisme; Essays in Honor of Dr. Henk Kossen*, ed. Arie Lambo (Amsterdam: Algemene Doopsgezinde Societeit, 1989), 201-14.

19. Michael Cartwright, for example, argues that "Yoder's consistently held assumptions about the 'voluntariness' of Jewish identity runs into conflict with the thickly woven practices of Jewish communities, including but not lim-ited to the rabbinical conversations about observance of (*halakhic* and *hag-gadic*) Torah." See Cartwright, "Afterword: 'If Abraham Is Our Father . . . ': The Problem of Christian Supersessionism *after* Yoder," in John Howard Yoder, *The Jewish-Christian Schism Revisited*, ed. Michael G. Cartwright and Peter Ochs (Grand Rapids, MI: Eerdmans, 2003), 266.

20. John Howard Yoder, *The Original Revolution: Essays on Christian Pacifism* (Scottdale, PA: Herald Press, 1971), 33.

21. Yoder, *Royal Priesthood*, 104.

22. Yoder, *Politics of Jesus*, 137. Yoder's understanding of the "powers" drew on the work of Jacques Ellul, William Stringfellow, and Hendrikus Berkhof, and bears comparison with the writings of Walter Wink. For a provocative critique of some discussion of the powers in contemporary theol-ogy, see J. Alexander Sider, "'Who Durst Defy the Omnipotent to Arms?': The

Nonviolent Atonement and a Non-Competitive Doctrine of God," in *The Work of Jesus Christ in Anabaptist Perspective*, ed. Alain Epp Weaver and Gerald Mast (Telford, PA: Cascadia, forthcoming 2008).

23. Yoder, *Politics of Jesus*, 143.

24. Ibid., 144.

25. Ibid., 145.

26. Ibid., 158.

27. Oliver O'Donovan is simply mistaken to claim that Yoder invokes the language of principalities and powers in order to "point up the demonic character of the state" (*Desire of the Nations*, 151). This characterization of Yoder fails to acknowledge Yoder's consistent stress on the goodness of the powers as part of God's creation and their subordination under the lordship of Christ.

28. Yoder, *Politics of Jesus*, 201.

29. Yoder, *Christian Witness to the State*, 75.

30. Yoder, *Priestly Kingdom*, 154.

31. John Howard Yoder, *Nevertheless: The Varieties and Shortcomings of Religious Pacifism*, revised and expanded edition (Scottdale, PA: Herald Press, 1992), 113.

32. Yoder, "The Anabaptist Dissent," 51.

33. Yoder, *Christian Witness to the State*, 36-37. Yoder's opposition to the death penalty stemmed both from his biblical exegesis and from the conviction that execution went beyond the "absolute minimum of violence" permitted the state. For his most concise discussion of capital punishment, see *The Christian and Capital Punishment* (Newton, KS: Faith and Life Press, 1961).

34. Ibid., 77.

35. Yoder, *Politics of Jesus*, 209.

36. See especially Guy F. Hershberger, *War, Peace, and Nonresistance* (Scottdale, PA: Herald Press, 1944).

37. Yoder, *Nevertheless*, 113. That Yoder's ecumenical spirit drove him to form alliances with Christian pacifists of various theological persuasions did not, of course, mean that he held back from criticizing what he viewed as the overly optimistic anthropology of many Christian pacifists. In his seminal response to Reinhold Niebuhr, for example, Yoder made clear that he joined Niebuhr in denouncing the high view of the human and the low view of sin characterizing the Christian pacifism of the Social Gospel movement. See Yoder, "Reinhold Niebuhr and Christian Pacifism," *Mennonite Quarterly Review* 29 (April 1955): 101-17.

38. Yoder, *For the Nations*, 101.

39. Ibid., 199.

40. See, for example, Yoder's respectful treatment of various effectiveness-oriented forms of pacifism in *Nevertheless*. Yoder's ability to engage in

thought-experiments is also evident in his consideration of what it would mean to make just war criteria effective. See Yoder, *When War Is Unjust: Being Honest in Just War Thinking*, rev. ed. (Maryknoll, NY: Orbis Books, 1997).

41. Yoder, *Christian Witness to the State*, 44.

42. Yoder, *Politics of Jesus*, 242.

43. Ibid., 204.

44. Yoder, *Royal Priesthood*, 204.

45. Yoder, *For the Nations*, 115.

46. Ibid., 27.

47. Ibid., 28.

48. Yoder, *Christian Witness to the State*, 72.

49. Yoder, *Priestly Kingdom*, 158.

50. Yoder, *Christian Witness to the State*, 73.

51. Ibid., 59.

52. This definition of "politics" comes from Heilke, who proposes the definition in order to oppose it to the "politics" of sixteenth-century Anabaptism. See Heilke, "On Being Ethical," 513.

Chapter 6
Parables of the Kingdom

1. Karl Barth, *Church Dogmatics* I/1, ed. G. W. Bromiley and T. F. Torrance (Edinburgh: T&T Clark, 1939), 74; hereafter *CD* I/1.

2. Variations of this approach include John Hick, *An Interpretation of Religion: Human Responses to the Transcendent* (New Haven, CT: Yale University Press, 1989), W. C. Smith, *Towards a World Theology* (Maryknoll, NY: Orbis Books, 1981), and the essays in *The Myth of Christian Uniqueness: Towards a Pluralistic Theology of Religions*, ed. John Hick and Paul Knitter (Maryknoll, NY: Orbis Books, 1987).

3. See, for example, Kenneth Surin, "A 'Politics of Speech': Religious Pluralism in the Age of the McDonald's Hamburger," in *Christian Uniqueness Reconsidered: The Myth of a Pluralistic Theology of Religions*, ed. Gavin D'Costa (Maryknoll, NY: Orbis Books, 1990), 192-212.

4. Karl Barth, *Church Dogmatics* IV/3.1, ed. G. W. Bromiley and T. F. Torrance (Edinburgh: T&T Clark, 1963), 86; hereafter cited in the text as *CD* IV/3.1.

5. Examples of these two approaches include Gordon Kaufman and Schubert Ogden, with Kaufman making the shift away from Jesus toward mystery, and with Ogden opting for a representative rather than constitutive Christology. See Gordon D. Kaufman, *In Face of Mystery: A Constructive Theology* (Cambridge: Harvard University Press, 1993) and Schubert M. Ogden, *Is There Only One True Religion or Are There Many?* (Dallas: Southern Methodist University Press, 1992).

6. Barth's use of the word "secular" should not obscure the fact that

Barth's argument that Christians can and do encounter God's one Word outside the church applies to the "religious" words and deeds of non-Christians.

7. Karl Barth, *Church Dogmatics* II/1, ed. G.W. Bromiley and T. F. Torrance (Edinburgh: T&T Clark, 1957), 319. [Hereafter *CD* II/1, 319.]

8. George Hunsinger, *How to Read Karl Barth: The Shape of His Theology* (New York: Oxford University Press, 1992), 242.

9. Ibid., 238.

10. Ibid., 261.

11. Yoder, "The Finality of Jesus Christ and Other Faiths," collected material from lectures and essays, reproduced in fall 1983 for the Associated Mennonite Biblical Seminaries course, Ecclesiology in Missional Perspective, 1983, 30. For a discussion of Barth's influence on Yoder's theology, see Craig A. Carter, *The Politics of the Cross: The Theology and Ethics of John Howard Yoder* (Grand Rapids, MI: Wm. B. Eerdmans, 2001), 61-90 and chapter 4 of Earl Zimmerman, *Practicing the Politics of Jesus: The Origin and Significance of John Howard Yoder's Social Ethics* (Telford, PA.: Cascadia, 2007).

12. John Howard Yoder, "The Basis of Barth's Social Ethics," in Yoder, *Karl Barth and the Problem of War, and Other Essays on Barth*, ed. Mark Thiessen Nation (Eugene, OR: Cascade Books, 2003), 147.

13. Hunsinger, 267.

14. Harmonization, of course, is not the same as repetition. One benefit of interreligious dialogue is the potential for Christian preconceptions concerning the content of Scripture to be challenged and undermined, thus bringing about new, fresh interpretations. For a discussion of how Barth's discussion of parables of the kingdom allows for a critique of scripture, see William Stacy Johnson, *The Mystery of God: Karl Barth and the Postmodern Foundations of Theology* (Louisville: Westminster/John Knox Press, 1997).

15. Karl Barth, *Church Dogmatics* I/2, ed. G.W. Bromiley and T. F. Torrance (Edinburgh: T&T Clark, 1956), 326. [Hereafter cited in-text as *CD* I/2.]

16. Yoder has perceptively noted that this section of the *Church Dogmatics* in which Barth analyzes the judgment of revelation upon religion is "epistemologically post-Constantinian" in its linking of political disestablishment to the church's renunciation of apologetics and to a noncoercive style of witness. See John Howard Yoder, "Karl Barth, Post-Christendom Theologian," in Yoder, *Karl Barth and the Problem of War and Other Essays on Barth*, 179.

17. See John Howard Yoder, "The Disavowal of Constantine: An Alternative Perspective on Interfaith Dialogue," in *The Royal Priesthood: Essays Ecclesiological and Ecumenical*, ed. Michael G. Cartwright (Grand Rapids, MI: Eerdmans, 1994), 242-61.

Chapter 7
The End(s) of Return
1. The advocacy work of ecumenical bodies such as the Washington, D.C.-based Churches for Middle East Peace (CMEP) and the Canadian organization KAIROS is representative of the type of advocacy about the Palestinian-Israeli conflict for which ending the Israeli occupation of the West Bank, East Jerusalem, and the Gaza Strip and the securing of a two-state solution to the conflict are central, even as an "inside-the-beltway" group such as CMEP, unlike some of its member churches, like the Presbyterian Church USA, has assiduously avoided association with divestment initiatives, perhaps fearing that promotion of such campaigns would harm its political effectiveness. The work of mainline Protestant advocacy groups like CMEP and KAIROS finds a counterpart in the efforts of groups such as Evangelicals for Social Action or Evangelicals for Middle East Understanding. See, for example, a July 27, 2007, letter from evangelical leaders to U.S. President George W. Bush urging U.S. involvement in securing a two-state solution to the conflict, available at www.esa-online.org/Display.asp?Page=LettertoPresident.
2. A point of nuance is in order here. CMEP, KAIROS, and, for the most part, the mainline churches, are on record as officially endorsing the right of return of Palestinian refugees. The churches' uncritical embrace of the rhetoric of the two-state solution, however, time and again means that refugee rights are de-emphasized or qualified, as in the so-called Geneva Initiative developed through second-track diplomatic efforts, by an affirmation of an abstract virtual "right" of return coupled with severe restrictions on any concrete realization of that right, with Israel's demographic "needs" accepted as non-negotiable. To the extent that the churches respond to the call of Palestinian civil society institutions to engage in boycott, divestment, and sanctions (BDS) initiatives, grappling with the refugee issue will become urgent, and unquestioned commitment to a two-state solution becomes problematic. After all, the Palestinian civil society's call for BDS explicitly names refugee return as one of the major goals of the campaign. A copy of the July 9, 2005 call by Palestinian civil society organizations for boycott, divestment, and sanctions against Israel can be found at www.bds-palestine.net/.
3. For a complementary analysis of different forms of Christian Zionism, see Rosemary Radford Ruether, "Christian Zionism and Mainline Western Christian Churches," in *Challenging Christian Zionism: Theology, Politics, and the Israel-Palestine Conflict*, ed. Naim Ateek, Cedar Duaybis, and Maurine Tobin (London: Melisende, 2005), 154-62.
4. The "Joint Declaration" of the 18th International Catholic-Jewish Liaison Committee Meeting can be found at www.vatican.va/roman_curia/pontifical_councils/chrstuni/relations-jews-docs/rc_pc_chrstuni_doc_20040708_declaration-buenos-aires_en.html.

The Chicago document, "What We've Learned from Each Other: A Report on a Jewish-Protestant Conversation about the Israel-Palestinian Conflict," can be accessed at http://divinity.uchicago.edu/news/spring_2005/jewish-protestant_conversation.pdf.

5. See, for example, "Time Is in the Palestinians' Favor: An Interview with Arnon Soffer," *Bitterlemons: Palestinian-Israeli Crossfire* (12 January 2004). Available at www.bitterlemons.org/previous/bl120104ed2.html#pal2.

6. Ephraim Yaar and Tamar Hermann, "The Peace Index: Demographic Fears Favor Unilateral Separation," *Ha'aretz*, 1 July 2004.

7. Quoted in Jonathan Shainin, "Letter from Israel," *The Nation*, 12 January 2004. See also Ari Shavit's provocative interviews with Burg, "On the Eve of Destruction," *Ha'aretz*, 15 November 2003, and "Leaving the Zionist Ghetto," *Ha'aretz*, 24 June 2007.

8. Benny Morris, "Mikhake le-barbarim [Waiting for the Barbarians]," *Ha'aretz*, 6 January 2004, quoted in Ahmad H. Sa'di, "Reflections on Representations, History, and Moral Accountability," in *Nakba: Palestine, 1948, and the Claims of Memory* (New York: Columbia University Press, 2007), 309.

9. For a perceptive analysis of the distorted binational reality in Palestine-Israel, see chapters 6 and 7 of Meron Benvenisti, *Son of the Cypresses: Memories, Reflections, and Regrets from a Political Life* (Berkeley: University of California Press, 2007). Israeli geographer Oren Yiftachel has developed the concept of ethnocratic regimes in his study *Ethnocracy: Land and Identity Politics in Israel/Palestine* (Philadelphia: University of Pennsylvania Press, 2006).

Chapter 8
The Ephesian Vision Against the Iron Wall

1. For a perceptive study of Ephesians that complements my reading of how the epistle addresses peace and reconciliation, see Thomas R. Yoder Neufeld, *Ephesians* (Scottdale, PA: Herald Press, 2002).

2. For Muslims, Jews, and ardent secularists, different images will of course be more resonant.

3. For a succinct discussion of how the Israeli occupation regime controls land and water resources, see Jad Isaac and Owen Powell, "The Transformation of the Palestinian Environment," in *Where Now for Palestine? The Demise of the Two-State Solution*, ed. Jamil Hilal (London: Zed Books, 2007), 144-66.

4. Ze'ev Jabotinsky, *Writings: On the Road to Statehood* (Hebrew) (Jerusalem, 1959), 251-60, quoted in Avi Shlaim, *The Iron Wall: Israel and the Arab World* (New York: W. W. Norton, 2000), 13-14. Jabotinsky advised that "the only way to achieve a settlement in the future is total

avoidance of all attempts to arrive at a settlement in the present" (quoted in Shlaim, *Iron Wall*, 14)—the insistence of contemporary Israeli politicians that "there is no partner" can be understood as a way of avoiding a settlement based on international law in order to impose a settlement upon the Palestinians that is more to Israel's liking.

5. For an overview of Israel's policies and attitudes toward Palestinian refugees, see Nur Masalha, *The Politics of Denial: Israel and the Palestinian Refugee Problem* (London: Pluto Press, 2004).

6. Hussein Abu Hussein and Fiona McKay have detailed Israeli restrictions on Palestinian land use inside Israel in their study *Access Denied: Palestinian Access to Land in Israel* (London: Zed Books, 2003).

7. Israeli political scientist Yossi Alpher observes that for many Israelis the wall appears to offer "a means of at least mitigating" what Alpher calls "the demographic threat." The separation wall can thus be viewed as an attempt to prevent a binational state from emerging. See Alpher, "The Fence Affects Demography, Too," *Bitterlemons: Palestinian-Israeli Crossfire*, 12 January 2004.

8. Quoted in interview with David Landau, "Maximum Jews, Minimum Palestinians," *Ha'aretz*, 14 November 2003. Olmert here simply echoed the rationale offered by the late Yigal Allon of the Labor party in defense of his Allon Plan to annex portions of the West Bank to Israel, namely, that it would produce "maximum security and maximum territory for Israel with a minimum of Arabs." Quoted in Eyal Weizman, *Hollow Land: Israel's Architecture of Occupation* (London: Verso, 2007), 58.

9. Quoted in Aluf Benn interview with Ariel Sharon, "Down in the Polls—But Not Down in the Dumps," *Ha'aretz*, 16 April 2004.

10. For discussions of the impact of Israeli practices on the Palestinian economy, see Sufyan Alissa, "The Economics of an Independent Palestine," in *Where Now for Palestine?* 123-43, and Sara Roy, *The Gaza Strip: The Politics of De-Development* (Washington, DC: Institute for Palestine Studies, 2001).

11. Quoted in Aviv Lavie, "Back to the Grassroots," *Ha'aretz Friday Magazine*, 16 April 2004, 7.

12. Ibid.

13. Abu Sway, who teaches Islamic studies at Al Quds University in Jerusalem, articulated this concept of *dar al-hiwar* at an informal talk sponsored by the James T. Shasha Institute of the Hebrew University in Jerusalem on June 4, 2004.

14. Regarding the Pauline (and patristic) notion of participation, I am following William T. Cavanaugh, *Theopolitical Imagination: Discovering the Liturgy as a Political Act in an Age of Global Consumerism* (London: T&T Clark, 2002), 13-14.

15. While Israeli and Palestinian supporters of binational solutions to the conflict remain minorities in their respective communities, their numbers are growing. Israeli historian Ilan Pappé poignantly suggests that the future lies, not with those who would suggest yet another project of partition, but with those who look for a future of mutuality. See Pappé, *A History of Modern Palestine: One Land, Two Peoples* (Cambridge: Cambridge University Press, 2004), 267-68. In addition to multiple essays by the late Edward Said, arguments in favor of binational approaches have proliferated over the past decade. These include Mazin B. Qumsiyeh, *Sharing the Land of Canaan: Human Rights and the Israeli-Palestinian Struggle* (London: Pluto Press, 2004); Tony Judt, "Israel: The Alternative," *New York Review of Books* 50/16 (23 October 2003); Meron Benvenisti, *Son of the Cypresses: Memories, Reflections, and Regrets from a Political Life* (Berkeley: University of California Press, 2007); Joel Kovel, *Overcoming Zionism: Creating a Single Democratic State in Israel/Palestine* (London: Pluto Press, 2007); Ali Abunimah, *One Country: A Bold Proposal to End the Israeli-Palestinian Impasse* (New York: Metropolitan Books, 2006); and Virginia Tilley, *The One-State Solution: A Breakthrough for Peace in the Israeli-Palestinian Deadlock* (Ann Arbor: University of Michigan Press, 2005).

Chapter 9
Thinking About Terrorism
1. Benjamin Netanyahu, *Fighting Terrorism: How Democracies Can Defeat Domestic and International Terrorists* (New York: Noonday Press, 1987).

2. Gideon Samet, "The Rogue Bull and the Gods' Blessings," *Ha'aretz*, 19 December 2001, 5.

3. Dov Tamari, excerpts from remarks made at Gush Shalom symposium on war crimes, "Israel on the Way to the Hague," January 9, 2002, in Tel Aviv.

4. Clyde Haberman, "Juice and Cookies Trip Alarms in Jerusalem," *International Herald Tribune*, 18 December 2001, 4.

5. Edward S. Herman and Gerry O'Sullivan, *The Terrorism Industry: The Experts and Institutions That Shape Our View of Terror* (New York: Random House, 1990), and Edward S. Herman, *Real Terror Network: Terrorism in Fact and Propaganda* (Boston: South End Press, 1998).

6. John Rempel, "Terrorism, International Law, and International Justice," *MCC UN Office Newsletter*, 10 October 2001. The Reuters news service refuses to use the word terrorism, declaring it too emotive and subjective.

7. Quoted in Gershom Gorenberg, "The T-Word: Its Use and Misuse," *Jerusalem Report*, 28 January 2002, 21.

8. Quoted in James T. Burtchaell, *The Giving and Taking of Life: Essays Ethical* (Notre Dame, IN: University of Notre Dame Press, 1989), 213.

9. Remarks at Gush Shalom symposium. See note 3.

10. Quoted in Nitzan Horowitz, "Terror—It's All in the Eyes of the Beholder," *Ha'aretz*, 18 November 2001.

11. Gideon Levy, "On the Way to School," *Ha'aretz*, 25 November 2001, 5.

12. Gideon Levy, "A Crime against the Innocent," *Ha'aretz*, 13 January 2002, 5.

13. Attacks on soldiers can appear to many people as less objectionable than attacks on noncombatants because soldiers are thought to have a degree of choice about being put into conflict's way. In the context of Palestine-Israel, Israeli settler-colonists in the occupied territories form an ambiguous group. Palestinians tend to view them as armed paramilitary groups, part and parcel of the military occupation. Israelis tend to view them as noncombatant civilians. Certainly Shalhevet Pass, the ten-month-old girl killed in Hebron, must be considered a noncombatant. I will simply note that one obvious reason the Fourth Geneva Convention prohibits an occupying power from settling its civilian population in occupied territory is to keep civilians out of harm's way. Adult settlers and the Israeli government choose to ignore and violate the Fourth Geneva Convention, placing civilians in a territory where armed resistance to a military occupation should not be unexpected.

14. Quoted in Amnon Barzilai, "Netanyahu: Iraq Is Next US Target," *Ha'aretz*, 19 December 2001, 2.

15. Figures from www.electronicintifada.net, compiled from Palestinian Red Crescent Society and the Union of Palestinian Medical Relief Committees.

16. Stanley Hauerwas, *Sanctify Them in the Truth: Holiness Exemplified* (Nashville, TN: Abingdon Press, 1998), 180. Hauerwas correctly observes that the "state of Israel was brought into power by an extended and very well organized terrorist campaign" (179).

17. Ibid., 181.

18. Peace meaning here simply a particular type of order with an absence of conflict. Clearly, different visions of "peace" in the earthly city compete with one another. Most if not all of these visions will also stand in tension with the peace that the church is called to embody and proclaim.

19. Stanley Hauerwas, *Sanctify Them in the Truth*, 180.

20. These tasks might have relevance in other conflict situations—others will be more qualified than I to judge if this is the case. I should stress that the "Christian pacifists" in Palestine-Israel include many Palestinian Christians who have been at the forefront of promoting nonviolence as a means of Palestinian struggle.

21. Ya'ir Hilu, "A Statement of Refusal on Grounds of Conscience," *Challenge: A Magazine Covering the Israeli-Palestinian Conflict* 71 (January–February 2002), 11.

22. Quoted in Akiva Eldar, "Counting the Days—and the Dead," *Ha'aretz*, 24 January 2002, 4.

23. Gideon Levy, "Defining Violence," *Ha'aretz*, 12 March 2001, 5.

24. Ed Nyce, "My Friends Are Not Terrorists," email update, May 22, 2001.

25. Lee Griffith, *The War on Terrorism and the Terror of God* (Grand Rapids, MI: Eerdmans, 2002).

26. For John Howard Yoder on "middle axioms," see *The Christian Witness to the State* (Newton, KS: Faith and Life Press, 1964), 72-73, 158.

27. Remarks made at Gush Shalom symposium; see note 3.

28. Ibid.

29. Amos Harel, "Security Brass: Targeted Killings Don't Work; No Military Solution to Terror," *Ha'aretz*, 19 December 2001, 2.

30. Jonathan Kuttab, "Nonviolence: A Powerful Alternative," 19 December 2001, distributed by Common Ground News Service.

Chapter 10
Remembering the *Nakba* in Hebrew

1. For photos of the site taken after the demolition of the schoolhouse, visit the Website of the Zochrot Association: www.zochrot.org/index.php?id=463.

2. For a brief overview of Miskeh, see the information collected on the Palestine Remembered Website, available at www.palestineremembered.com/Tulkarm/Miska/index.html. See also the relevant entry in *All That Remains: The Palestinian Villages Occupied and Depopulated by Israel in 1948*, ed. Walid Khalidi (Washington, DC: Institute for Palestine Studies, 1992), 558-59.

3. Walid Khalidi and his colleagues in *All that Remains* count 413 destroyed and depopulated villages and towns. Salman Abu Sitta, however, argues for the higher figure of 531. See Abu Sitta, *From Refugees to Citizens at Home* (London: Palestine Land Society, 2001).

4. Laleh Khalili, "Places of Memory and Mourning: Palestinian Commemoration in the Refugee Camps of Lebanon," *Comparative Studies of South Asia, Africa and the Middle East* 25/1 (March 2005): 30.

5. Ahmad Sa'di, "Catastrophe, Memory, and Identity: Al-Nakbah as a Component of Palestinian Identity," *Israel Studies* 7/2 (Summer 2002), 194-95.

6. Lena Jayyusi, "Iterability, Cumulativity, and Presence: The Relational Figures of Palestinian Memory," in *Nakba: Palestine, 1948, and the Claims of Memory*, ed. Ahmad H. Sa'di and Lila Abu-Lughod (New York: Columbia University Press, 2007), 108.

7. Jonathan Cook offers a perceptive discussion of the status of Palestinians inside Israel in his book *Blood and Religion: The Unmasking of the Jewish and Democratic State* (London: Pluto Press, 2006).

8. For more on the Jewish National Fund, see Walter Lehn and Uri Davis,

The Jewish National Fund (London and New York: Kegan Paul International, 1988). For an account of the systematic destruction of still-standing remains of Palestinian villages starting in 1965, see Shai Aron, "The Fate of Abandoned Arab Villages in Israel," *History and Memory* 18/2 (Fall/Winter): 86-106.

9. For more on internally displaced Palestinians, see the essays collected in *Catastrophe Remembered: Palestine, Israel and the Internal Refugees*, ed. Nur Masalha (London: Zed Books, 2005). For more on Palestinians inside Israel, see As'ad Ghanem, *The Palestinian-Arab Minority inside Israel, 1948-2000: A Political Study* (Albany: SUNY Press, 2001); Nadim Rouhana, *Palestinian Citizens in an Ethnic Jewish State: Identities in Conflict* (New Haven, CT: Yale University Press, 1997); and Dan Rabinowitz and Khawla Abu-Baker, *Coffins on Our Shoulders: The Experience of the Palestinian Citizens of Israel* (Berkeley: University of California Press, 2005).

10. I will note briefly here that other Zionisms could be and were envisioned, Zionisms that were not tied to exclusivist control over land but instead offered visions of a binational future of coexistence within one state. One thinks, for example, of Martin Buber or Hannah Arendt.

11. Quoted in Nur Masalha, *Expulsion of the Palestinians: The Concept of "Transfer" in Zionist Political Thought, 1882-1948* (Washington, DC: Institute for Palestine Studies, 1992), 94-95.

12. Ibid., 131-32.

13. Ibid., 134.

14. For some of the best recent scholarship on the question, see the essays collected in *The War for Palestine: Rewriting the History of 1948*, ed. Eugene L. Rogan and Avi Shlaim (Cambridge: Cambridge University Press, 2001). See also Ilan Pappé, *The Ethnic Cleansing of Palestine* (Oxford: Oneworld Publications, 2006) and Benny Morris, *The Birth of the Palestinian Refugee Problem Revisited* (Cambridge: Cambridge University Press, 2006).

15. The "Jewish state" delimited by the UN Partition Plan (UNGA 181), one should note here, would have had a 50 percent Palestinian Arab population and thus would not have been "Jewish" in the spatial-demographic sense advocated by Weitz and most Zionists of both the left and the right.

16. Ghazi Falah, "The 1948 Israeli-Palestinian War and its Aftermath: The Transformation and De-Signification of Palestine's Cultural Landscape," *Annals of the Association of American Geographers* 86/2 (June 1996), 281. For Hanafi's discussion of spacio-cide, see his article, "Spacio-cide and Bio-Politics: The Israeli Colonial Conflict from 1947 to the Wall," in *Against the Wall: Israel's Barrier to Peace*, ed. Michael Sorkin (New York: New Press, 2005), 158-73.

17. Planting, uprooting, and telling stories about trees, Carol Baderstein notes, have been key acts through which Palestinians and Israelis have sought

to restore a ruptured "people-land" bond, acts that "have significantly shaped their respective collective memories and identities." See Baderstein, "Trees, Forests, and the Shaping of Palestinian and Israeli Collective Memory," in *Acts of Memory: Cultural Recall in the Present*, ed. Mieke Bal, Jonathan Crewe, Leo Spitzer (Hanover, NH: University Press of New England, 1999), 149.

18. Eitan Bronstein of the Zochrot Association explains that the presence of some ruined buildings on the landscape, rather than speaking to the Israeli consciousness of the erased Palestinian presence, actually helps contribute to that erasure, since it "gives the impression that the place is ancient, deeply rooted in the soil—even though the roots belong to people who no longer share this space; they simply remain faceless." See Bronstein, "The *Nakba* in Hebrew: Israeli-Jewish Awareness of the Palestinian Catastrophe and Internal Refugees," in *Catastrophe Remembered: Palestine, Israel and the Internal Refugees*, ed. Nur Masalha (London: Zed Books, 2005), 219.

19. Meron Benvenisti, *Sacred Landscape: The Buried History of the Holy Land since 1948* (Berkeley: University of California Press, 2002), 229-30.

20. Ibid., 57.

21. Ibid., 269.

22. Palestinian identity, Dan Rabinowitz observes, has hinged "on the experience of dispossession and exile throughout the twentieth century—its zenith being the 1948 defeat by Israel known as *al nakbah* (the disaster) and *al ghurba* (the exile) which ensued." See Rabinowitz, "The Common Memory of Loss: Political Mobilization among Citizens of Israel," *Journal of Anthropological Research* 50/1 (Spring 1994): 28.

23. Ilana Feldman contends that the "circulation of memory through refrain has in fact helped to keep the tragic realities of Palestinian history from utterly destroying Palestinian community and political life." See Feldman, "Home as Refrain: Remembering and Living Displacement in Gaza," *History and Memory* 18/2 (Fall/Winter 2006), 40.

24. Susan Slyomovics, *The Object of Memory: Arab and Jew Narrate the Palestinian Village* (Philadelphia: University of Pennsylvania Press, 1998), 16-17.

25. Mahmoud Issa, "Oral History, Memory, and the Palestinian Peasantry," *Al-Majdal* 32 (Winter 2006-2007), 7-8. UNRWA stands for the United Nations Relief Works Agency, the agency tasked with providing humanitarian assistance to Palestinian refugees. The United Nations Conciliation Commission for Palestine (UNCCP), charged after the 1948 war with resolving the Palestinian-Israeli conflict, including work on behalf of Palestinian refugee return, maintains archives in New York of Palestinian land records from before 1948 but has been otherwise inactive for more than five decades. Palestinian refugees fall outside of the remit of the UN High Commission on Refugees and thus do not have an international body that

works on their behalf for durable solutions of return, repatriation, resettlement, and restitution.

26. Salah Mansour, "Lessons Learned from PalestineRemembered.com's Oral History Experience," *Al-Majdal* no. 32 (Winter 2006-2007), 31.

27. Both Issa and Mansour replicate the insufficiently critical understanding of oral history advanced by Paul Thompson in which oral history's task is primarily one of unearthing new "facts" to be added to the historian's archive. They seem to assume that oral history is primarily about excavating buried facts from the past and not equally as much about present realities. Thompson, *The Voice of the Past: Oral History* (Oxford: Oxford University Press, 1988). Neither Mansour nor Issa, moreover, discusses how the ideological framework of the interviewer shapes the interview. In other words, they do not display an awareness, well articulated by Alessandro Portelli, that "oral history is basically the process of creating relationships: between narrators and narratees, between events in the past and dialogic narratives in the present." See Portelli, *The Order Has Been Carried Out: History, Memory, and Meaning of a Nazi Massacre in Rome* (New York: Palgrave Macmillan, 2003), 15. For an insightful discussion of the pitfalls and challenges of bringing oral history testimonies into a positivist legal framework, see the discussion by Samera Esmeir of the legal, historical, and epistemological issues in the libel case raised by Israeli veterans against Theodore Katz, an Israeli graduate student in history whose master's thesis at the University of Haifa used oral testimonies of refugees to describe a massacre allegedly carried out by the Zionist Alexandroni Brigades against civilians in the village of Tantoura in Esmeir, "1948: Law, History, Memory," *Social Text* 21/2 (2003): 25-48.

28. Diana K. Allan, "The Role of Oral History in Archiving the Nakba," *Al-Majdal* 32 (Winter 2006-7): 10.

29. Ibid., 11.

30. Diana K. Allan, "Mythologizing al-Nakba: Narratives, Collective Identity and Cultural Practice among Palestinian Refugees in Lebanon," *Oral History* 33/1 (Spring 2005): 51.

31. Allan, "Role of Oral History," 10.

32. Lori Allen, "The Polyvalent Politics of Martyr Commemoration in the Palestinian *Intifada*," *History and Memory* 18/2 (Winter 2006): 109. See also Salim Tamari and Rema Hammami, "Virtual Returns to Jaffa," *Journal of Palestine Studies* 27/4 (Summer 1998): 65-79, in which two Palestinian sociologists from Jaffa accentuate the private dimensions of memory that escape the limits of nationalist accounts.

33. Allan, "Mythologizing al-Nakba," 55. Allan's contention regarding how various media shape perceptions of the past mirrors the argument advanced in Tessa Morris-Suzuki, *The Past within Us: Media, Memory, History* (London: Verso, 2005).

34. Helena Lindhom Schulz explains that for many Palestinians "to be *a'idoun* represented action, to go back to where one came from, as opposed to the term 'refugee,' which implied being a passive victim of things that happened rather than an active producer of one's own life." See Schulz, *The Palestinian Diaspora: Formation of Identities and Politics of Homeland* (London: Routledge, 2000), 131.

35. Slyomovics, *Object of Memory*, xiii.

36. Ibid., 3.

37. Khalidi, *All That Remains*, xvii.

38. Slyomovics, *Object of Memory*, 13.

39. Quoted in Bronstein, "The *Nakba* in Hebrew," 217.

40. Quoted in Baderstein, "Trees, Forests," 148.

41. Pierre Nora, "Between Memory and History: *Les Lieux de Mémoire*," *Representations* 26 (Spring 1989): 12.

42. Nora, "Between Memory and History," 19; Sa'di, "Catastrophe, Memory, and Identity," 177.

43. Elias Sanbar, "Out of Place, Out of Time," *Mediterranean Historical Review* 16/1 (June 2001): 90.

44. Kerwin Lee Klein, "On the Emergence of Memory in Historical Discourse," *Representations* 69 (Winter 2000): 145.

45. Dayan's statement in the April 20, 1969, issue of *Ha'aretz* is quoted in Edward Said, "Afterword: The Consequences of 1948," in *The War for Palestine: Rewriting the History of 1948*, ed. Eugene L. Rogan and Avi Shlaim, 206-19 (Cambridge: Cambridge University Press, 2001), 218.

46. Maurice Halbwachs, *Collective Memory* (New York: Harper and Row, 1980), 86.

47. Zochrot director Eitan Bronstein states that Zochrot's main objective is to "Hebrewise the *Nakba*," to speak the Arabic word *Nakba* in Hebrew discourse ("The *Nakba* in Hebrew," 220).

48. Bronstein, "The *Nakba* in Hebrew," 221.

49. Morris-Suzuki, *The Past within Us*, 238.

50. Ibid., 241.

51. While the village visit, with its testimonies and signposting, is Zochrot's main activity, it carries out other forms of public memory related to the *Nakba*. At www.zochrot.org/, for example, Zochrot is constructing an interactive Hebrew-language map and database through which destroyed Palestinian villages are put back on the Israeli maps from which they have been erased. In Rabin Square in the heart of Tel Aviv, meanwhile, Zochrot has staged an interactive performance in which passersby are given cards bearing the names of destroyed Palestinian villages, cards that are coded to squares on a grid-map of Palestine-Israel, and then encouraged to place the cards on the map. Zochrot has also undertaken political and legal challenges to Israeli

erasure of Palestinian traces from before 1948, such as petitioning a regional planning council to oppose a proposed suburban development on the remains of Lifta, west of Jerusalem and mounting a successful legal challenge in Israeli courts to force the Jewish National Fund to post signs at the "Ayalon-Canada Park" at the western entrance of the Jerusalem corridor, marking that the park was built over the remains of Yalu and Imwas, villages in the so-called Latrun salient destroyed in 1967. For more on Zochrot's actions regarding Lifta, see Bronstein, *Studying the* Nakba *and Reconstructing Space in the Palestinian Village of Lifta* (Florence, Italy: European University Institute, 2005) and Malkit Shoshan and Eitan Bronstein, "Reinventing Lifta," *Monu: Magazine on Urbanism* 4 (2006): 64-69.

52. Bronstein, "The *Nakba* in Hebrew," 215.

53. Ibid., 229.

54. Eitan Bronstein, "Position Paper on Posting Signs at the Sites of Demolished Palestinian Villages," available at www.zochrot.org/index.php?id=343.

55. Eitan Bronstein, "The Nakba—An Event That Did Not Occur (Although It Had to Occur)," available at www.palestineremembered.com/Articles/General/Story1649.html/.

56. Bronstein, *Studying the* Nakba, 9.

57. Ibid., 17.

58. Links to Hebrew and English-language coverage in the Israeli press of Zochrot's activities can be found at www.nakbainhebrew.org/index.php?id=329. Aviv Lavie's article in *Ha'aretz*, "Right of Remembrance" (12 August 2004) is a particularly thoughtful introduction to Zochrot's work. Available at www.zochrot.org/index.php?id=340.

59. Cited in Lavie, "Right of Remembrance."

60. The theft and vandalizing of signs in Canada Park provide an interesting case study of the Israeli establishment being forced to signify the erasure of the Palestinian presence from the landscape, followed by new efforts at erasure, efforts that ironically drew further attention to the absence. After a two-year battle in the Israeli courts, the JNF agreed that Zochrot had the right to post signs in Canada Park commemorating Yalu and Imwas, along with Dayr Ayub, destroyed in 1948. The JNF, along with the Civil Administration and the "Military Commander in Judea and Samaria," then posted signs in Hebrew that read: "The Military Commander—Judea and Samaria. The Ayalon-Canada Park is replete with historical sites . . . including the remains of a church from the Byzantine period and the remains of a crusader fortress. During the monarchic period, in 1268, the tomb of Sheikh Ibn-Jamal was built. The village Dayr Ayub, which overlooked the road leading up to Jerusalem, existed in the area of the park until the War of Independence. The villages Imwas and Yalu existed in the area of the park until the year 1967. In

the village of Imwas there lived 2,000 residents, who now reside in Jordan and in Ramallah. Near the remains of the village is a cemetery. In the village of Yalu there lived 1,700 residents, who now reside in Jordan and Ramallah. There remains a spring and a number of wells in the village." See http://zochrot.org/index.php?id=434. One of these two signs was later stolen and another was vandalized, with all of the text about Dayr Ayub, Imwas, and Yalu covered over with black paint. See http://zochrot.org/index.php?id=460 and http://zochrot.org/index.php?id=435.

61. For more on this action, see the report at http://zochrot.org/index.php?id=175.

62. For a brief description of the event with photos, see www.zochrot.org/index.php?id=486.

63. See http://news.nana.co.il/Article/?ArticleID=410335&TypeID=1&sid=126.

64. A report on this action can be found at http://zochrot.org/index.php?id=489.

65. Bronstein, "The *Nakba* in Hebrew," 218.

66. Ibid., 225.

67. Bronstein describes this heterogeneous space with reference to Michel Foucault's notion of *heterotopia* ("The *Nakba* in Hebrew," 237).

68. See www.zochrot.org/index.php?id=213.

69. For more detailed description and photos of this activity, see www.zochrot.org/index.php?id=213.

70. Description and photos of this activity available at www.zochrot.org/index.php?id=466. Earlier in the month, Zochrot director Bronstein had written to Yaron Bibi of the ILA, asking why the structures had been demolished and petitioning for their reconstruction. Bibi's response exemplifies how state power is used to erase names from the landscape and to threaten those who try to create heterogeneous spaces:

From: District Manager's Bureau
August 30, 2006
To: Mr. Eitan Bronstein, director of Zochrot organization
Subject: Your letter from August 1, 2006

I am not familiar with the organization you manage or with the purpose of your petition.

I understand, out of an examination I arranged, that you refer to the buildings which were destroyed in an orchard near Moshav Mishmeret, that you name "the schoolhouse of the destroyed village Miske."

The land where the buildings stood is under the management of the Israel Land Administration, and it is leased by a leasing contract as required to the lessees.

The lessees have addressed us with a request to help them prevent illegal activities in the territory they lease, since people from the area have invaded their land, have tried to reconstruct the destroyed buildings, have held protests and gatherings while trespassing, have tried to plant trees and to fence the buildings.

All of these activities are illegal activities and some of them even constitute criminal offenses.

To the request of the lessees, a permission to demolish the buildings has been issued by the Local Committee for Planning and Construction of the Southern Sharon district.

The permission for the demolition had been given by the above mentioned committee during meeting no. 200603 on February 14, 2006. You could probably receive a copy of the permission from the Local Committee.

As representatives of the land owners, we have helped the lessees with their actions to prevent trespassing and with the execution of the demolition of the buildings in accordance with the law and we will act in the same way in the future.

Regards,

Yaron Bibi

District Manager

(A copy of this letter is available at www.zochrot.org/index.php?id=471).

71. Nora, "Between Memory and History," 19.

72. These types of memory performances can usually, it should be stressed again, only be carried out today by internally displaced Palestinians inside Israel, given the walls, checkpoints, and travel restrictions that prevent Palestinian refugees in the West Bank and the Gaza Strip from visiting the sites of their former homes. Palestinian refugees in Lebanon, Syria, and Jordan, of course, typically also cannot travel to Israel, making return visits impossible. I emphasize this point to underscore the fact that social, economic, and political conditions all shape the forms and ends of memory work. Acts of memory by Palestinian refugees in, say, camps in Lebanon will most likely not have the character of performing a binational future: this should not be a surprise, nor should it be taken as a criticism of, or a moral judgment on, the different modalities that Palestinian refugee memory work takes, from nostalgic reflection, to fragmented, personal recollections, to insistent demands for justice and a reclamation of property.

73. For an analysis of Palestinian refugee rights in the context of international law, see *Survey of Palestinian Refugees and Internally Displaced Persons, 2004-2005* (Bethlehem: BADIL Resource Center for Palestinian Residency and Refugee Rights, 2006).

74. Bronstein, "The *Nakba* in Hebrew," 236.

75. Edward Said, "Afterword: The Consequences of 1948," 217.

Epilogue

1. Gillian Rose, *Mourning Becomes the Law* (Cambridge: Cambridge University Press, 1996), 10.

2. William E. Connolly, "Pluralism, Multiculturalism and the Nation-State: Rethinking the Connections," *Journal of Political Ideologies* 1/1 (1996): 58.

3. Talal Asad, *Formations of the Secular: Christianity, Islam, Modernity* (Stanford: Stanford University Press, 2003), 179.

4. John Milbank, "Against the Resignations of the Age," in *Things Old and New: Catholic Social Teaching Revisited*, ed. F. P. McHugh and S. M. Natale (New York: University Press of America, 1993), 19.

5. Asad, *Formations of the Secular*, 179.

6. Daniel Boyarin, *A Radical Jew: Paul and the Politics of Identity* (Berkeley: University of California Press, 1994), 248-49.

7. Asad, *Formations of the Secular*, 180.

8. Connolly, "Pluralism, Multiculturalism and the Nation-State," 61.

9. Eyal Weizman, *Hollow Land: Israel's Architecture of Occupation* (London and New York: Verso, 2007), 178.

10. See, for example, Jeff Halper, *Obstacles to Peace: A Re-Framing of the Palestinian-Israeli Conflict* (Jerusalem: Israeli Committee against House Demolitions, 2004).

11. Siegfried Kracauer, *History: The Last Things before the Last* (Princeton, NJ: Markus Wiener Publishing, 1995), 8.

12. Nigel Parry, "British Graffiti Artist, Banksy, Hacks the Wall," *Thresholds: MIT Department of Architecture's Critical Journal of Architecture, Art, and Media Culture* 32 (October 2006).

13. Ilan Pappé, "Zionism and the Two-State Solution," in *Where Now for Palestine? The Demise of the Two-State Solution*, ed. Jamil Hilal (London and New York: Zed Books, 2006), 46.

14. For a haunting reflection by one Ta'ayush activist, see David Shulman, *Dark Hope: Working for Peace in Israel and Palestine* (Chicago: University of Chicago Press, 2007).

Index

The Author

Alain Epp Weaver served for eleven years with Mennonite Central Committee in the Middle East, including as an English teacher in the northern West Bank village of Zababdeh; as development coordinator for the Gaza Strip; as program administrator in Jerusalem; and, most recently, as representative for Palestine, Jordan, and Iraq.

The author of numerous articles in academic journals, Epp Weaver has also published many essays in church publications and other popular periodicals. He has edited several books, including *Under Vine and Fig Tree: Biblical Theologies of Land and the Palestinian-Israeli Conflict* (Cascadia and Herald, 2007). He co-edited *Borders and Bridges: Mennonite Witness in a Religiously Diverse World* (Cascadia and Herald, 2007) with Peter Dula, and *The Work of Jesus Christ in Anabaptist Perspective* (Cascadia and Herald, 2008) with Gerald Mast.

Alain grew up in Lincoln, Nebraska, and is married to Sonia K. Weaver, with whom he has two children, Samuel Rafiq and Katherine Noor. He is a member of First Mennonite Church of Bluffton, Ohio.